Living Our Religions

Living Our Religions

*Hindu and Muslim South Asian American
Women Narrate their Experiences*

By

Anjana Narayan and *Bandana Purkayastha*

with

Shobha Hamal Gurung, Selina Jamil, Salma Kamal,
Shweta Majumdar, Bidya Ranjeet, Shanthi Rao, Aysha Saeed,
Monoswita Saha, Neela Bhattacharya Saxena, Parveen Talpur,
Elora Halim Chowdhury, and Rafia Zakaria

Kumarian Press
An Imprint of Stylus Publishing

Living Our Religions: Hindu and Muslim South Asian American Women Narrate their Experiences

Published 2009 in the United States of America by Kumarian Press
22883 Quicksilver Drive, Sterling, VA 20166 USA

Copyedit by Publication Services
Proofread by Beth Richards
Index by Anjana Narayan
Design and production by Rosanne Schloss, NY
The text of this book is set in 11/14 Adobe Sabon

Printed in the USA on acid-free paper by IBT Global.

∞ The paper used in this publication meets the minimum requirements of the American National Standard for Information Sciences—Permanence of Paper for Printed Library Materials, ANSI Z39.48-1984.

Library of Congress Cataloging-in-Publication Data

*Living our religions : Hindu and Muslim South Asian American
    Women Narrate their Experiences* / edited by Anjana Narayan and
    Bandana Purkayastha.
        p.   cm.
    Includes bibliographical references and index.
    ISBN 978-1-56549-270-7 (pbk. : alk. paper) — ISBN 978-1-56549-271-4
    (cloth : alk. paper)
    1. South Asian American women—Religious life. 2. Hindu women—United
States—Social life and customs. 3. Muslim women—United States—Social life
and customs. I. Narayan, Anjana, 1976– II. Purkayastha, Bandana, 1956–
    E184.S69L58   2008
    305.40954—dc22

                                                                    2008028263

Contents

Acknowledgements

Though this appears to be an edited book, all the authors were co-participants in this project. This book would not exist without their passion, dedication, and long-term commitment. And to all of you who are part of the South Asian Tree network, who "demanded" a book of this kind, thanks!

Anjana Narayan and Bandana Purkayastha would like to thank their mentors and friends Mark Abrahamson, Roger Buckley, Davita Glasberg, Myra Ferree, Nazli Kibria, Kathryn Ratcliff, Ron Taylor, and Gaye Tuchman. Anjana would also like to thank Laurie Roades, Gary Cretser, Mary Danico, Barbara Way, Sharon Hilles, Tara Sethia, Nirmal Sethia, Lise-Helene Smith, and all at Cal Poly Pomona for their constant support. A special thanks to Ramani and P. Balakrishnan for their help and encouragement, and to Mini Krishnan for sharing her valuable insights on religion. Bandana is grateful to all the mentors at Vivekananda Nidhi who taught her about different religions.

Many friends—Christian, Jewish, Muslim, and Hindu—keep us grounded in the positive aspects of religions; to them we give our thanks. And most of all, our gratitude to our families—Daddy, Shashi, Mummy, Manju, Vinay, Amma, and Achan—for their love and resolute support, and to Indra and Aheli who read multiple drafts and cheerfully shouldered a million tasks as we were writing this book. This book would not have been completed without them.

1

Introduction

Anjana Narayan and Bandana Purkayastha

Row upon row of girl children—little tots all, sitting cross-legged on the ground, facing the brazen goddess . . . . [T]his is a day-school of piety. These babies are learning texts—"mantrims" to use in worship—learning the rites that belong to the various ceremonies incumbent upon Hindu women. . . Women pray first as to husbands; then to bear sons. Men must have sons to serve their souls (Mayo 1925, 137).

No feminist works emerged from behind the Hindu purdah or out of Muslim harems; centuries of slavery do not provide a fertile soil for intellectual development or expression (Schneider 1972, xiv).

Islamic culture explains, in large part, the failure of democracy to emerge in much of the Muslim world (Huntington 1998, 4).

The persistence of these ideas, through the twentieth century, with the repeated themes about homogenous, non-modern civilizations, the subordinated position of women in these civilizations, and the ongoing role of violence—force, slavery—in sustaining these civilizations, raises an important question. What do women who live these religions have to say about their experiences?

Mayo, Schneider, and Huntington have been very influential in shaping public opinion, policies, and academic theories for years.[1] Their overgeneralized, ahistorical ideas have intersected with media depictions of Hindus and Muslims. We have been deluged with images of US-hating Muslim and Hindu fundamentalists and terrorists

1

and stories about veiled, raped, harassed, and subordinated Hindu and Muslim South Asian women. The American mainstream has become familiar with Osama bin Laden and bands of ultramasculine, Islamic terrorists, but they have not become familiar with social justice activitists such as Khan Abdul Gaffar Khan or Mohammed Yunus. Mukhtaran Mai and Phoolan Devi, shown primarily as rape victims of oppressive patriarchal cultures, have been widely featured by the Western media, but the Muslim cleric who first protested Mukhtaran Mai's rape is invisible. Few lead stories feature Bachni Devi, Sehba Hussain, Shabana Azmi, or Ela Bhatt, who have defined and claimed economic and social human rights and contributed to building peace in the world.[2] These orientalist features about certain kinds of Muslim and Hindu women and men, and the invisibility of other kinds, create persistent ideas about these groups and cultures; they maintain the imagined distinction between the subordinated women of "their cultures" and the liberated women of the cultures of the pundits, and, consequently, the hierarchy between civilizations (Said 1979).

In the United States, there has been a great deal of public discussion about how to control the "bad guys" who violently resist modernization and how to save the oppressed women of these cultures. These questions have taken on a real urgency as we deal with the horrors unleashed by recent Islamist terrorist attacks. This urgency is also related to a demographic reality. Since the mid-1960s large numbers of new Hindu and Muslim migrants have arrived in the United States.[3] After September 2001 these Muslims and "Muslim-looking" groups—such as the Hindus and Sikhs—have became central to US national and local discussions about security and assimilation. The right to practice different religions *as a principle* is not generally questioned in the United States, although fundamentalist Christian groups periodically mobilize to bring Christian principles more centrally back into public affairs. As in earlier periods of ethnic history—when Catholics, Jews, and Native Americans struggled, with various degrees of success, to practice their religions—there are many contemporary questions about how, where, and under what rules and restrictions these practitioners of other religions are to be included in American civic life (e.g., Sarna and Dahlin 1997; Simon and Alexander 1993). Although we assume all Americans are free to practice their religion in family or community arenas, a range of laws, policies, ideologies, and discourses of the public world shape what is possible in these private spaces. Racialized "others" are subject to many extra restrictions on their freedoms (Glenn 2002). For instance, over the last several years, local, state, and national governments have been acting on the oft-circulated ideologies about Muslims, Hindus, Sikhs, Christians, and others to create racial profiles to classify some groups as potential threats to the security of nations and others as good citizens. These policies and initiatives shape whose phenotypes and cultures are to be used for racial profiling and whose movements and actions—communications, charitable giving, and so forth—should be subject to extra scrutiny (e.g., Santos 2008).

The anxiety about new immigrants and their religions intersects with the scrutiny of women's positions. Because the treatment of women informs us about any religion and culture, a particularly important part of this discussion has focused on women in minority religions. The perceived treatment of women—inferred from the stereotypes powerfully proclaimed by pundits—is often used to gauge immigrant groups' ability to assimilate into modern US society. Although some have seen no contradiction between religions and cultures of new immigrants and their ability to assimilate (Levitt 2007), others have expressed concern about minority women who are "locked" into these other cultures and have suggested that it would be better for women if they simply assimilated into more modern progressive Western cultures (Okin 1999).

There is another urgent reason for exploring the experiences of women. A great deal of recent scholarly literature has documented the growth of religious fundamentalisms around the world (Van der Veer 2003; Sarkar and Butalia 1995). Christian, Islamic, Hindu, and other fundamentalist groups are engaged in creating homogenized, simplistic forms of faith-based, militant, nationalistic, religious identities. In order to win supporters among people who practice "their" religion, all fundamentalists rely on two tropes. They claim it is important to return to a purer form of religion through a literal reading of original texts, such as the Bible or the Koran, or to traditions and authentic pasts, such as Ramrajya/Golden Vedic age, in the case of Hinduism. Using a variety of sophisticated, modern methods—

Web-based organizing, conference-style proselytizing, direct marketing appeals to buy ethno-religious artifacts, religious heritage tourism, and merchandizing and marketing religions through a wide variety of media—fundamentalists propagate a return to tradition in order to draw ethnocentric boundaries between "us/believers" and "them/nonbelievers."

Like the mainstream pundits, fundamentalists use gendered racialized ideologies and practices to maintain their power. All fundamentalists talk about the essential natures of men and women. In these proclamations, men are bread-winners and protectors, and women are the protected home-makers or, at best, community care providers. The repeated appeal to tradition infuses their reinvented discourse with a sense of authority and timelessness. Fundamentalists promote the notion of the pure woman of "our" religion and the servile, sexually exploited, or over-sexed women of "their" religion.[4] Assertions about Western women's uncontrolled sexuality by Muslim and Hindu fundamentalists, Muslim woman's servile status by Christians and Hindus, or Hindu women's servile status by Christian and Muslim fundamentalists arise from exactly the same objective: the use of women as symbols to draw boundaries between religions.

Both mainstream pundits and fundamentalists support the idea that religion uniquely determines the lives of women. But, as Nobel Laureate Amartya Sen (2006) has argued, few women (or men) are solely Hindu or Muslim (or Christian, Buddhist, Jew, Sikh, or Jain)—they are also parents, spouses, siblings, scientists, musicians, teachers, activists, students, migrants, and citizens, people with many cultural, social, economic, political, and national affiliations and interests. This book reflects this perspective. We offer a counterpoint to the ahistorical, overgeneralized constructions of Hindu and Muslim women by mainstream pundits and religious fundamentalists. We assume that any individual's religious practices reflect particular social, political, and economic histories. Because we present experiences of women in today's world, we do not assume that their lives are being determined by their local communities; in a globalized world, people maintain ties with family and friends in different parts of the world, their economic and political lives spanning multiple countries. The opportunities and barriers they encounter in living their religions work through these transnational structures and affiliations.

In order to move away from simplistic definitions of religions and unidimensional explanations of the connections between religions and women, in this book we asked Hindu and Muslim women how they *live* their religions. What kind of opportunities and barriers do they encounter? Which religious ideologies and practices do they reject? Which ones do they value? What do they change? How do their experiences differ from others of their linguistic, cultural, and political communities? How does religion intersect with other dimensions of their lives? What are their views about the institutions—families, communities, nation-states—through which they live their religions?

Through the Lens of Living Religions

Going against the grain of the powerful imagery of subordinated Hindu and Muslim women, this book presents everyday, personal, ethnographic accounts of women of South Asian origin. We offer a corrective to the orientalist and fundamentalist claims by presenting the voices from the middle.

Mainstream declarations and fundamentalists claims have led people to examine whether religious texts and ideologies are favorable or oppressive to women. Some have linked religious precepts to the subordination of women (e.g., Ali 2007; Kamguian 2004); others refute such claims (e.g., Ahmed 2002; Barlas 2002). Instead of adding to the existing debate, we choose to focus on the act of *living religions*. The living religions frame allows us to present the ways in which women weave beliefs, choices, and practices; the changes they initiate, the opportunities they perceive; and the barriers they encounter.

Mainstream pundits and fundamentalists are rarely able to acknowledge diversity; such acknowledgement would dilute their power to speak authoritatively for the whole group. But a focus on living religions reveals significant diversity within each religion. Even when we listen to highly educated women, their experiences reflect the multidimensionality and dynamism of religions. Bringing women of other socioeconomic backgrounds into the dialogue would increase the diversity exponentially. Analyzing these women's experiences shows us that despite repeated claims to clashing civilizations—a frame that has been a staple of mainstream pundits *and* fundamentalists—the boundaries between religions are often blurred through everyday practice and a shared acknowledgement of a common humanity.

Although many discussions of religions focus exclusively on "the religion" as a force untouched by other processes in the real world, our frame of living religions directs attention to the interplay between situated context and religious practices of groups. When we look through the lens of living religions, we find that people's religious practices reflect particular histories and social circumstances. This is true of Islam, which is organized according to the directions in the Koran (Moghadam 2003; Imam 1991); it is also true of Hinduism, which has no single book that codifies its values and principles (Swami Nirvedananda 1979; Purkayastha and Narayan, forthcoming). Hinduism does not look the same in different parts of India, Nepal, and Bangladesh; Islam does not appear the same in Pakistan, Bangladesh, and India.

And, just as we move away from an exclusive focus on the influence of one set of texts, beliefs, mosques, and temples, we do not confine ourselves to what happens within a single nation at one point in time. We describe how individuals' religious lives are woven through the histories, politics, and cultures of many nations; these histories cumulatively shape the opportunities and restrictions they encounter in their everyday lives. We present accounts of religions as they are lived in homes and communities, in formal places of worship and through social justice activism in secular spaces, as individual values and as collective practice, as ongoing ritualized practices and as practices evoked sporadically during life changing events.

By unlinking the idea of religions from its familiar text-dependent, faith-based, church–mosque–temple moorings, we problematize the idea of traditional religions and the corresponding implication that traditions are always an impediment to progressive causes. Instead, we show how some religious traditions act as inspirations for social justice activism, and how others become less relevant in the midst of changing socioeconomic and political settings. Thus, contrary to how most people have been taught to think, this book does not show any linear progress from tradition to modernity (or from modernity back to tradition), the idea that is central to the ethnocentric frames.

This is a book by and on women. It is for people who wish to move beyond the stereotypes and gain more knowledge about these religions. Given the incendiary politics around women and religion, these descriptions of living religions, in a context spanning South Asia and the United States, offer an alternative way to understand how religions are lived through transnational social and political worlds in multidimensional ways.

Studying Religions:
Questions of Tradition and Gender

Academics have long assumed that carefully fashioned scholarly studies provide a sufficient counterpoint to the simplistic overgeneralizations that pervade many public discussions. But it does not always work that way. As we demonstrated earlier, some of the public discussions have drawn on scholarly studies by Mayo, Huntington, and Schneider. And, very frequently people interpret scholarly work to fit their frames of understanding; they ignore dictums about limitations and generalizability of studies, and they pick portions that support their views. Who reads the scholarly work, how they interpret it, and how much power they have to widely disseminate *their* interpretations is germane to understanding how the accounts of Hinduism and Islam are being constructed in the scholarly world. Because questions about tradition—how such traditions affect women—are central to public discourse and policy-making in multicultural America, we provide a brief overview of how this concept has been addressed in the scholarly literature. Then we focus on questions of gender, the intersecting ideological, interactional, institutional processes that construct and sustain differences between diverse women and men.

Religion and Tradition

The long-established, plentiful literature on religions and religious philosophies focuses on the interpretations (and translations) of texts and traditions of Hinduism and Islam (e.g., Barlas 2002; Beane 1977; Coburn 1991; Eck 1993; Kupperman 1999; Miller 1986; Saxena 2004).[5] The excellent scholarship on texts demystifies many of the values and symbols of these non-Christian religious traditions, explaining different ways of thinking about human lives and the universe. Yet there is an unintended consequence of this prolific scholarship on religious texts. People who seek to understand "new" religions—the religions of newer immigrants—often focus on these texts *alone* to draw conclusions about how contemporary groups live their life according to tradition. Casual reading of these books alone reveals little about the specific historical periods when many texts were generated, who translated them and why, and to what extent the language of these translations is accurate by today's standards.[6] Furthermore, because many of the religious texts featured in scholarly discussions are authored by males, these discussions create the impression that males have directed the norms and that women have lived by them. The relationship between these texts and the people who interpret, imagine, and construct their religious lives in a variety of social and historical contexts are not readily apparent. Consequently, tradition tends to assume a changeless form when people focus solely on texts to understand religions.

A second area of scholarly focus, an area that has been growing very rapidly in the last few decades, is the study of fundamentalisms. This literature examines the sources, organizations, and methods through which fundamentalisms are organized and propagated (e.g., Hansen 1990). Because fundamentalists of all religions are involved in reinventing and asserting their version of tradition and the need to return to a pure way of life, the emphasis in the social movement literature is to decode how fundamentalists claim and assert tradition (Bachetta 2004; Sarkar and Butalia 1995; Racial and Ethnic Studies, Special Issue, May 2000). However, as Moghadam (1994) points out, many other scholars and non-scholars continue to assume that fundamentalism is a predominant expression of culture and an independent influence that overrides differences in economies, nation-state systems, and local histories. And, because studies of fundamentalism do not typically explain the pervasiveness of the trends, it is often an easy step to elide fundamentalisms with the entire religion. Thus, along with the religious textual analyses, the social movement literature inadvertently contributes to the misperception about the overwhelming, often negative, influence of religious tradition on women.

A third, relatively small but growing literature focuses on the religions of new immigrants to the United States. The religious practices of Asian Americans and Latino groups are examined, often focusing primarily on Christianity, or studies of Hinduism and Islam may focus on single religious sites (Carnes and Yang 2004; Ebaugh and Chafetz 2000; Rayaprol 1997). A common objective of these studies is finding out whether new immigrants are assimilating into the United States. Specifically, to what extent have they moved beyond their traditions and become more modernized and globalized in the United States? These studies have typically examined representation of women in temple or mosque executive boards in order to understand whether women have become more modernized and are taking on public roles in religious institutions in the United States (Yang and Ebaugh 2001). But by focusing on congregation nodes of religions that are not congregationalist in character, this strand of research has documented only a part of how these two religions are lived in the United States. Most accounts of what immigrants do in temples or mosques rarely answer the prior question of why *these specific* groups choose *these* practices in *these* places. Only a few recent studies (e.g., Joshi 2006; Kurien 2007) have begun to move the discussion beyond temples and mosques to examine the opportunities and restrictions on religious practice and religious identity in civil society.

Few studies on fundamentalism or immigrant religions showcase the diversity of the religions. Hinduism is a case in point. Practiced by a growing number of immigrants in the United States (a few thousand in 1970 to close to a million in 2000), it is not a religion that is based on a book or on one major figure, but it is practiced in many thousands of ways in India and other parts of the world. Scholarly work has rarely focused on why and how Hinduism is being recreated as a centralized homogenized religion in the United States. Compared to the vast US-based literature on the metaphysics of Hinduism and on treatises and descriptions of traditions of Hinduism by religious scholars, empirical work on the social organization or lived aspects of Hinduism has focused mostly on Hindu fundamentalisms (Maira 1999/2000; Prashad 2000) or on Hinduism in temples (Rayaprol 1997). The literature on Islam reveals a similar pattern. Islam is the fastest growing religion in the United States, attracting adherents from immigrant and nonimmigrant communities. Yet the rapidly growing books on Islam focus mostly either on the politics of Islamist groups (e.g., Abuza 2006; Bergen 2001; Hussain 2007; Saikia 2004) or on the principles, beliefs, and traditions of Islam (e.g., Ali 2007; Kamguian 2004). Only recently have gender scholars addressed other issues such as varieties of jurisprudence (Imam 1991), differing interpretations (Mernisi 1987; Barlas 2002; Hassan 1995), and diverse practices.

Religion and Questions of Gender

The ideologies, interactions, and institutions that create and sustain gender hierarchies are central to the project of living and remaking religions. Although religions vary in the ways in which the original roles of women and men are explained, in most religions males have generally been able to garner more power to speak authoritatively about religions. However, these ideas about gendered symbolism and structuring of religions do not translate automatically to less freedom for Third World Muslim and Hindu South Asian women than for their Christian peers in the developed world; indeed, many historians would argue the opposite is true (e.g., Forbes 1996; Ramusack and Seivers 1999). Actual statuses of women (and men) of all religions are far more complex, emerging through their symbolic and achieved and ascribed roles and statuses in family, community, and nation-states.

Engaging with Western Feminism

The growing influence of feminist scholarship and its insistence on considering the experiences of women has permeated to different fields of inquiry. Indeed, part of the impetus in new immigrant religion studies arises from the wish to focus on women's absence or presence in institutions. This book, with its emphasis on women's experiences, is part of the larger endeavor to include women's voices and their experiences in discussions about religion. However, this book departs theoretically and methodologically from the mainstream feminist scholarship on women and religion in Euro-America by *examining* the experiences of Hindu and Muslim women instead of assuming we know what these experiences are likely to be.

The significant point of departure of this book is its rejection of a Western feminist perspective. We use the term *Western* with a capital *W,* to problematize the type of scholarly work that takes the experiences of women of the dominant group (in terms of their race, class, nativity, religion, and other social characteristics) in a society as the norm for understanding gendered experiences of other women. The most influential Western feminist work, which is based on the experiences of white women, relies on a hierarchical understanding of liberated Western women versus subordinated non-Western females. This work makes the hegemonic economic, political, and ultra-nationalist processes that contribute to their positions of privilege relative to the lack of privilege of other women invisible (see Mohanty 1991 and Oyewumi 1996 for two powerful critiques of Western feminism). Western feminism does not include all scholars who live in Euro-America, nor does it exclude scholars who live in other parts of the world, especially those scholars whose work consistently privileges the experiences of middle class women of the majority group in their societies.[7]

There are many scholars who are geographically located in the west (with a small *w*) who do not reify Euro-American middle class white experiences. In fact, these multiracial scholars have challenged the ideological construction of "women" as an undifferentiated category that makes the intersecting influence of race, class, and other social hierarchies invisible (e.g., Amos and Parmer 1984; Baca Zinn and Dill 1994; Brah 1996; Espiritu 1997; Glenn 2004;

Hill Collins 1990; Oyewumi 1996). Scholars located in other parts of the world have developed perspectives that look beyond ahistorical depictions of male–female dichotomies to consider class, race, caste, national background, colonial status, culture, and other locally extant social hierarchies germane to the study of gender (e.g., Ahmed 2002; Chakravarty 2003; Kishwar 1998; Kumar 1993; Omvedt 2006; Sen 1990; Vanita 2002).

A primary drawback of Western feminism in Euro-America for studying women in Islam and Hinduism is the lack of reflection on terms such as *modernity* and *traditionalism*. It is often taken for granted that the gender hierarchy in other religions is likely to be worse because their religions socially support the extreme subordination of women. This view was reflected in Schneider's quotation at the beginning of this chapter. Tripp's recent discussions of the nature of Western feminist interventions in the Amina Lawal case in Nigeria, the rape of Muslims and Croatians in the former Yugoslavia, genital cutting issues in Africa, and the saving of burqa-clad women in Afghanistan are stark reminders of continuing orientalism in the twenty-first century (2006). There is also a continuing trend in feminist literature to take Western, white Christian experiences and project these as women's experiences. For instance, in a recent summary of feminism and religion, Andersen (2005) lists the following arenas of feminist scholarly contribution to our understanding of women and religion: feminist scholarship on the historical relationship of women, religion, and feminism; women's religious beliefs and status within churches; the role of churches in minority communities; and new perspectives inspired by feminist spirituality and theology. There is little recognition that some religions may actually support gynocentric ideologies (Saxena 2004), may not be church- and congregation-based with attendant notions of centralized authority and hierarchy and homogenized practices and beliefs (Ahmed 2002), with one book as the source of all beliefs and ideologies.

Complex Feminism

Our theoretical framework for this book is based on more complex ideas of feminism. First, the editors and authors of this book are well aware that for centuries women have organized themselves in their countries of origin and have challenged patriarchal practices and ideas in their communities; we are unwilling to cede the lineage of feminism solely to Euro-America. Second, we do not accept the ahistorical idea about a linear progress from tradition to modernity, which many Western feminists tend to take for granted. Traditions and modernities coexist in social locations. Our knowledge horizons stretch over many countries; we share Kishwar's horror of trying to fit into pure isms (1999). Thus we weave different strands of prior theories to fashion our frame for this book.

As "women of color" in the United States, we have benefited from the work of feminists who have challenged the earlier Western feminist gender-only notions of patriarchy and moved the field to consider the intersections of race, class, and gender. We draw on their insights about dominant and minority social locations and material bases of gender hierarchies to reflect on how this intersection of different factors affects the living of religions. Similarly, postcolonial scholars who have emphasized the continuing influence of neoliberal, imperialistic state-formation processes, help us to frame complex feminisms within situated "glocal" (global + local) contexts. By drawing on both these strands of scholarship, we avoid the missteps of both groups. Multiracial feminism is focused mostly on the United States and has not systematically discussed how other religions have become the markers of race differences in the United States and the world. We also extend our perspective beyond political/economic/social post-colonial conditions to examine how these affect women and men's ability to traverse overlapping secular and sacred realms. Along with these two strands of scholarly work, we look to scholars who have studied religions. We have been inspired not only by Ahmed's seminal book *Gendering the Spirit* but also by the work of Barlas (2002), Imam (1991), Mookherjee and Khanna (1977), and Saxena (2004), who have demonstrated ways to understand the role of feminine principles in religion.

As a result, we start with the assumption that there is no dearth of strong women or strong women's symbolism in either religion, even though patriarchal voices might choose to contest this view. Hinduism offers one model. It is brimming with imageries of goddesses who are warriors, destroyers, creators, guardians of wealth and education, and ultimate liberators. In Hinduism, god is neither man nor women; s/he is *ardhanariswara* (half woman half man) and, in reality, beyond such male/female dichotomies based on physical bodies or essential natures. Such symbolism, as well as the relative freedom given to individuals to choose preferred ways of worship (forms that are not mediated by a male priestly hierarchy in religious institutions), constructs religious freedom for women and men in very different ways than freedoms embedded in congregation-type religions. Islam offers a different model but still offers freedoms to women. As Barlas (2002) and Hassan (1995) have documented, the central principles of Islam are gender neutral. Islam is replete with the traditions of Sufi women such as Rabe'ah (ninth century) and Hiyati (early nineteenth century) who have challenged masculinist versions of Islam (Nurbakhsh 1990). Mernissi has pointed out that because "Islam is no more repressive than Judaism or Christianity, there must be those who have a vested interest in blocking women's rights in Muslim societies" (1987, vii). Theoretically we expect the influence of women to be reflected in our co-participants' chapters.

In the United States, Katzenstein (1996) has documented how women in churches have tried to create "woman church" outside the centralized patriarchal authority of mainstream churches. These women have not only created alternate spaces for living their religion, but they have also begun to alter symbols to create a more feminine face of god. But women's religious spaces have been very much alive in South Asia, in both religious traditions, for centuries. Thus the equivalent of "women's churches" in South Asia is often a long-established tradition rather than a Western feminism–inspired project-in-the-making. The accounts of medieval Bhakti saints, whose roots were in Islam *and* Hinduism, include women such as Mirabai, Andal, Sahojo-bai, and Daya-bai who emphasized faith-based, boundary-breaching religions (Sen 2005). The history of religious change in South Asia shows that many women religious leaders were of the working class and that their revolutions radically challenged the hierarchies of their times, popularizing the idea of non-priest/imam-mediated, non-religious-institution-specific ways of living religions. Many contemporary women religious leaders exist as well (e.g., Narayan, this book; Ahmed 2002). This awareness of women's traditions and the need to go beyond sharply defined religious and sex boundaries shaped our theoretical perspective.

Our complex feminism framework leads us to recognize the physical, social, and psychological repressions that women are subject to in any society. Therefore, we recognize and are committed to showcasing women's "creative engagement with religion in which faith and different types of sacred and secular knowledge reinforce each other" (Ahmed 2002, 8) amid these constraints. Consistent with our epistemological roots in complex feminism, we follow a slightly unusual methodology in this book. We did not use the well-established process of interviewing participants and writing a research monograph. Instead we asked our co-participants in this project to write their own accounts of religion, leaving them free to define religion and what they chose to emphasize as they reflected on their lives in South Asia and the United States. (The advantages and drawbacks of using this method are discussed in the appendix.) Many of the chapters may not appear to be feminist in the conventional (Western) sense of the term, but they are consistent with the perspective we outline here. Each account shows ways in which women continue to define religion, negotiate boundaries, and sustain changes through their everyday practice; they reflect enactments of historical possibilities.

Overview of Chapters

This book can be read in multiple ways. Readers who are primarily interested in learning about the diverse ways in which Hinduism and Islam are practiced in South Asia and the United States can read the personal accounts in each chapter, beginning with chapter 2. For those interested in Hinduism in India, chapters by Anjana Narayan, Bandana Purkayastha, Shanthi Rao, and Neela Bhattacharya Saxena describe a variety of practices in the north, east, and south of India. For those interested in Hinduism in Nepal, Bidya Ranjeet and Shobha Hamal Gurung offer two different accounts based on practices of their communities. Providing accounts of Islam in Pakistan,

Aysha Saeed, Parveen Talpur, and Rafia Zakaria offer three types of experiences that do not fit the homogenized versions of Pakistani Islam that are featured in the media. Elora Halim Chowdhury and Selina Jamil describe Islam in Bangladesh. As with the differences between Hinduism in India and Nepal, there are differences in the living of Islam in Bangladesh and Pakistan. Collectively, these chapters show significant diversity of beliefs and practices and offer glimpses of the different sociohistorical circumstances in which these practices developed.

Equally important, the chapters depict blurred religious boundaries. Bidya Ranjeet's chapter is particularly important because her community—the Newars—is not only Hindu but also Buddhist. Even though we have classified chapters according to accounts of Islam or Hinduism, there is significant overlap, for instance, between Bandana Purkayastha's chapter on Hinduism and Selina Jamil's chapter on Islam. Similarly, Neela Bhattacharya Saxena's account of folk religions showcases, as does Ahmed's work (2002), a continuum of practices in Hinduism and Islam.

All of the chapters—those listed above and the chapters by Salma Kamal, Shweta Majumdar, and Monoswita Saha—describe the authors' experiences in the United States. The authors live in the American East, Midwest, and West, and the politics of these locales are evident in their accounts.

Readers who are interested in situating these personal ethnographic accounts within academic debates can read the subsection interpretative intervention chapters (chapters 9 and 17) for the theoretical framework. These two chapters and the concluding chapter on human rights and religion provide ways of fitting these accounts into academic debates.

The chapters are presented in two sections to highlight two overlapping dimensions of gendered experience; however, the chapters were not written to emphasize one or another aspect of experience. Just as interviews are arranged and presented to support or challenge some theoretical viewpoint, the chapters are organized to insert a theoretical framework for reading these accounts. From the chapter authors' perspective—even though many of them are well known academics themselves—the emphasis is on communicating the lived experience of their religion.

Because boundaries are central to discussions of traditions and gender, the first set of chapters are arranged to illustrate boundaries. The chapters by Bandana Purkayastha, Selina Jamil, Parveen Talpur, and Bidya Ranjeet blur boundaries between religions. Neela Bhattacharya Saxena further describes the syncretism evident in folk traditions that contribute to this idea of blurred boundaries not only between religions but also between religious and secular life. These five chapters, along with the chapters by Salma Kamal and Monoswita Saha, reflect the sociopolitical boundaries that are relevant for understanding religions. Kamal's and Saha's chapters additionally highlight their experiences as American citizens after the immigrant generation, who are, nonetheless, racial outsiders in the United States.

The second set of chapters dwells on religions, practices, and resistances, often focusing on changing boundaries. Chapters by Anjana Narayan, Shanthi Rao, Shobha Gurung, Elora Chowdhury, Aysha Saeed, and Rafia Zakaria describe how religious traditions are a source of disciplined action in a variety of social justice issues. They describe and emphasize a common theme, reaching out to people of different cultures, religions, and race groups and establishing common ground with them. Some of the activism is familiar, such as working for pan-ethnic groups, participating in organized protests, and working to challenge domestic violence; other forms are more unobtrusive, such as resisting incursions of authoritarian forms of religion in community life or learning to quietly share multiple religious traditions within the same household. In addition, a chapter by Shweta Majumdar shows how Dalit (low-caste Hindu) groups are organizing in the United States and worldwide to claim their human rights, including the right to religion.

Notes

1. Katherine Mayo's book *Mother India*—with its descriptions of Indian male sexual predators and servile female victims—not only provided an argument for continued British colonial presence in India, but also influenced how legislators considered "Hindoo" migrants—a race term used to classify present day Indians, Pakistanis, and Bangladeshis—during discussions of the Citizenship Bill in the US Senate (Sinha 1998). Mayo's book continued to be

published as recently as the 1980s (Sinha 1998). Miriam Schneider's book, a classic of second-wave feminism, influenced academic theories for decades. Despite recent shifts in feminism toward intersectionality, the idea of the subordinated Third World woman who is a victim of her patriarchal culture and who needs to be assimilated into modern social norms continues to frame many academic discourses. The continuing popularity of Deepa Mehta's film *Water* (2005), which shows the condition of a specific group of Bengali Hindu widows in the early twentieth century, is a commentary on Indian women in women's studies circles and is a testimony to the continuing power of the racialized, gendered frameworks popularized by Mayo and Schneider. Huntington's thesis, which emphasizes a similar framework for looking at the world, is grounded in more contemporary events. His ideas are relentlessly discussed in the media, and have been used as a justification for foreign and domestic surveillance and security policies. The power of Huntington's selective ideas is apparent in some recent events. Liptak (2008) reports, "[T]he Archbishop of Canterbury [said] recently that a Western legal system should make room for the Shariah, or Islamic law. When the archbishop, spiritual leader of the world's 80 million Anglicans, commented in a radio interview that such accommodations were unavoidable, critics conjured images of stonings and maimings, overwhelming his more modest point." (3) The Archbishop did not propose to introduce Islamic criminal laws to Britain, he was simply talking about divorces where both sides have to agree to the arbitration of a religion tribunal, which is similar to the arbitration by Christian and Jewish tribunals that already operate in Britain. The press coverage of Ayaan Hirsi Ali's statements such as, "Islam is a political ideology . . . it is expanionist and totalitarian. . . . The liberals and moderates are in jail and in exile" (Conde Nast Traveller 2008, 14), or the repeated use of Barak Obama's middle name Hussein (Luo 2008), are examples of this same pattern of rejection.

2. Abdul Gaffar Khan, also known as the Frontier Gandhi, led nonviolent protests of Muslims against the British (Khan 2007). Nobel Peace Prize winner Mohammed Yunus, the founder of the Bangladesh-based Grameen Bank, is the pioneer of micro-credit lending to women. Mukhtaran Mai is the fearless woman from Pakistan who challenged her rapists through the courts and by bringing international attention to the cause of other voiceless, invisible victims of hypermasculine norms (see Mukhtaran 2007). Bachni Davi is one of the leaders and initiators of the Chipko movement in India, a nonviolent struggle against environmental degradation and human rights to uphold local knowledge systems (see Sen 1990). Sehba Husain is one of the organizers of the female chickaan workers in Lucknow as part of the Self Employed Women's Association (SEWA) in India. Ela Bhatt is the Gandhian lawyer and trade unionist who helped shape and establish SEWA (Rose 1993). Shabana Azmi is an actress, public intellectual, and Member of the Indian Parliament.

Among her many public acts of activism was her challenge to conservative mullahs as they tried to impose outdated interpretations of the Koran.

3. Although Hinduism and Islam are perceived as new immigrant religions by most people, Indian migration to the United States occurred in the nineteenth and early twentieth centuries. Most of the migrants were Sikh males. Encounters with Hinduism appear in the work of transcendentalists such as Emerson and Thoreau, and Swami Vivekananda lectured on Hinduism in many parts of the United States in the late nineteenth century (Burke 1986; Purkayastha and Narayan forthcoming). However, a ban on Asian—including Hindoo—migration virtually stopped Hindus, Muslims, and Sikhs from migrating to the United States from 1917 to 1965. Thus, the recent South Asian American Hindus and Muslims appear to be new migrants. Muslims now make up 0.6% of the American population and Hindus 0.4% (Pew Forum 2008). According to some estimates there are 6 million Muslims in the United States, 33% of Muslims are from South Asia originally (CAIR 2003; Mujahid 2001). There are approximately 2 million South Asian ethnic people in the United States, according to the data of the 2000 Census.

4. Fundamentalist groups use different ideologies to maintain gender hierarchies. Some fundamentalists, such as Al Qaeda or Taliban, eschew the sight and presence of women outside the confines of homes. Enforcement of veiling, restriction of mobility, and control of sexuality become central ways in which gender hierarchies are maintained (Imam 1991; Mernissi 1987). Other fundamentalists insist on the "essential nature of women" and "traditional family values" to define the role of men as protectors and guardians to maintain gender hierarchies. Some Hindu fundamentalist groups use a different tactic, such as asserting the strength and symbolic importance of "their women." Although the widespread availability of strong goddess symbols is an accurate reflection of Hinduism, an analysis of how this strength is supposed to be exercised in real life shows that women are supposed to be strong because they are keepers of tradition. In this role they are expected to react ferociously, even violently, against the practitioners of other religions (Narayan 2006).

5. Because a vast, multilingual literature on religious texts and related issues has been produced over centuries in South Asia, our lack of focus on texts in these countries should not be seen as a lack of existing literature in that region.

6. For instance, a seminal book by Tagore, which several authors refer to in this book, is titled *Religions of Man*. When it was translated in the early twentieth century, "Man" was the common term for people. The original Bengali term is best translated "Religion of Humans," which would also be more appropriate in today's world.

7. Because Hindu and Muslim fundamentalist groups often use the term *Western feminism* (which is used to indicate all feminism) to construct a vision

of "foreign influences" on all women's groups that agitate for empowerment, it is important to point out that our theoretical classification of Western feminists does not rely on ethnocentric boundaries. Instead, it points out how, in any society, some women are privileged and restricted because of their class, race, ethnicity, citizenship, religion, and related statuses, and how their academic work becomes problematic if they do not examine how they generalize their positions onto all women.

PART I

*Religion, Gender,
Boundaries*

2

Transgressing the Sacred-Secular, Private-Public Divide

Bandana Purkayastha

This fall, like the previous 22 years of my residency in the United States, I spent a weekend celebrating Durga puja with other Bengalis in Connecticut and Massachusetts. This *sarbojanin* puja (worship by a collective) is mainly celebrated in public spaces in Kolkata, although, prior to the independence of India in 1947, there were more home-based Durga pujas. The partition of India into Hindu and Muslim majority nation-states led to massive relocations of people and the destruction of the social and economic networks that supported home-based pujas. In independent India, with a few exceptions, people of different localities contribute money for their *sarbojanin* Durga puja. Intricately decorated bamboo and cloth edifices (*pandals*) are built on public roads, and the images of the goddess and her family are worshipped for four days.

We have managed to enact the public part of this puja in the United States, by organizing it in church halls or school auditoriums that we rent for a weekend. We decorate the hall on Friday evening, temporarily making it a Bengali space. We play Bengali music, and women and men set up the images for the next day. The priests are people from the community. The last priest was a medical doctor; the current priest is a scientist. Many years ago, one priest wanted to restrict the helpers of the priest to Brahmins only.[1] This priest was promptly replaced by another person who would not make such caste distinctions. The pujas are performed on Saturday morning and Sunday afternoon. The puja is led by a male priest; the *stree achar* (women's rituals) are led by women. On Saturday evening, we organize cultural programs; Bengalis (Hindus and Muslims) perform in and attend this event. On Sunday afternoon, people ritually embrace each other, and younger people touch the feet of elders. Plaintive songs of farewells are played on the audio system. Then the decorations are dismantled, and the images returned to their wooden containers and transported back to someone's house for safekeeping until the next year.

I have been asked why Bengalis choose to hold their pujas outside temples, even when there are temples nearby. There are cultural and spiritual reasons for this. First, the image of the demon-slaying Durga does not fit easily with the benign gods and goddesses featured in most Hindu temples in the United States. Second, Bengalis are non-vegetarian, and no compromise needs to be made when ordering festive foods to accommodate vegetarian Indians who predominate in US temples. Third, and this is the core principle, holding the puja in a neutral public space makes it easy for Bengali Muslims (from India and Bangladesh) to come to the cultural function because it is not in a Hindu-designated place. Some Muslim families come to the pujas; some help out preparing the Prasad. Muslim and Hindu Bengalis still share a culture, and keeping the avenues open to foster this relationship is more valuable than building larger temples and mosques. Thus, the boundaries between sacred spaces and secular ones (temples vs. school or church halls), between who is Hindu and who is Muslim, who is Indian and who is Bangladeshi, who is Brahmin and who is not, is diluted in this form of religious practice.

This event should not be interpreted as a triumph of multiculturalism in modern United States, but a testimony to religious freedom in the West that is the staple of discourses about clashing civilizations. Although we have been able to work out ways of sharing space for Durga puja with churches or schools, this essentially is a private arrangement between principled parties. This year we allowed a Christian group to hold their prayers on Sunday morning in the hall we rented because they had no place to go. But this sharing is not a general trend. We also have been asked to leave another facility where officials were unhappy about the smell of curry after we had our event dinners. More importantly, unlike the well-recognized

Christmas holiday, we have no right to take a day off from work (unless we use one of our personal days) to celebrate this much-loved community event on the actual days according to the Bengali calendar. As I discuss later, we have only managed to negotiate interstitial social spaces to practice our religion.

I begin my essay with these observations because I had not expected to encounter any barriers to living my religion when I moved to the United States from India. I was raised in a nonfaith-based, nonritualistic Hindu tradition that does not require regular gathering at any temple, mediation of priests, any specific set of rituals, or adherence to a set of rules defined in a book. My way of practicing religion is to live according to a core principle I share with other Hindus. We all acknowledge the centrality of *dharma*—a word implying the essential nature of things (as a noun), and a moral duty (as a verb). The religion of humans, *manava dharma* (or in Bengali colloquial terms, *manusher dharma*), is about understanding and practicing how to become more human by getting in touch with the divine in ourselves. This is not divinity in the sense one becomes a *superior* being; it means the individual has to cultivate and express those qualities that take her/him beyond narrowly defined physical and social selves. Dharma implies living life in a way that reflects our connectedness to a greater essence/energy/universe called Brahman (Nirbedananda 1979).[2]

Since I do not need any exclusivist congregation to practice Hinduism, I had not thought about the many ways in which sociopolitical rules can impose on religious freedoms until I came to the United States. Having come up against such boundaries, I am very conscious of the way in which my religious freedom is impeded. In order to explain these boundaries, I begin with an overview of the practices with which I was raised and the principles by which I expect to live. My account of being a Hindu is interspersed with the easy cosmopolitan and radical intellectual culture of Kolkata (formerly Calcutta) where I was raised. It is also interspersed with the history, politics, and culture of Bengal, the cultural region that is now split between India (West Bengal) and Bangladesh. I conclude with an account of trying to fit Hinduism within the religious landscape of the United States.

Blurring the Sacred and Secular

Naming a religion often gives it a degree of exclusivity. The Hinduism I practice (in India and the United States) has blurred boundaries; it does not fit neatly into bureaucratic definitions of religion. My parents did not believe in religious orthodoxies.[3] My father was involved in the nationalist uprising against the British. Like his peers in the movement, he rejected class- and caste-based distinctions because he saw such rejection as a valued political principle for postindependence Indian society. His political principles overlapped with my mother's family's way of practicing religion. They followed the teachings of the Ramakrishna-Vivekananda-Sarada order (also known as Ramakrishna Mission) ever since my grandfather received *dikhsha* (initiation as a follower) from Sri Ma Sarada. This movement had begun to influence Bengali religious ethos since the late nineteenth century, challenging all forms of religious, caste, and gender exclusiveness. Ramakrishna was a Brahmin; his principle spokesperson, Vivekananda, was Sudra. Vivekananda and Ramakrishna's wife, Sarada Ma, and their followers accepted people of all different castes as their disciples. Ramakrishna's Hinduism is concisely expressed in one homily: That which quenches our thirst is called water or *pani* or *jal;* religion is one, and people give it different names. Vivekananda insisted on putting service to people above rituals and dogmas. This idea of service to people emanates from the fundamental principle of dharma, and it is a way to realize and link one's life to the greater universe of life forms to be a part of it.

This overlap of secular and sacred principles led my parents to reject rituals and customs that maintain distinctions and hierarchies. My sisters and I received very little formal exposure to faith-based ritualistic forms of religion, yet we were well aware of multiple ways of practicing religion within the same family. We had a set of *thakurs* (a sex-neutral term for gods and goddesses) on a shelf at home. These thakurs—a panoply of deities, real people such as Ramakrishna, Sarada Ma, and Vivekananda, our grandparents, as well as inanimate objects like a tub of Ganga water—were used mainly by a bachelor uncle for *his* daily rituals. My father often recited from the Upanishads (in Sanskrit) at dawn. Although knowledge of Sanskrit and the Vedas or Upanishad are the purview of Brahmin men in more orthodox families, we just picked up these gender-neutral prayers because we heard him so regularly. When we were little children, we also accompanied my maternal grandmother on her visits to Belur Math, the main center of the Ramakrishna Mission, to meet the monks and attend the evening *aarti* at the temple. This temple, as Swami Tattwajnananda (2001) has described, is situated on the banks of the river Ganga (Hooghly) and is explicitly syncretic in design, combining the architecture of Buddhism (the gate), Islam (the domes), Hindu (the circulating paths leading to the center), and Christianity (the congregation hall). Among the hundreds of books we possessed were children's stories about the Ramakrishna movement and children's versions of the Hindu epics, Ramayana and Mahabharata, which many Hindus venerate. My mother had a healthy disrespect for Rama (the hero of Ramayana) for abandoning his wife Sita for political expediency; therefore, unlike many other Hindus, we never thought of these books as sacred. Thus, without any overt lessons about challenging caste and gender distinctions, our parents managed to impart a series of humane principles to us through their everyday practice.

Outside of our family, we encountered many other ways of practicing Hinduism. Some of our Hindu neighbors practiced more ritual-dependent forms of Hinduism, and they organized regular pujas in their homes. And, throughout the year, we were drawn to the public pujas. In Bengal, all the public pujas focus on female deities.[4] The year began with worshipping Saraswati, the goddess of learning, in the spring. She is widely worshipped in individual homes as well. Little children are formally introduced to writing after a ritual called *hathe-khari* (literally, chalk-in-hand). Older students give their books to the priest who puts them in front of the goddess. The books, musical instruments, and other tools of learning are worshipped as an extension of the deity. The biggest and most elaborate was Durga puja (the one I described in the previous section). In preparation for this puja, skilled craftsmen of Kumartuli (a specialized caste of people) in Kolkata spend months creating images of the goddess and her family. Depending on the resources of the group that commissions the images, each image can be double or triple the size of the average human. In Hindu mythology, Goddess Durga is the embodiment of strength and power. According to a legend, when one particular *asur* (demon) got too strong for the male gods, they collectively appealed to Durga to vanquish the demon. They showered her with their most potent weapons, and she left to confront the evil force that was overpowering the gods. The form of Durga that is worshipped in Bengal represents this tableau: Durga—standing on her attendant lion and her 10 hands carrying different weapons—with the virile Asur—who has partly emerged from the body of a buffalo that is pinned down by the force of her trident—is semiprone at her feet. This tableau also shows Durga's children: Lakshmi, the goddess of wealth; Saraswati, the goddess of learning; Kartik, the god of war; and Ganesh, the god of benevolence. Each deity is shown with the animals and plants associated with them, symbolizing a deep environmental message about the interconnectedness of the universe.[5]

Durga puja was popularized in Bengal in the nineteenth century as part of a radical transformation of society (Kumar 1993). In order to break away from the caste control of Brahmins who presided over the sacred precincts of temples, Durga pujas were organized to create a space for people of all backgrounds. To this day, with rare exceptions, Durga is never a permanent deity in a temple in Bengal. Her clay image is created before each puja, ritually invested with divinity, and, at the end of five days, the image is divested of divinity and immersed in the waters of a river as a symbolic immersion with the core elements of the universe. Even though the priest is a Brahmin, Durga's worship includes roles for people of different castes (those who make the image; those who provide the materials for the puja; those who make music and art, etc.) and different groups of men and women. The puja requires water from five rivers and earth from various locations, including the doorstep of prostitutes. Symbolically and functionally, the puja emphasizes three messages: the connections of humans to other animate and inanimate things in the universe; the need to transcend socially created hierarchies in order to recognize interconnections with *all* human beings; and the need to understand that gods are imagined by humans and that these gods are merely reflective of an undifferentiated Brahman. In a quiet way, this puja has contributed to the dilution of gender, class, and caste boundaries among Bengalis.

During Durga puja, each neighborhood and club in Kolkata tries to outdo one another through the form, material, and beauty of the images and pandals they commission. The city shuts down for several days, and all schools and workplaces are closed for a couple of weeks. As young children, we received new clothes from relatives to wear each day (a different outfit in the morning, and one at night if we were lucky); and our parents bought clothes for our younger relatives as well as a large number of needy people. Like thousands of people who tour the city in their finery viewing images of the goddess, we were allowed to go out in groups, without adult supervision, at a fairly young age; so Durga puja also represented a symbolic rite of passage toward adulthood. After the *dashami* (the fourth day of these public celebrations), these images are taken off in a procession and immersed in the river Hooghly. The pandals are left standing for one more week to celebrate Lakshmi puja. After the ritual immersion of Lakshmi, the whole edifice is dismantled. Between dashami and Kali puja, families and friends visit each other for *bijoya,* a ritual time for renewing ties of love and caring; young people formally visit and ritually touch the feet of all their older relatives and close family friends. Each family prepares special foods to welcome the visitors. Thus, the celebrations stretch for several days.

The religious celebrations would end with a bang, literally, with Kali puja in November. Kali is the dark, naked goddess who is worshipped with a garland of skulls around her neck. Associated with the Tantra tradition, Kali has become "the" patron goddess of Bengal. Her temple in Kolkata is one of the significant points of pilgrimage for Hindus. Kali also represents strength and power of a more fierce, unrestricted variety than Durga's power. Kali puja means a night or two of incessant fireworks. We would light our own silent sparklers on our rooftop, while the more intrepid young men would ignite noisemakers on the streets.

However, our religious awareness did not stop at any exclusive Hindu boundary. The religious landscape of Bengal consists of several public celebrations, patterns of worship within religious buildings (temples, mosques, churches, gurudwaras, fire temples, viharas, etc.), and, depending on the religion, home-based rituals. We were raised in an area where Hindus, Muslims, and Christians lived in close proximity. The roads in the neighborhoods were not exclusively Hindu public spaces. There was a mosque behind our house, and we awoke every day to the sounds of the muezzin calling devout Muslims to prayer at dawn. Shia processions to commemorate the deaths of Imam Hussain during Muharrum were very much a part of our regular life. Like Durga puja, roads were closed to make way for the bigger processions. Eid prayers, greetings, and meetings often spilled into the streets. Firecrackers during Shab-e-barat were as much a part of our taken-for-granted world as the firecrackers during Kali puja.[6] So too with Christian celebrations, we were very used to hearing church bells on Sundays and seeing a crèche set up at the end of our street during Christmas.

We grew up assuming it was natural for people of all religions to have the formal time and access to public spaces to celebrate. We shared in these varied festivities because people generously shared their special foods with us. We looked forward to eating mutton biriyani during Eid and cake and special cookies during Christmas. Since we went to an English medium school with Muslim, Parsi, Jewish, Christian, and Sikh children, we were often invited to partake in their feasts. I remember being amazed at the order and organization of a Sikh Langar when hundreds of people are fed—served with a great deal of humility and respect—by members of the community regardless of their economic status. By the time I was in college, I had gone to Christian church services, the Golden Temple (the main Sikh gurudwara in Amritsar), Buddhist temples, and the places commemorating a number of Sufi saints, such as Hazrat Nizamuddin's tomb in Delhi (also see Sengupta 2006).[7]

Hinduism: Working out a Personal Version

I discovered Hindu philosophy as I read Nobel Laureate Rabindranath Tagore's essays on religion, humanism, and ultimately his translations of the Upanishads, Kabir, Baul songs, and Sikh bhajans during my Bengali literature class in high school (Tagore 1961a). During my years at Presidency College, I had the opportunity to travel to many corners of India for fieldwork, thus experiencing India's immense religious and cultural diversity.[8] Later, I was fortunate to encounter a remarkable network of college students, physicists, university and management professors, corporate executives, homemakers, and a monk at Vivekananda Nidhi, an organization that had embarked on a unique study and activism project to rekindle a focus on holistic values, which were deeply ecological in character, to get beyond narrow religious boundaries. We studied religious texts—Hindu, Buddhist, Zen, Islam, Sikhism, Christian—and a range of other books, such as Fritjhof Capra's treatise on the links between the world of quantum mechanics and subatomic particles/waves and Asian philosophical thinking (Yuktananda and Guha 1989).

These varied experiences helped me develop a more nuanced understanding of the idea of dharma as connectedness, and of the Upanishadic principle *Tvat Tamasi* ("That Art Thou"), which implies being one with Brahman (Prabhabananda and Manchester 1957). I also discovered that these principles, expressed in gender- and caste-neutral language, do not identify any religious, gender, or caste boundaries that exclude anyone from its purview. It was equally clear that at any given time, Hinduism represents a dynamic constellation of diverse perspectives and practices on living dharma.

Tagore's perspective (as opposed to the writings of other religious scholars) not only distills the highly erudite Upanishads, but—breaking away from a narrow, rigid Vedic perspective—it draws from folk sources to explain the essence of dharma. Among his principle sources were the Bauls, often uneducated men and women. Tagore was equally drawn to Sufi saints and Sikh seers. In his collection of essays, Religion of Man (*manusher dharma*/religion of humans in its original Bengali), Tagore emphasizes the connections between the abstract Brahman and the sacredness of everyday life, and about conscious, joyful living. Such joyful living brings us closer to sat-chit-ananda (knowledge-consciousness-bliss). Individuals and groups choose different paths for achieving this state of joyful living.

A Hindu man in a village in India might acknowledge his ties to Brahman by praying to the rishis (seers), devas (gods), pitri (forefathers), nri (human), and bhuta (plants and animals) each day, while the scientific-minded cosmopolitan woman might dwell on the image of a universe of swirling atoms, which, in spite of the apparent chaos, represents connections and stability (Tagore 1961b, 1913a).

Most of all, Tagore spoke out repeatedly against barriers imposed by religions, narrow nationalisms, ethnocentrism, racism, casteism, gender dichotomies, and other such social exclusionary forms, even when they were disguised as freedom. Tagore argued that rather than focusing on "timeless traditions" or reifying rituals conducted in specially designated spaces ("bhajan pujan sadhan aradhana, somostho thak pore, andhokare ghorer kone keno achesh ore?"/Why do you sit in a dark corner by yourself chanting these prayers?), humans are invited each day to participate in a joyful universe ("jogote anando jogge aamaer nimartran"). It is up to the individual to develop the ever-searching soul of a bride who seeks her union with her lover/destiny/god amid the mundane routines of each day ("poran aamar, bodhur beshe chole, chiro swamayambora"/my soul, dressed as a bride, travels forever for her union with her chosen lover) (Tagore 1913b).

In sum, there are four aspects of Hinduism that grew into the central pillars of my religious life. First, I value the blurred religious boundaries, the tradition drawn from Buddhism, Hinduism, Islam, and other religions. It teaches, above all, to value connectedness with the continuum of living and nonliving aspects of the universe. Second, overlapping with the first point, this religious framework teaches an individual to live with diversity. In religious matters, it talks about four ways of attaining dharma depending on a person's emotional and intellectual bent and her/his stage of life: An individual may follow the path of faith and worship (bhakti-yoga), or one of regulated practice (raj-yoga), or through excellence in work (karma-yoga), or through the acquisition of knowledge (gyana-yoga). And I am expected to understand and appreciate the fact that these paths may characterize any religion; hierarchies and ethnocentric thinking about the superiority of *my religion is better than your religion* has no place in this scheme. Third, I value the amalgam of lessons from female and male seers, which valorize principles such as care, compassion, and sobriety that are associated with feminine principles, over hyperrational, glamorous, and masculine religious traditions (Nandy 1993). I value the gender- and sexuality-transcending symbolism of *ardhanariswara*, the merging of feminine and male principles in each person. Fourth, it is a religion embedded in a life of pleasures and pains; it requires no edifices, no gatekeepers, no separation of sins and good deeds, and no rejection of the pleasure or diverse experiences of life. And it expects us to change during different stages of our lives—as students, as people forming families, as householders transferring family responsibilities to others, and in the last stage, as individuals who disengage from all family obligations—recognizing the dynamism of humans in a changing universe. As these four points indicate, this version of religion is more universal than reflective of any exclusively bounded religion. This is what makes my description of religion similar to Selina Jamil's (see her chapter on growing up in Bangladesh), though we are from different countries, and we outwardly belong to different religions.

Reconstructing Religion in the United States

Since I was not brought up in a faith-based religious tradition, I expected my migration to another secular democracy—the United States—to be a nonissue in terms of my ability to practice Hinduism. I was aware of the Ramakrishna Mission centers—Vedanta Societies—that had been gradually established after Vivekananda's visit to the United States at the turn of the twentieth century (Burke 1996; Radice 1999; Sen 2000). I knew there were some temples in New England, but I did not feel any need to visit temples regularly. I did not expect to become so conscious of a bounded religious identity that would constantly define me, regardless of my own beliefs and practices. As a sociologist, I can identify several factors, some arising from the US mainstream and others from practices among sections of the Indian American community, which contribute to the kinds of boundaries I experience as a Hindu in America.

The Limits of US Secularism

I recall realizing, with great surprise, that I no longer had religious holidays for my events in the United States. Without ever giving it much thought, I simply assumed that, as a secular country, the United States would provide the same institutionalized opportunities for minorities to practice their religion. I was influenced by the Indian version of secularism that allows diverse groups equal freedom (see Bhargava 2005 for a discussion on different kinds of secularisms). Despite being a society where the vast majority of people are Hindus (much as the United States has a vast majority of Christians), small groups in India—Muslims who make up 10–15% of the population along with Christians, Sikhs, Buddhists, Zorastrians, and Jains who make up less than 2% of the population each—get holidays to follow their practices. And they have the right to worship in designated places or on the streets and follow their religio-cultural practices surrounding births, marriages, and inheritances. For instance, when people die, they can cremate, bury, or leave their dead for the birds. That lack of insistence on a homogenized set of rules for all religions provides a great deal more freedom than the assimilating framework in the United States, where people are forced to live according to the organizational structures preset by the dominant religious group.

Similarly, the laws against practicing religions in public spaces makes sense if worship is solely seen as something that happens within defined private spaces, such as churches (or homes). Religious practices that are not church-, mosque-, or temple-based—for instance Durga puja or Muhharam processions—are legislated out of the public sphere. These restrictions on public celebrations means children (and adults) in the United States get too few opportunities to savor the sights, sounds, smells, colors, and sheer joy of the festivals of different religious groups that was so much a part of the lives of many contributors of this book.

The lack of recognized holidays for other religions adds to this marginalization. Those of us who practice minority religions have to contend with the invisibility of our religions in public discourse (beyond linking these to questions of national security or debates about clashing civilizations), and we have to work twice as hard to celebrate our religious events. We have compromised by reducing Durga puja to two days over a weekend, because most people do not have the autonomy to seek time off from work for religious events on the appropriate days according to the Bengali calendar. Most people, young and old, are under pressure to conform to school, college, and work deadlines. Even when they are able to negotiate private arrangements to take time off, there is a continuing penalty for being part of another religion: We have to work harder to make up for lost time. Every time another colleague organizes a weekend event that is in my field of academic expertise, without bothering to check about possible conflicts with religious events, I am reminded of my position as a member of a minority religion, since my status as a professor does not seem to extend to respecting my religiocultural human rights. The absence of the particular type of secular tradition and freedoms that many contributors of this book and I were raised with—the taken-for-granted assumption that there are at least seven or eight religions, that people worship differently, and that it is right and proper that they have the equal rights to do so—keeps me very aware of my religious outsider status in the United States.[9]

The restrictions embedded in the US type of secularism often become burdensome because of continuing racism in this country. This racism operates through the efforts of some overzealous, bigoted groups and individuals. I continue to be pursued by evangelical groups who operate on the assumption that, as a person of Indian origin, I have to be an ignorant, subservient woman. Such groups try hard to convince me to go to their church and learn about "the true religion that would empower me." They have lectured me on their version of the true nature of Hinduism where women-killing (sati and dowry deaths), false-idol worship, and pre-modern animism are key components. They are unable to comprehend that I am extremely knowledgeable about gender and religion (theirs and mine). It is also futile for me to point out that incidents of sati in India in the last century are a thousand-fold lower than incidents of polygamous marriages—for instance, among Mormons—in the United States. Such groups are determined to save my soul based on their absolute faith; their orientalist beliefs do not change because of an immigrant woman's opinion.

Although I have developed a whole range of ways to rebuff such people, I worry about the lack of contact these people have with people and practices of other religions in public space. Their ideas remain enmeshed in the ethnocentric stereotypes because it is *solely* created and sustained by whatever is imagined within their closed communities. Other radical church leaders, who ignore the lessons of Christianity about humility, respect, and tolerance, continue to spew their hate-filled messages about other religions, such as Hinduism, Buddhism, and Islam, often characterizing these as religions of darkness (Grillo 2001). People like myself are always in a bind in the United States: Our protests against hate-filled messages bring more publicity to these messengers, and they revel in the publicity; if we choose silence, the stereotypes they circulate appear to be true. And we always remain aware that any politicized campaign by these groups against the people who let us rent spaces for Durga puja could result in our losing the facility for the following year.

The racial imagery about Third World women (subordinated, nonempowered women) that is circulated endlessly through secular media and some sections of academia also erodes our authority as Third World females to speak on our religions. As Neela Bhattacharya Saxena points out in her chapter, unless we present ourselves as victims of patriarchal religious practices, we are almost never asked to speak publicly about our religions. It is as though our continued affiliation with our ("not-quite-modern") religion is a sign of our traditionalism, subordination, and lack of understanding of real empowerment. The press invariably prefers to talk to temple-based male leaders as "the authority" on matters of religion. Academic studies focus on the lack of women in temple hierarchies, without any attempt to find out how important temples are to the lives of Hindus. And academic scholarship, which increasingly focuses *only* on Hindu fundamentalism, or Hindu-Muslim riots, without studying the mechanisms through which Hindus and Muslim continue to sustain peace, often unwittingly contribute to sustaining the orientalist tropes about our religions.

Recent political efforts to erode the walls between faith-based religion and state affairs has exacerbated these structural constraints.

Since faith-based groups are now being allowed to become a primary conduit for social justice efforts, it erodes the space for other kinds of groups. The current political initiative requires each of us to define our faiths, even if we do not follow faith-based paths. Such requirements confer disproportionate authority to Hindu temples and temple-based leaders to get these monies and act for the Hindus, while eroding the legitimacy of diverse practices that make up the Hindu world. And, people's faith and national origin also is being used for security profiling in ways that keep us constantly aware of our religious identities (e.g., Kelly 2001; Khanna 2001; Sengupta 2006).

Temples, Hierarchies, and Reconstructionists

Ever since their migration in large numbers in the mid-1960s, Hindus have been establishing temples in the United States to carve out spaces where they can practice their religion. For many Hindu groups in India, as Shanthi Rao's chapter describes, going to temples is part of their regular routine; for them temples are an appropriate religious space for their faith-based worship. But because of the insistence that all religious matters be moved to temples (or mosques or churches), temples face the additional challenge of balancing the needs of all kinds of Hindus with very diverse deities and religious events. There are usually long periods of negotiations about which gods and goddesses are to be represented in each temple. In the end, few temples feature the unrestricted power of female goddesses, represented by Durga and Kali; only benign versions of goddesses are depicted, usually as wives of gods.

The overwhelming dominance of male deities with female consorts in American temples reflects two intersecting forces. In many parts of India, it is more typical to worship male deities, and the laws of averages lead to the overrepresentation of male deities. The other reason is that temple boards self-censure with an eye to how they are going to be received by the mainstream. If, for instance, a temple featuring the goddess Kali—with her nakedness, her garland of dripping skulls, and her stance on the male god Shiva—made the headline news in the local media, how would the worshippers of such a deity be perceived? So the depictions of tradition in temples reflect the intersections of patriarchy and racism.

Temples are places for faith-based worship. In the absence of the right to practice religion elsewhere, temples become the de facto community centers for many Hindu Indians. People send their children to learn how to do puja as told by a Brahmin man, or how to lead a Hindu life as taught through Hindu Sunday schools set up in the temples. And a series of traditions, many of which are no longer widely practiced in the area of India I come from, such as the sacred thread ceremony for Brahmin men, are reemerging in the United States, much to the astonishment of my friends and family in Kolkata who consider such rituals to be early twentieth century relics. And Hindu practices are increasingly being presented as Indian culture, ignoring the right of other religionists to make such a culture.

Temples offer few spaces for most women to become authority figures. In India, female gurus coexist with temple priests and command the loyalty of thousands of people, as Neela Bhattacharya Saxena and Anjana Narayan describe in their chapters, but established temples are spaces where high-caste male authority prevails. While a few women are in prominent places on the boards of American Hindu temples (which has been interpreted as a sign of waning traditionalism by some academic scholars), there are typically very few professionally successful women in these positions. There are no American female gurus that I am aware of (though some female gurus from India visit their followers periodically). Professionally successful men, with few obligations to contribute to a second shift at home, often take on spokesperson roles in such organizations. Much of the organizing, cooking, cleaning, and community activities remain women's tasks. Overall, the altered social organization of Hinduism in the United States, where temples become the sole representatives of Hinduism, contributes to renewed class, caste, and gender distinctions that, in India, are balanced by the thousands of other choices people have to practice their versions of Hinduism.

The structural conditions in America, which encourage homogenized sets of practices and centralized authority through congregations, have been used by a rapidly growing religious industry that is hawking its brand of Hinduism. Mislabeled Hindu fundamentalism—a mislabeling because there is no singular set of fundamentals in Hinduism—these Hindutva proponents attempt to market a virulent brand of ultramasculine, authoritarian religiopolitics under the guise of establishing authentic Hinduism. There is a virulent strain of Hindu-ist politics in parts of India that has grown for the same reasons as Christian fundamentalism has grown in the United States and Islamic fundamentalism in the Middle East (Nandy 2005, 1993; Sarkar and Butalia 1995; Sehgal 2007). In the United States, Hindutva proponents use the feelings of dissatisfaction among Hindus who encounter unequal freedom to practice their religion to propose a new global Hinduism (Joshi 2006; Narayan 2006). They fund hate in India (Stop funding hate 2008) and are actively organizing in the United States to claim the voice of Hinduism. The relentless messages about subordinated women in the media serve as a central rallying principle of the Hindutva movement. Their Web sites discuss how authentic Hinduism (Hinduism undiluted by Islam or other religions) uniquely supports very high status for women. Such seemingly affirmative presentations of Hinduism are attractive to those who find few other outlets to challenge the racist images circulating in the mainstream (Kausalya 2006; also see Anjana Narayan's chapter in this book). Their actions violate the most basic human rights (for an example, see IIJG's Threatened Existence 2003).

The Hinduism of the Hindutva movement is exclusivist and ethnocentric. Going against Hinduism's dictum about diversity and connectedness, it encourages its practitioners to be antagonistic toward other religions, particularly Muslims. Their ethnocentric, masculine version of gender empowerment emphasizes different rights of women and men (a modern day "separate but equal" hierarchy). This model of gender is very different from the lessons of fluid Ardhanariswara (god as half-man, half-woman) in Hinduism. And, their version is directly opposite to the central principle of dharma (interconnection) expressed through the dictum *Tvat Tamasi,* or Tagore's notion of a joyful universe, or Vivekananda's call to serve *people* as the primary way of practicing dharma. Hindutva proponents often quote Vivekananda selectively by focusing on his exhortation to defend Hinduism to evoke the idea of a religion-under-siege. Conveniently overlooked in this version is Vivekananda's central message about serving *all* people (and, his temple at

Belur, which I described earlier, that enshrines the influence of many religions).[10] Nor is Vivekananda's dictum to serve all people followed when Hindutva proponents lash out against Dalits (see Shweta Majumdar's chapter). The kind of Hinduism I practice, with a conscious acknowledgment of the messages of Buddhist, Sufi, Sikh, and other saints, is exactly the kind of Hinduism the Hindutva proponents would like to stifle. Unable to control unruly Hindus who don't join their folds, Hindutva proponents have begun to demand that local school boards revise their history books to reflect a Hindutva version of true history of Indic civilizations as a way to influence future generations (Lal 2006).

Much like the religiobusinesses run by TV evangelists who have created new profitable religious consumer markets, there is a new industry for selling new texts, holding conferences and Hindu camps, and marketing artifacts of Hindu culture such as "om" signs. Thus far, the success of the Hindutva movement—to transform Hinduism from a decentralized, variegated practice-driven, change-oriented system of practicing spirituality to a masculine religion with a homogenous set of practices, distinctive boundaries, one congregation, recreated versions of single sacred texts, and a centralized authority structure—is restricted by an audience that still upholds the idea of diverse practices.

It could be argued that, given the varied nature of Hinduism, this emerging Hindutva can be accommodated under a broad umbrella of practices. These newly invented practices should coexist with the older, more androgynous principles and inclusive forms of practices that I have described earlier. But set as a minority religion within a context where faith-driven initiatives are becoming the framework for mainstream politics, and where the efforts of radical Christian fundamentalists to impose their beliefs in a variety of arenas breaks our everyday world into fragments by narrow domestic walls, such strident oppositional religious movements develop a certain resonance. And, as religion (and phenotype) becomes the new marker of demarcating true natives from naturalized citizens and new-generation natives, it becomes harder for people to maintain a set of religious practices with blurred boundaries embracing humanity in general instead of identifying with narrowly defined religiocultural groups.

Possible Religious Horizons

Given the multiple sources of religious bigotry I described above, is humane religious life still possible? Many of the values I hold dear—such as respect for multiple religious traditions, constantly striving to serve people (including activist work to reduce inequalities), finding ways to practice peaceful and mindful living, and not having to subordinate my intellectual understanding of the universe to a framework of unquestioning faith—are shared by a network of friends from Hindu, Christian, Jewish, Muslim, Buddhist, and other religions. My criticism of fundamentalist Christianity does not make me blind to the humane practices of other Christians. I am inspired by the history of social justice efforts by some Christian groups on behalf of the poorest, voiceless immigrants. The vast majority of the participants in the civil rights movement were inspired by the messages of humanity spread through black churches; their efforts and sacrifices opened the doors for me to come to the United States. The Quakers who went voluntarily to internment camps for the Japanese Americans were practicing these same Christian principles. These groups did not use the proximate suffering of others as an opportunity to proselytize about their religion as some groups have done recently (Baron 2006). Instead the motivation was to share in a common humanity, including the pain of injustices and deprivations. Such histories of doing are synonymous in my mind with living dharma. Whether it is an historical memory of Gandhi's marches in India in the early twentieth century, or those of the civil rights movement in the United States in the mid-twentieth century, or the sacrifices made by anti-apartheid participants—Christian, Muslim, atheist, Hindu—in the late twentieth century in South Africa, I can see dharma being enacted in a million ways.

Many religions teach me lessons in connecting with others. Each year, about the same time as Durga puja, I marvel at the humane principle that leads all Muslims who are more than 12 years of age, all over the world, regardless of class and sex, to participate in a month of dawn-to-dusk fasts so that they can actually experience some of the pains of deprivation felt by the poor. It always has seemed to me to be a more principled way of engaging in subsequent charitable contributions. Although I often contribute to humanitarian or charitable causes prompted by pity for the suffering of distant others, I do not meet the same high standard that prompts so many Muslims to try to experience the pain of living a deprived life as part of the act of giving. Recently my daughter participated in Ramadan fasts, for a very short period of time, when some Muslim students at her college suggested this might be an appropriate way to link their interest in blurring the boundaries between religions with their attempt to raise money for Darfur. Since she was not able to come home for Durga puja, she interpreted this fast as a way of enacting a principle, i.e., making an effort to reach beyond the boundaries she normally lives by to consciously identify with a larger humanity. Such activism, grounded in religion and humane in substance, helps us to combine the sacred and the secular in meaningful ways.

We try to uphold this principle through our own family practices; we continue to participate in a variety of religious practices—Satyanarayan pujas, visits to Ramakrishna Mission–inspired gatherings, Christmas celebrations, and Eid celebrations—even though we do not follow rituals ourselves. And we are proud of the fact that our combined families include Hindus of many castes, as well as Sikhs, Muslims, and Christians.

How do feminist principles fit into these religious horizons? I am very comfortable with situating myself within the long history of *formal* activism for women's rights and social justice that dates back at least to the early nineteenth century in India. This movement was not an exclusive movement of Hindus, nor was it a movement that was exclusively by women. Unlike the feminist movements in the United Kingdom and United States, the Indian movement always considered narrow nationalism, state roles, and colonialism as central influences in constructing gender hierarchies. As a woman of color in the United States, understanding the complex sources of the barriers I encounter are important to me. I have been fortunate to develop networks of feminist and human rights groups in several countries; groups that attempt to make sure human justice principles and actions are not framed in narrow nationalistic, civilizational, and ethnocentric terms. As a Bengali Hindu, I was raised, almost exclusively, with Durga, Kali, Lakshmi, and Saraswati. The symbolism of Shakti (female strength/power)—and the force of regeneration that arises from the twin forces of creation and destruction—colors my feminism with its specifically Hindu roots. The idea of ardhanariswara, a symbol of god as half-man, half-woman that insists I move beyond atomized notions of essentialized women and men, is very important to my thinking in militating against gender hierarchies.

These religious/spiritual ideas intersect with my academic training to hone my secular intellectual capacities to recognize and challenge the multiple ways in which many women's lives are restricted and injured in the name of religion. I can knowledgeably criticize sections of Hindus—men and women—who continue to evoke the thirteenth-century laws of Manu or other traditions to justify their violent behaviors toward women. I challenge Hindutva groups who finance and practice genocide against Muslims and lower-caste groups and try to frame it in terms of correcting history or establishing religion. I am equally critical of Islamic fundamentalists. Recently a friend's father was murdered by such a group for speaking out against growing fundamentalism in Bangladesh; it served as a stark, personal reminder of the dangers of the growing power of fundamentalism in different South Asian countries. I recognize the virulence of Christian fundamentalists in the United States, and I denounce their activities, too. As a sociologist, I can trace the paths through which their hate-filled actions get enacted as "neutral" public policies. My religious principles and my academic training overlap to shape my interest in understanding and exposing the inhumanity of exploitive economic systems. As I watch contemporary LGBT groups struggle for rights in the United States, I am reminded of the fluid sexuality described in Hindu traditions (Ruth 2000); perspectives that are largely invisible in the strident heteronormative claims by different groups of fundamentalists in the United States. Because I believe in human freedoms, I cannot be anything but a feminist. Hinduism structures how I think of my connections to a boundless universe. I practice Hinduism *and* feminism, finding these non-antithetical and without any need to guard the boundaries of versions that are linked to any exclusive foundations in a selected history.

The more universal, boundary-less *manusher dharma* shapes how I think about human ties and humane freedoms. The ongoing challenge is to resist exclusionary boundaries while holding onto humane principles and translating them into everyday action in multiple realms.

Notes

1. Euro-American textbooks typically describe the caste system as a four-fold, Hindu social hierarchy with Brahmins (typically the teachers, scholars) at the pinnacle, followed by the Kshatriyas (administrators, soldiers), the Vaishyas (traders, business people), and at the lowest rung, the Sudras (menials, servants, laborers). Caste distinctions started as a system of occupational specialization, but it quickly became a birth-defined hierarchy. One cannot achieve caste, so many Western scholars conclude there is no chance of moving up socially. The system, as it works on the ground, is more complicated. First, each caste is divided into hundreds of jatis whose exact social status depends on the local cultural region (see Srinivas 1962). A brahmin who performs pujas at funerals does not hold the same power as the Kshatriya king. At a social organizational level, caste is about power, and how much power a group can control depends on the landscape of power at the local level. Historically, Brahmins have controlled the power of knowledge, Kshatriyas political power, and Vaishyas the finances. These three have wielded enormous power over the last group, especially when they acted together, as they frequently have, to protect their social privileges (Kaviraj 1991). In modern India, the combination of caste-based organizing and the ability to gather political power adds another dimension to the operation of the caste system (Kothari 1970). This is why caste-like social organization is evident among Christians and Muslims in India (Kurien 2004; Syed 2002). Second, caste is also a patriarchal system. Women's caste is mainly based on the husband's or father's caste; in other words, half the population has the potential to take on and change castes. Arrangement of marriages is the primary means of gate-keeping for caste exclusivity. Third, caste-based distinctions are officially banned in India; however, the human rights violations against Dalits continue with impunity in parts of the country. Thus, caste, like other forms of social hierarchy, is a dynamic system that adapts itself to contemporary conditions to maintain the privileges of the powerful.

2. Words such as dharma or Brahman do not translate into English, because there is no equivalent social understanding that might be expressed through language.

3. There were several other caste/gender challenging rituals my parents, a Brahmin and a Baidya, rejected. Though they were Brahmins, my cousins were not initiated into sacred thread ceremonies to initiate them to male, caste-based statuses because my parents, as the eldest in the family, were responsible for setting the family norms. Dowry taking or giving was not allowed. When my father died, my mother performed the funeral service for him, while we—the female children—performed it for our mother.

4. The only male god who is worshipped is Biswakarma, the god of instruments and instrumentality. But Biswakarma puja is only performed in factories and workshops; it is not a puja for householders or neighborhoods. Biswakarma puja is marked by kite duels such as the one described in Khaled Hosseini's book *Kite Runner*.

5. Saraswati's attendant is the swan, which, supposedly, can filter the good from the filth, a quality essential for learning. Lakshmi's attendant is the owl, which can see in the dark, a skill necessary for handling wealth. Kartick's attendant is the peacock, which is gorgeous and deadly in its attacks. Ganesh's mouse reminds us of the value of the lowly rodents in the environmental chain.

6. Shab-e-barat is celebrated as a day of accounting of past deeds and a day of atonement in preparation for Ramadan by Indian Muslims. Houses are illuminated, firecrackers burst, and sweets are widely distributed. Sunnis commemorate this day as the day the Prophet Muhammed entered Mecca, whereas Shias celebrate it as a day of birth of their last imam. For more on this event see Shab-e-Barat 2006.

7. While we certainly experienced some elements of utopia during our childhood, I do not mean to romanticize the experience. I remember a sense of acute fear during a Hindu-Muslim riot sometime in the 1960s in our neighborhood, which had to be quelled by special squads of armed police—a sight unthinkable in Calcutta. And many of our Hindu neighbors continued to mourn the loss of family and possessions because they were forced to move as refugees after India's and Pakistan's partition. (They rarely had much to say about the suffering of Muslims who had to move in the opposite direction). Many of our neighbors also would not venture through the Muslim-dominant parts of Calcutta. The partition of India and Pakistan, and the move to India, must have been traumatic to our parents' generation, but thanks to our parents, it did not cast long shadows of hatred in our minds. Our parents had very respectful relations with Muslims, Christians, and Sikhs. We were not subjected to any restrictions on eating anything or with anyone, the main process through which social and emotional distance is built up at the individual and community level. Nor did our parents fuss about the foreign missionaries who would come to our school to proselytize. I now think their matter-of-fact reaction to the presence of these missionaries helped reduce the missionaries' messages to white noise (the kind of background noise on planes).

8. This diversity arises because there is no single Hindu-definitive holy book. Four Vedas are the oldest known texts, composed about 2000 B.C.E. The Upanishads are a distillation of the end part of the Vedas, the Vedanta. Epics like the Mahabharata (especially the section called the Gita) and Ramayana are considered to be sacred by some people. Others live by the Manusmriti, a set of rules of social behavior devised in the tenth century C.E. by a Brahmin called Manu. Yet others follow the teachings of locally relevant spiritual leaders or lessons handed down through oral sayings. A vast panoply of practices makes up the diversity of Hinduism.

9. The wave of multiculturalism that has opened up some space for cultural rights of different groups in the United States does not solve this problem, though it has made people somewhat more aware of different religious and cultural traditions. I have discussed the problems and prospects of multiculturalism for South Asians in my book *Negotiating Ethnicity* (Purkayastha 2005).

10. Vivekananda's message is about interactions between religions: He repeatedly talks about the ideal of having a Hindu mother and Muslim father; his poetry emphasizes the commonalties between the Vedas, Bible, and Koran; and he designed the overtly syncretic design of the Belur temple that I mentioned earlier. Vivekananda's talks about valor were a challenge to Western missionary and political leaders who attempted to justify colonization and Christian conversions in India (see Burke 1983; Radice 1999; Sen 2005).

3

The Interconnecting Humanity: Connections Between Our Spiritual and Secular Worlds

Selina Jamil

Although I thought I was dropping into an interminable abyss of uprooting when I left what I called "home" in Dhaka, Bangladesh, two decades ago and came to the United States as a graduate student, I now realize that my vertiginous perch was the catalyst that forced me not to simply plunge into an ever-deepening, ever-changing secular world of intellectual oysters and corals, but also to develop the consciousness of an ever-expanding, ever-changing spiritual world of mystic ether. As I ponder the years, I find that although I have hopped from state to state (Michigan, Connecticut, Texas, and Maryland, to be precise), this world of contemplative flexibility continues to beckon me with its eclectically multidimensional hues and its fluid song of syncretic freedom. For the more I glimpse the appalling faces of war, ethnocentrism, racism, and other forms of bigotry and prejudice, the deeper and wider grows my secular-spiritual world. This chapter is my attempt to hold the mirror up to this world of religious freedom.

My secular-spiritual world originated in Dhaka, where growing up was like being in a little earthen pot on the ledge between a latticed, prism-forming window and sun-soaked, breeze-fluted curtains. My gaze at the world outside was not so much barred or tinted as it was trellised into appreciating a multidimensional view, and my gaze at the world within was not so much scorched or buffeted as it was swathed into appreciating a multihued receptivity. That is my picture of the warm, liberal, progressive, dynamic, prismatic flexibility that I grew up in as a child and young adult in my parents' home. And it is this home within the breeze-fluted curtains that connected me with a world beyond the prism-forming window where, like me, other individuals breathed the air of secular liberalism, and thus where the discussion, impact, or practice of religion meant seeing interconnectedness between different faiths and realizing that these different creeds continually come together to weave a singular tapestry of the love of humanity. Thus I learned to belong in a world where to act meaningfully was to interconnect. And it is this flexible and dynamic world of Bangladesh that propelled me into the flexible and dynamic world of the United States. I continued learning to look out my window and creating my place in a world that was the fluid product of an unending, ductile dialogue between secular and spiritual concerns.

True to my desire to see the connections in different religions and thus to connect with practitioners of different faiths, as a doctoral student I once welcomed a few Mormons into my home when they knocked on my door sometime in the early 1990s. Having been thoroughly impressed by a liberal, intellectual milieu, where my professors abounded as much in wit and wisdom as in humility and geniality, and where my fellow students were not lagging far behind, I naively found the arrival of the young Mormons with a text in hand (in a neighborhood meant only for graduate students and their families) not entirely suspect. They were polite and friendly, and they wanted to take a little of my husband's and my time to discuss some chapters of the Bible, and I was curious about the Mormon faith. Accordingly, we spent two or three afternoons discussing chapters they brought to our attention. Then these young missionaries knocked on our door again, inviting us to visit their church on a particular Sunday. We politely declined, but I could not help wondering why they wanted us to visit the church. Thus they announced that they wanted to have us baptized. Struggling between bewilderment and amusement, I told them that our whole purpose of meeting with them was not to make exclusive ties but to broaden and deepen our circumscribed world by transcending exclusiveness. But my quest for breadth and depth went unheeded. The young prose-lytizers left without even attempting to veil their disappointment at the stubborn erroneousness of two straying sheep that refused to enter the fold. I must add, in all fairness to them, that they used neither this hackneyed image nor any other presumptuous image as they departed; but their wilting, drooping gaze of resignation was curiously mottled with obvious displeasure and tranquil conde-scension. Hence they left me pondering the strange irony about the ways in which people erect walls as a result of their attempt to dis-mantle divisions. Breadth and depth indeed! There I was, near the end of the twentieth century, contemplating the flushed sky after sunset but also spiraling down the historical screw that connected an episode of my life and my world with episodes of the lives and the worlds of the natives of colonial Bengal.

My own world within my parents' home in Dhaka, Bangladesh, until the 1980s may have been epistemically tiny, but it showed clear traces of a cultural diversity that can be found in the homes of most urban Bengali middle or upper-middle class Muslim fami-lies. For the air in such a home was saturated with the works of Ra-bindranath Tagore, Jibanananda Das, Kazi Nazrul Islam, Bankim Chandra Chatterji, and Swarat Chandra Chatterji, on the one hand, and those of William Shakespeare, the English Romantics, Voltaire, Thomas Hardy, and Leo Tolstoy, on the other hand. But the musty smell of old books was forever courting the contemporary gloss of my father's volumes of the *Reader's Digest* and my eldest brother's volumes of *Soviet Culture,* a Soviet literary magazine in English, and of *Desh,* an Indian literary magazine in Bangla. And the air in such a home was perpetually enlivened with *Rabindra Sangeet* (Tagore's songs), especially because my father's gramophone and col-lection of records, which he managed to salvage from his younger days, had become cherished old friends in our home. But such a home also was infused with English and American rock music. (Among my own favorite singers were Cat Stevens and Paul Simon, Elton John and Joni Mitchell, Rod Stewart and Joan Baez, George Harrison and Don McLean, and among my favorite bands were Pink Floyd and Fleetwood Mac, Genesis and the Eagles, Supertramp and Chicago, etc.) In such a home the radio, cassettes, or the television also would animate the air with Indian classical music and the songs of Nazrul Islam, as well as Bengali folk (specifically Baul and Bhatiali) and devotional music. But listening to music on BBC and Radio Australia, or to talk shows and plays on BBC and All India Radio, also was a regular phenomenon in my home. And just as we would watch local programs, we also would watch British and American shows on television. But the television also regularly aired readings from the Koran and the *Bhagavad Gita*, the *Tripitaka* and the Bible. And even though I must confess that as a child I did not find myself glued to the television during these programs, I must also add that they helped me develop a sense of interdenominational synchronicity in the multidimensional world that I inhabited.

Breathing the air that was infused simultaneously with works of secular liberalism and with verses from sundry religious texts ever since childhood, it seemed to me that the differences between one religion and another were more about cultural and expressional differences than about doctrinal ones. As I see religion, it is a fundamental concern for and expression of the role of the sacred in the life of an individual and of the culture in which the individual belongs, and it demonstrates the individual and cultural search for a morally fulfilling order. Clearly, in such an environment, where the windows, verandahs, and rooftop always opened out to the wonders of an infinite sky, secular circumstances never conflicted with religious considerations. For me the voice of the Hindu priests and chime of temple bells were as full of the unfathomable and refreshing beauty of a mysterious God's elusive touch as was the sound of the *Azan* that would glide into the crisp early morning air and blend into the blossoming lilac-peach of the waking sky. And, although the sounds of chiming temple bells or chanting priests at the Buddhist temple—where I went once or twice for the *Buddha Purnima* (the birth anniversary of the Buddha)—apparently had nothing to do with faith in God, these chants and chimes were full of the dulcet rhythms of spirituality. Between the chimes and chants were the tenuous nuances that held the inexpressible peace and beauty of a silence that articulated the voice of the interconnecting humanity; and hence they invoked in me a fleeting sensation of the divine music of ineffability.

Indeed, in those early years of my adolescent life, particularly the years that followed 1971,[1] I would occasionally experience a poignant ecstasy that throbbed with the divine passion of life when I would hear my *ustad*'s rendition of a raga. As an adolescent I took voice lessons at a performing arts school on weekends in the years following the unspeakably terrifying ordeal and devastation of the Liberation War of 1971. Even now I continue to marvel at the un-fathomable phenomenon that manifested itself in the most grue-some forms of violence that Elora Chowdhury describes in her chapter later in this book.

Like many other Bangladeshis who had survived the genocide, at the end of the war I found myself staring subliminally into the paradox of an abysmal chaos like the black hole of a collapsed star but that simultaneously churned up an opening of life like an ever-expanding universe. That serene but passionate feeling of being poised at the brink of a sudden, mystical, cosmic beginning started to grow in me when I had the splendid fortune of being a student of Ustad Akhtar Sadmani, a noted and reputed classical vocalist of Dhaka. Once in a while at the end of a day's lesson, he would, ac-companied by the tabla player, yield himself to a burst of inspira-tion as though he had caught sparks of the cosmic fire of eternal energy. Most of the time the lyrics had no mention of God, and sometimes they were about regular, mundane affairs of the every-day world, but the sound of his invigorated voice would fill the room as though ether were gliding out of Shiva-Nataraja's cosmic drum. Needless to say, we, his awed, speechless students, would sit transfixed and flushed, oblivious of everything but a monumental and instinctive brush with the profoundly powerful bliss and pain-fully burning fire of creativity. As I connect this act of listening in my past with the act of writing at this present moment, I am reminded of a point that one of my favorite professors, Dr. Douglas Peterson, a Shakespearean scholar, impressed upon me about the inseparable connection between the world of work and the world of play that transforms recreation into re-creation. As my worlds of work and play merge in this act of writing now, so my worlds of work and play merged in the act of listening then, to transform my passive recre-ation into an active sense of renewal. And although I could not have articulated the feeling at the time, through my ustad's creative act in a little room of a two-story building in the heart of a war-ravaged, overcrowded, squalid city, I had, poised beyond illusions and dis-illusion, found boundless moments of the immutable, inexplicable, intangible, ethereally fresh breath of divinity on the fleeting, spat-tering, passionately heaving breath of humanity. Thus, quite early in life, it seemed to me—as it seemed to many others in my social environment—that to develop a sense of religion was never to be-come enmeshed in the abstruseness of an abstract quest for an in-tangible entity.

But it was only after having come to an entirely different world, the United States, that I turned to exploring the teachings of the Buddha and the *Bhagavad Gita* for an easy access to intellectual wealth. I came upon Eknath Easwaran's translation of the *Bha-gavad Gita,* where Krishna warns Arjuna that "[s]elfish action im-prisons the world," and urges him to "[a]ct selflessly, without any thought of personal profit" (*Bhagavad Gita* 3:9). "You should never engage / in action for the sake of reward, nor should / you long for inaction. Perform work in this / world, Arjuna, as a man established within himself—without selfish attachments, and / alike in success and defeat" (*Bhagavad Gita* 2:47–48). Clearly, the point that the *Gita* makes is to free oneself from *all* kinds of "selfish attachments," and hence not simply to move beyond desiring material "reward," but also to transcend spiritual "reward," for only then can one ex-perience the peace of being "alike in success and defeat." As the Buddhist mystic, Osho, observes, and as we have seen all too often, many "religious" people can be just as materialistic as worldly peo-ple. Just as worldly people often desire power and wealth in life, so do certain "religious" people desire power and wealth that "no-body can take [. . .] away, not even death" (*Bhagavad Gita* 124, 127). The problem is certainly not with seeking spiritual wisdom, nor is it even with the ability to exercise spiritual power. But the problem is with "any motivation of self" (Osho 2004, 132). The problem, then, is allowing selfish desires for power to infect spiritual concerns. The problem also is the inability to perceive the treacher-ous manner in which secularism tends to dominate religion. As Ashis Nandy (2002) argues, the true practice of religion has never produced intolerance: "Religious communities in traditional societies *have* known how to live with each other" (Nandy 2002, 79). And as Nandy asserts, secularism poses a threat to religious believers in that "it guarantees no protection to them against sufferings inflicted by the state in the name of its ideology. On the contrary, with the help of modern communications and the secular coercive power at its command, the state frequently uses its ideology to silence nonconforming citizens" (Nandy 2002, 75). It is the exercise of this "coercive power" against the believers that turns them toward "fanaticism and violence" because it arouses "a sense of defeat" and "feelings of impotence" in them (Nandy 2002, 75–76). Indeed, what passes as fanaticism or fundamentalism "is often only another form of westernization becoming popular among the psychologically uprooted middle classes in South Asia" (Nandy 2002, 77). "Most postcolonial societies," with their brands of "defeated civilizations," have constructed a certain concept of "Western Man" as "an invisible reference point" (Nandy 2002, 76–77). The point I wish to make is our need to transcend this "reference point" and listen to the dialogue between the secular and spiritual worlds in order to appreciate the exchanges between them. What we need to appreciate, then, is the interconnection between these two worlds that colors and shapes our horizon.

Indeed, the more I see the plight of our selfish world of global ambitions, the more I wish to emphasize the need to see our human connections. Hence, I turn to the Krishna who teaches Arjuna the meaning of freedom from selfish attachments (*Bhagavad Gita* 12:18–19). As I see the question of self-fulfillment, the answer lies in the attainment of peace in life; but peace with oneself is inseparable from peace with others. Indeed, the thought that my own sense of spiritual or religious experience has increasingly hinged upon me—especially in light of the throes of Middle Eastern tension and in the wake of the September 11, 2001, disaster—is the simple (but elusive) truth that there can be no peace in any kind of selfish desire. Time and again we read the same message of the dangers of self-absorption, but time and again, trapped in the widening gyre of our karma that whirls "friend and foe" inseparably, we unleash the same violent chaos in the world; and the hollow sound of a confused and self-absorbed soul that turns an internal war into an external war becomes increasingly cacophonous (*Bhagavad Gita* 12:18).

Hence, as I read religious texts in the context of wars, I see this same warning against the self-absorbed soul's deluded need to indulge in self-righteousness. In the *Gita*, Krishna urges Arjuna to "[a]ct selflessly, without / any thought of personal profit" (3:9), and exhorts him to "participate in this battle against / evil" (*Bhagavad Gita* 2:33). Hence, the battle of the Kurukshetra where the Pandavs fight their relatives, the Kauravs, is inseparable from and metaphorical of the battle raging within the human soul: "Use your mighty arms to slay the fierce enemy / that is selfish desire" (*Bhagavad Gita* 3:43). Here I am reminded of the Sufi saint Bawa Muhaiyaddeen's story about the meaning of "jihad": When Prophet Muhammad's followers (who flee with him to Medina in order to avoid being persecuted by the Meccans) seek his permission to fight the Meccans because they have heard stories about the latter's persecution of their relatives in Mecca, they tell him that they have been disgraced and dishonored: "We are warriors, and we have been disgraced. How can we live in this world with such dishonor?" (Muhaiyaddeen 1987, 77). But, as Muhaiyaddeen (1987) suggests, the Prophet realizes the significant use of the words "disgrace" and "dishonor," and thus he sees the problematic connection between defeatism and self-absorption. For Allah tells the Prophet: "O Muhammad, tell your companions to begin the holy war in their hearts to sacrifice the evils in their own hearts" (Muhaiyaddeen 1987, 77). The true enemy, as the Prophet tries to impress upon his followers, is not outside but inside. Hence, to engage in a "holy war" is not to engage in violence. Likewise, in the *Gita*, Krishna advises Arjuna to "fight!—but stay free from the fever of the ego" (*Bhagavad Gita* 3:30). To "fight" with the purpose of freeing oneself from "the fever of the ego" is to be "equally disposed to family, enemies, / and friends" (*Bhagavad Gita* 6:9). And through a story about the Prophet's son-in-law, Ali, Muhaiyaddeen (1987) encapsulates this same message of the interconnecting humanity that fights the enemy within: "After overcoming an opponent in battle, Ali refuses to kill the man. The opponent does not understand Ali's action, and, in an attempt to hasten the end, spits in Ali's face." At first Ali becomes angry, but then he removes his foot with which he has been holding down his enemy; he puts his sword aside, saying that he and his opponents are not the real "enemies." "The real enemies are the evil qualities within us. You are my brother, yet you spit in my face. When you spat upon me, I became angry, and the arrogance of the 'I' came to me. If I had killed you when I was in that state, then I would be a sinner, a murderer. I would have become the very thing I was fighting against" (Muhaiyaddeen 1987, 83). Indeed, it is this self-absorption ("the arrogance of the 'I'") that turns the individual to violence or to any quest for power. As in the *Gita,* and as in this story about a Muslim's holy war, the point then is to dismantle the rampart of self-absorption and confront the war within. But time and again we build a bulwark of self-absorption with which we fortify our confused and deluded connections between morality and power.

Hence, I turn to the method of attaining peace by substituting love for self-love that makes Sufi poetry particularly engaging. As Carl W. Ernst defines Sufism, it is a path that moves from "ordinary external life" toward "the inner reality of God" (1997, 26). As such, Sufism is the path of "mystical annihilation (*fana'*) of the ego" that recognizes the connection between the spiritual and the secular worlds (Ernst 1997, 60). For the path of *fana'* of the ego, as the thirteenth-century Sufi poet Rumi asserts, is the path of love. Indeed, the Sufis' concern is to connect the perceiving individual to the dynamic world with love. As Fadiman and Frager (1997) remark, "[o]ne basic Sufi principle is to live in the world and still pursue the highest mystical goals. To serve others is, in a real sense, to serve God" (Fadiman and Frager 1997, 17). I would add that the power of love that the Sufis have so well understood is the magic of connecting the spiritual world with the secular world. Indeed, having been raised in Bangladesh, where the influence of Sufism has permeated the culture since the mid-eleventh century, I find myself peculiarly drawn to the Sufis. According to Raisuddin (2005), Sufism, which has "influenced the literary and cultural life of the land," has "not only helped the spread of Islam in Bengal, but it [has] also influenced the indigenous religions. The ideal of Sufism, attaining the love of God through love of His creation, has greatly influenced the [. . .] mysticism of the Bauls" (Raisuddin 2005, 3).

Indeed, the songs of the most famous Baul—Lalon Shah (or Lalon Fakir), who shows an obvious Sufi influence—have a peculiarly poignant resonance in my heart as in the hearts of most Bangladeshis. As Edward Dimock asserts, "[t]he doctrinal and poetic similarities between Bauls and Sufis are plentiful" (1996, 258). Like the Sufi poets, Lalon, the nineteenth-century Baul, in a song that Abu Rushd translates as Song No. 17, sings of the mystical annihilation of the ego: "Rise from the grave / is the command of the Lord / and 'I' merges with the I" (Shah 1964, 16–18). When the "I" becomes "'I'" (the difference is in Lalon's use of inverted commas), the ego constructs barriers and thus separates the self from God. The "'I'" shows that the self is consumed by notions of individuality, self-identity and distinctness, and hence is trapped in isolation and separation. But the Sufi saint, Mansur al-Hallaj (who claims "I Am the Truth") accomplishes the complete annihilation of the ego, the complete absorption of the self ("'I'") into God ("I"): "The saint Mansur / knew the truth" (Rushd 1964, 12–13). Mansur al-Hallaj has lost his "'I'" and become absorbed in "I." That is, in claiming "I Am the Truth," he means that God is the Truth. Hence, Lalon begins his song with the line: "I am the end of all knowledge," and goes on to explain that "the real I" is not "'I'" (Rushd 1964, 1, 3, 6). As Lalon interprets, Mansur receives special "bless[ings]" because he does not imprison himself in the forms (rituals) of worship: "So he is blessed more than the undiscerning reader / of the holy book" (14–15). Indeed, as Lalon would have known, the Koran warns readers against ritualism. To quote from Dawood's translation, "[r]ighteousness does not consist in whether you face towards the East or West" (Koran 21:174).

In his own pursuit of righteousness and truth, Lalon is continually emphatic about the connections between Hinduism and Islam. "To the Baul, there is no difference between Hindu and Muslim" (Dimock 1996, 264). As Lalon would have been aware, the Koran does not sanctify Prophet Muhammad above other prophets or messengers instrumental in the birth of other religions. To quote from Dawood's translation, "We [God] have sent apostles before you [Muhammad] to other nations" (Koran 16:63). "[N]othing is said to you [Muhammad] that has not been said to other apostles before you" (Koran 41:40). As the Koran emphasizes, "[a]n apostle is sent to every nation. When their apostle comes, justice is done among them; they are not wronged" (Koran 10:47). Indeed, in a song, which Abu Rushd translates as Song No. 3, Lalon shows interaction between Hinduism and Islam as he blends the Hindu concept of God, who can release one from *samsara* (the cycle of birth and death) and hence from reincarnation and karma, with the Muslim concept of God as the merciful creator: "Several times in a round / a man is born. / This time be careful / to remember the name of Allah" (Rushd 1964, 6–9). Clearly, divine mercy is inseparable from divine justice. Hence, just as God metes out "Just[ice]," so does karma (Rushd 1964, 1). To "remember the name of Allah," then, is to "contemplat[e]" God, and hence to work out of the self-absorbed "immers[ion] in loss and gain" and be absorbed into God (Rushd 1964, 5). As the Koran articulates, the successful quest for God is in the act of unselfish generosity: "[H]e that does good works for the sake of the most High only, seeking no recompense," receives God's blessings (Koran 92:12). Likewise, the *Gita* teaches that to be "completely" devoted to God is to "act without selfish attachment," and this "free[dom] from ill will for any creature" is the way to "enter into" God (*Bhagavad Gita* 11:55). Thus, as the *Gita* emphasizes that to be "[u]nited with the Lord" is to "attain nirvana in Brahman" (*Bhagavad Gita* 5:24), so does Lalon, who alludes to God as the savior and refers to the concept of reincarnation and karma. Further, if like the Sufis, Lalon sings of God as Allah, so like the Vaishnavs, he sings of God as Krishna, as in the song that Carol Salomon translates as Song No. 1: "I long for the Dark Moon, / hoping to become his maidservant" (Salomon 1995, 5–6). Not only does Lalon rise above seeing any difference between the Hindu and the Muslim, but he also rises above gender biases to focus on the life that throbs in the human heart.

Life comes and goes, but just like Lalon's Achinpakhi (unknown bird), it flits mysteriously out of one cage and into another, connecting the individual to humanity in a ceaseless and unfathomable act of renewal despite death. Indeed, Lalon sees the human soul as the mysterious expression of an elusive, unknowable Infinity: Achinpakhi. "Says Lalon, forcing the cage open, / the bird flitted away to no one knows where" (Salomon 1995, 12–13). Clearly, Lalon, who wants to cage the Achinpakhi and yet "forc[es] the cage open," realizes the intermingling between the spiritual world of the soul's ethereality and the secular world of the body's corporeality. And using Lalon's metaphor of the Achinpakhi in his discussion of Bangladeshi theater, my eldest brother, a drama scholar, writes about "a chilly winter full-moon night" when "the magic of a [rural] performance . . . enchants the spectators. What is it like? It is like the Achinpakhi—the Bird Unknown—soaring in the infinite sky" (Ahmed 2000, 2). He wishes his Western audience to realize that in a country that has so often been labeled as "[a] country of Islamic fanatics" who want "to hang an iconoclast woman [Taslima Nasreen]," he has "seen performances in the interior villages where *Allah is physically represented*" (Ahmed 2000, 1, 2). Like Lalon, he wishes to articulate the "magic" of "human existence" that emanates from the delicate, fluid, and sublime reciprocity between the secular and the spiritual worlds of Bangladesh as he "attempt[s] to unfold the infinite variety of the Achinpakhi" in his discussion of Bangladeshi drama, which constitutes both religious and secular performances (Ahmed 2000, 2).

It is a little of this "infinite variety" that I aspired to unveil to a classroom audience, when I once accepted an invitation from a student (albeit not one of my own students), who was working on a class project, and who requested that I deliver a talk about some aspects of South Asian culture in 2002. During the fall and spring of 2001–2002, I was teaching at a university where, despite the devastating shock of 9/11 and the sudden chaotic outbursts in its wake, I did not feel as though my South Asian presence caused any particular anxiety or unease as I walked in and out of classrooms. Indeed, the general atmosphere at the university seemed to be unruffled by either overt or simmering tension. And so one tranquil morning, draped in a sari, I walked into a classroom to deliver my talk, which was mostly about South Asian religious and social customs. I took with me a jamdani silk sari, a few statuettes, a small

naksi katha tapestry, etc. to give the classroom audience some con-
crete examples of Bangladeshi culture. At the end of my talk came
the question-answer session. And one or two of the questions revealed the audience's curiosity about South Asian women's social
and political status. As I answered the questions, I tried to make my
audience glimpse a specific world of specific circumstances. And I
tried to make my audience realize that an impalpable set of parallels between the patriarchal world of the United States and that of
South Asia lay beneath an obvious veil of contrasts. After this session I was profusely thanked both by the student, whose project I
had participated in, and by her instructor; and I saw in these thanks
my cue to depart. But behind my retreating figure boomed the voice
of the instructor, who began by expressing delight at the presentation but then quickly shifted gears to impress upon her students the
need to remember how "lucky" they were to have been born as
Americans unlike the "oppressed" women of Third World countries. And thus she implicitly drew a binary opposition between the
women of the Third World (non-Western women who presumably
were all "oppressed") and American women (Western women who
presumably were all privileged members of the First World). But, to
quote Chandra Talpade Mohanty, "[i]f this ['self-presentation' of
Western women as 'secular and liberated'] were a material reality,
there would be no need for feminist political struggle in the West"
(Mohanty 1994, 215). I had walked into that classroom armed
with a naivete that grew out of all the favorable impressions I had
received from two or three sagacious, open-minded, mindful, and
sensitive colleagues in my own department with whom I had begun
to develop close contact. But as I was walking away from that classroom, my naivete suddenly sputtered into a nonplussed imagination, and it seemed as though the booming voice behind me had
transformed itself into a whizzing Corvette that announced its phenomenal presence by coursing right through (and thus covering itself with) the muddy contents of a gutter. As Mohanty would have
told me, in their approach to non-Western women, Western feminists often replicate the colonialist stance of hegemony: "It is in the
production of this 'Third-World difference' [that 'stable, ahistorical

something that apparently oppresses most if not all the women' in the Third World] that Western feminists appropriate and colonize the constitutive complexities which characterize the lives of women in these countries" (Mohanty 1994, 198). Such a colonialist discourse of hegemony "reinforces the assumption that people in the Third World just have not evolved to the extent" that their Western counterparts have (Mohanty 1994, 214).

But I remember an instance of the subtle power exercised by an "oppressed" Third World woman that I wished I could have shared with this particular Western feminist. As a child I once witnessed a most unusual event from the verandah of my parents' home in Dhaka. A young woman (presumably returning home from college) had just descended from a rickshaw when a gray-bearded but curiously sprightly old mullah (Muslim cleric) almost pounced upon her and vigorously slapped her back as he rebuked her for not covering the back of her blouse with the end-piece of her sari. Although blissfully unaware of his own sensual eye, he must nevertheless have been so severely afflicted by an obvious inability to control his lustful impulses (and by his prejudiced notion of other males as equally unable to control their lasciviousness) at the sight of a slim feminine back that he sought to escape them by spilling out his envenomed distress on the young woman herself. She, however, after being initially startled by the old mullah's preposterously shallow and misguided concern for propriety and modesty, turned around and faced him with a silence that spoke of the tolerance of a refined sensibility, which took note of a self-styled neighborhood patriarch whose appalling coarseness was unspeakably lamentable. And then she turned away from the scene with her head held high. The quiet dignity and courage of a young woman who refused to break down in tears or to hasten away with lowered head, and who calmly picked her way with steady steps, first perplexed the old patriarch into speechlessness and then reduced him into incoherent mutterings. But certain Western feminists, perhaps, wouldn't have paid attention to the second half of this story, because presumably they would have found the first half well suited for their inquiry into the condition of the "oppressed" Third World woman, who is so "different" from the liberated First World woman.

Indeed, whether I live in a Midwestern and Northeastern state, or whether I live in a southern or mid-Atlantic state, my identity as a Third World woman invariably seems to exude the amazing properties of erecting a barrier of condescension that separates me from the nuanced world of mainstream America. Not surprisingly, while teaching a course on non-Western literature at a college some time ago, I discovered another manifestation of the determined refusal to see parallels between the West and non-West in one or two of my students. I never read Achebe's *Things Fall Apart* (1959) in Bangladesh, where, at the Dhaka University's English Department the curriculum did not include non-Western literature. As an educator in the United States, however, I discovered a whole new world of Asian and African literature and culture, and plunged into it with zeal and passion. And I tried to bring the same to my students. Our focus was on Achebe's topic of religion and its connection to the Umuofian community's sacrifice of a young man, Ikemefuna. Achebe's portrayal of the native religion reveals that the Ibo clan of Umuofia, which sees a close connection between the natural and the human worlds, conceives of elemental forces as gods and goddesses who are deputies of the creator God. One of these gods (the Oracle of Hills and Caves) is understood to have ordered the "kill[ing]" of Ikemefuna, who is chosen by his own community to be given to Umuofia in order to avoid the violence and bloodshed of war (Achebe 1959, 57). Ikemefuna soon overcomes his initial fear and becomes a loved and loving member of the protagonist Okonkwo's family, and hence Okonkwo's surrogate son. But as soon as the process of Ikemefuna's adoption into a new family and new home is complete, the community understands that the Oracle has ordered Ikemefuna's death. As far as violence is concerned, this community never goes to war unless "its case" is "clear and just" (Achebe 1959, 12). Clearly, Achebe points out that in this culture where violence is not encouraged, the violent death of the young, innocent Ikemefuna causes heart-wrenching pain. And, through the sacrifice of Ikemefuna, this Ibo clan shows its profound understanding of the significance of the individual in the community and of turning the enemy into the family.

As I tried to impress upon my students, we (like Achebe's Umuofians) may not condone the practice of human sacrifice, but we may not dismiss it as reflective of a simple-minded and ignorant culture, because it demonstrates the Ibo community's understanding of the complex movement of life that shows the tension between contradictory forces and impulses. And most of my students were able to see that if a culture has strengths, it also has weaknesses, just as all other cultures. But for a few of my students, this story confirmed the superiority of Christianity to the native religion because Christianity does not advocate human sacrifice. Never mind Achebe's implied parallels between Umuofia's decision to sacrifice Ikemefuna and Abraham's decision to sacrifice Isaac. And never mind Achebe's implied parallels between the death of Jesus, who sacrifices his life to bring salvation to humankind, and the death of Ikemefuna, whose sacrifice saves two Ibo clans from bloodshed and teaches them the meaning of self-sacrifice and that of the inseparable connection between opposites. For these students—in whose eyes Christianity is superior to a non-Western religion, and despite the fact that the post-9/11 world is an intermingled, interconnected world—their world remained one where binary opposites situate them at the height of civilizational eminence.

As William James observes, "nothing is more congenial, from babyhood to the end of life, than to be able to assimilate the new to the old," and to resist any new concept that "threaten[s]" to "burst" or change "our well-known series of concepts" (James 1900, 328). As we need "to assimilate the new to the old," we also need to assimilate the old to the new. Nevertheless, two most important aspects of our human identity are our abilities to choose and to contemplate. And it is with these abilities that we need to engage in a ceaseless dialogue (and thus to draw a dynamic connection) between the old ideas or ways and the new ones. Only then can we grow beyond Robert Frost's treacherous and artificial "wall" of traditions and borrowed convictions ("Mending Wall"), and stand under the measureless sky that colors the horizon with the subtle hues of an interconnecting humanity and that perceives and forges connections between the spiritual and the secular worlds.

Note

1. This year is of peculiar significance to all Bangladeshis or Bangladeshi Americans because of the War of Liberation, which transformed East Pakistan into Bangladesh. Also known as the India-Pakistan War of 1971, it lasted for nine months. And although all the members of my immediate family and most of the members of my extended family miraculously survived this war, it resulted in a genocide that, according to the Bangladeshi government, swept away the lives of approximately 3 million people, including the most eminent scholars and other prominent professionals.

4

Islam through a Mosaic of Cultures

Parveen Talpur

Islam in the American Post-9/11 Era

In the aftermath of the horrifying attacks on New York's World Trade Center on September 11, 2001, many Muslims in the United States found themselves in a quandary. They feared the hate crimes within the United States, and they shuddered at the idea of going back to their countries of origin. For many Muslims, the misinterpretation and distortion of Islam in several countries had made life uncomfortable and prompted them to migrate in search of a more peaceful life. The post-9/11 interpretations of Islam in the United States media also made people, like myself, vulnerable to the hate crimes that were erupting in America.

Soon after the attack, the FBI reported 350 hate crimes against Muslims and people resembling Muslims. In a few cases, Sikh males were mistaken for Muslims because, as Kaur's recent film *Divided We Fall*[1] documented, their beards and turbans were taken as markers of terrorists. Today, seven years after the incident, Islam is still identified with terrorism by many people, and the Muslim world continues to be perceived as a primitive civilization compared to the progressive civilization of the West.

In October 2007, for example, *Newsweek* featured a cover story showing Pakistani students chanting anti-American slogans. The title described Pakistan as the most dangerous country in the world. While the activities of *those* male students may have been represented accurately, the portrayal of those students as representative of all students in Pakistan and the rest of the story—which focused on a resurgence of militancy—contributed yet another building block to the widespread media images of a homogenous Islam in places where anti-Americanism or anti-Western feelings are rampant, one which is promulgated by young traditional militant men and where women are invisible. Though I live in a place thousands of miles away, such images impinge on my peaceful life as a researcher in Ithaca. Such discourses also silence histories of diverse Islam and Islamic civilizations around the world. In this chapter I attempt to describe the larger tapestry of distant histories and contemporary events that have shaped my life.

Whose Islam?

Ahmed Rashid, the well-known writer on Islam and Central Asian Affairs, observed in 2001, shortly before 9/11, many Western commentators do not particularize the Taliban, but condemn Islam wholesale for being intolerant and anti-modern. The media relentlessly focus on "traditional practices" without ever questioning how these "traditional practices" are sustained. Rarely are the political and economic systems that sustain authoritarian groups in positions of power ever questioned. And, as scholars focus a great deal of attention on fundamentalism as a subject of study, their work appears to match what the media portray, even though the objective of scholarly writing on fundamentalism may be different.

As a Muslim woman, I am part of a "civilizational" discourse on women in Islam. Widespread audiences know about Muktaran Mai's gang rape[2] to protect family honor. I have tried to interpose, as I do now, that it was a local *male cleric* who first spoke out against this atrocity, this un-Islamic practice, and many Pakistani women's groups were organized to protest her treatment. Similarly, as many people in the West equate the veil with the servile status of Muslim women, I would like to point out that the adoption of this custom in Muslim societies needs some clarification. The veil, *chador* or *hijab* or any head covering that Muslim women wear, is not a religious requirement in Islam. Two generations ago, it was almost in disuse in large segments of the Muslim world or, at least, it was not used as a head covering, as is done now. There were a few exceptions: Saudi Arabia made the veil mandatory and so did Iran after the Islamic revolution led by Ayatollah Khomeini, whereas Afghanistan followed these models after the Taliban took over the government. In Pakistan and in India (where Muslims are the largest minority), it has always been a common practice among rural women to cover their heads with veils. However, the veil is by no means an Islamic compulsion. Hindu women cover their faces and heads with a veil (as do peasant women in Italy with a scarf). When urban women in Pakistan draped veils around their necks and shoulders, it was a fashion statement rather than a traditional head cover. However, in the late 1980s, the younger generation of Pakistani women began to cover their heads. Far from this being a symbol of suppression, the *hijab* was meant as a symbol of rebellion against their parents and as a way to show Muslim power. Within the home, it was a symbol of teenage defiance, as it was a novelty to the mothers and many of them objected to its use. In the 1980s, the *hijab* was more likely to be worn in America than among middle-class women in Pakistan. In Bangladesh and Indonesia (which, along with Pakistan, are the three major Islamic countries of the world), widespread veiling is of even more recent vintage, beginning sometime in the late 1990s. In each case, a combination of political and economic circumstances intersected to create the resurgence of this practice. And, much like jeans and tank tops, *hijabs* may carry very different social meanings in different countries. Yet, because of the history of recent conflicts and the resurgence of a variety of modern authoritarian masculinities, the *hijab* has come to be widely regarded not as a variable, recent trend that requires explanation, but as a "traditional symbol" of the sufferings of Muslim women.

Islam in the United States

I am a first-generation Pakistani American. My experience of post-9/11 America is from the perspective of a resident of the college town of Ithaca, New York. Ithaca, because of Cornell University, has a constant flow of international scholars and students. Its residents, excluding the academia, are mainly farmers and local business owners who are quite used to foreigners, including the various Muslim sects. Because of their very small numbers, Muslims in Ithaca do not have a mosque, and they perform their Friday and Eid prayers in the secular halls of Cornell. On this limited platform, my participation could be described as minimal. Coming from a family that worships at home, I have never been a frequent visitor to these gatherings. So, in view of the demography and the psyche of this town and my own limited social life, I did not directly experience any significant negative effects of 9/11.

Yet, like the rest of humanity, I, too, was touched by the tragedy of the event. I was awestruck by the way death visited those enormous towers, and I was angry that this large-scale murder had been committed in the name of religion. Night after night, I wrote imaginary letters addressed to unknown names and scribbled poems to pay tributes to the departed souls. Although the events did not affect me directly, I noticed that an Indian restaurant, which originally advertised Pakistani and Indian food, erased the Pakistani part of it. A man who prayed publicly disappeared. The few familiar faces wearing *hijabs,* whom I often saw on the streets and in the stores, did not discard their *hijabs,* but they were less visible. I was concerned about air travel, as I knew that the sight of a Middle Eastern man at the airport or on board would make me uncomfortable.

Recent commentaries on Islam have notable omissions. The way Muslim women live their religion in the United States varies from individual to individual, depending upon their outlook, their personal history, their family constraints, and their socioreligious context, but all this has not been much emphasized in the new literature. The diasporic Muslim communities scattered across the globe have developed their own identities. Yet, for the most part, Americans judge the status of women by the degree of their segregation in the mosques; this attitude also is internalized by several post-immigrant generations. A younger generation Muslim American author wrote in 2000:

> Living in the United States is positively affecting the lives of American Muslim women . . . If it weren't for American culture that emphasized Sundays as a gathering day for everyone in the family, American Muslim women might never have gained leadership roles in the mosque. (Gull Hasan 2000, 116)

Yet, a year later, the situation was very different. For instance, a woman who fled from Afghanistan when the Taliban took over her country had opened a restaurant in America. A few days after 9/11, her restaurant was trashed. The attackers had left behind a mess of graffiti and ignorance; one piece read, "You guys destroy my country." Those who assaulted the property were perhaps not aware of the gender of its owner. However, the public read the news, not the graffiti, and such news terrified Muslim women. It was only logical that the wearing of the veils should become an issue, and many women felt their social life being disturbed as they minimized their visits to the mosques and the community centers.

In the immediate aftermath of 9/11, I drew some solace from the fact that whereas the Islamic revolution in Iran and the Taliban regime of Afghanistan were creating an image that Islam was violent and conservative in matters of religion, many Americans, by converting to Islam in the past few decades, were proving Islam's flexibility and adaptability to new geopolitical locales and to changing times. Prior to 9/11, there was a definite dearth of quality, updated material on Islam, yet it attracted a large number of converts, which proves Islam's accommodating nature. Of the total Muslim population in America, 50% consists of native-born Americans.

American converts to Islam learned about their new religion through the 1,500 or more mosques that are spread across the United States. In most cases, the heads of these mosques had no academic training in Islam. Any training they did have was from the Islamic institutions of the Muslim countries, mainly Arab countries, which were the biggest sponsors of these mosques and were undoubtedly the most conservative. However, regardless of their orthodoxy or training, these clerics were able to preach an Islam that can be adapted to the American lifestyle, proving that Islam can thrive in American conditions. There is, however, another statistic that might appear to contradict this statement. A large number of Muslims in the United States do not participate in the religious/social activities of the mosques, although this number mainly includes Muslim settlers from other countries. The Muslim population in America is roughly estimated to be between 6 to 7 million. Of these, only about 2 million attend the mosques. The average attendance of these Muslims is once or twice a year. This low number actually indicates that there is a growing number of progressive/moderate Muslims who, unlike the new converts, are not interested in listening to a conventional sermon on Islam.

In terms of number, women's attendance in the mosques is much lower than the men's. This may become even lower as the younger generation of Muslim women, born and raised in the United States, find it degrading to pray in the segregated conditions of the mosques. This already has provoked some of them to action; Asra Nomani's much-publicized refusal to enter the mosque through its "back door,"[3] and the resolve of a few other women to lead the prayers, are just two radical steps taken against the tradition of segregation in the mosques.

South-Asian American Muslim women are aware of the equal rights of women. Many educated women are well aware that the United Nations Millennium Development Goals plan to empower women in every sphere. They also know that the sociopolitical conditions of the Muslim countries keep female representation to a minimum. The majority of Muslim women living in America look forward to a life defined by the global standards of women's rights, and not by the misinterpreted Islamic tradition of the clerics. The progressive Muslim women and men in the United States already have begun to look for alternate institutions that meet their standards. Some of them have begun by establishing their own organizations, interpreting Islam in a moderate way. I believe that this will cement the formation of a progressive/moderate Islam in America, in which Muslims will be able to stress their American thinking. With the passage of time, this outlook will shape the identity of a future Muslim America. The new Muslim America will certainly be tolerant, as it will be born out of a mosaic of cultures.

Half of this mosaic, as mentioned earlier, comprises indigenous Americans, while the other half consists of 25% South Asians, 12% Arabs, and the remaining percentage of the Muslims from West Asia, Central Asia, Southeast Asia, and North and West Africa. According to one forecast, by the year 2010 this number will multiply and make Islam the second largest faith in America, after Christianity. Perhaps this Muslim America will be able to influence the world. There is a hope that as moderate Muslims, who are educated, wealthy citizens of the sole Superpower, will be able to influence Muslim countries toward moderation and progress. One of the positive outcomes of this Islam would be that the interfaith dialogue between the Muslim and Jewish communities and between Muslims and Hindus would increase and, hopefully, accelerate the peace processes in the Middle East and South Asia.

Reflecting on Islamic History

A study of Islamic history provides further reason for hope. There is a discernable pattern that went with the territorial aggrandizement of the early Muslims as they came in contact with new cultures. On one hand, Muslim clerics were tailoring the Islamic concept of leadership to the new demands that mainly required an autocratic ruler; on the other hand, due to political expediency, Islam itself was adapting to new cultures by following pragmatic policies. At one point in its expansion, the Islamic empire spread from Europe to China. It had conquered diverse people and encountered a variety of cultures. Therefore, to accurately reflect on Islam, one cannot overlook the cultural diversity in Islamic thought and practice. Unfortunately, this has not been emphasized in the West. Americans mainly identify all the Muslims with the *Wahabi* Islam, which is limited to Saudi Arabia and is undoubtedly orthodox in nature. Arabs are more identifiable by their headdress and loose white robes rather than the beard. The beard is more common among Iranian males, due to the Islamic Revolution of the 1970s, and is also common in Afghanistan, as the Taliban forced men to grow beards. Yet, for most Americans, the beard remains a common feature of Muslim men (much as the veil remains the characteristic of the suppression of Muslim women).

Many Americans are unaware that Islam itself is a divided religion, because the Arabs and the Iranians practice two different sects of Islam, the *Sunni* Islam of the Arabs and the *Shiya* Islam of Iran. If the war in Iraq has made people aware of these divisions, few know exactly what the difference is. It is also important to remember that Islam tends to merge with the cultural traits of a given society. In the past, there has been the Indianization of Islam, the Africanization of Islam, and the Europeanization of Islam. Hence, there is hope of an Americanization of Islam. The flexibility of Islam has been used and misused in its recent history; the best case of its misuse is under the Taliban in Afghanistan. The destruction of the images of Buddha, which had survived for more than 20 centuries, documents the long history of acceptance of these symbols, as well as the recent violent rejection.

Islam's early history, in a place not too far from Afghanistan, shows a very different trajectory. In eastern Afghanistan, on the Arabian Sea coast, lies Sindh, which was a fiefdom of Afghanistan in the eighteenth century and is now a province of Pakistan. Coming from Sindh and being a South Asian historian, I will describe Islam as practiced in Sindh to showcase another face of Islam. Sindh is known as *Bab-ul-Islam*, the Gateway to Islam, as Islam entered India and South Asia through Sindh. In 711 C.E., Sindh was conquered by the famous Arab conqueror, Mohammad Bin Qasim. The first port town he conquered came to be known as Debal to Arab historians. In the folk literature of Sindh, this port town is known as Bhanbhore and is better known for the love story of Sassui and Punhoon. Although the fate of Sassui-Punhoon was a tale of unfulfilled love (like the story of Laila-Majnu of the Arabian Desert, Shireen-Farhad of the Persian Empire, and Heer-Ranjha of the fertile plains of Punjab), the story testifies that the ruins of Bhanbhore witnessed the Sindhi Sufi tradition of eternal love. The pre-Islamic cultural levels revealed at Bhanbhore, and at many other sites in Sindh, indicate that Aryans, Iranians, Greeks, Scythians, Parthians, and several lesser-known nations already had conquered it, and some of the greatest religions such as Jainism, Buddhism, and Hinduism already had sanctified it.

The Arabs must have had some degree of respect for this past, because they followed a pragmatic policy in Sindh. Apart from the destruction that is part of warfare, they did not vandalize the Buddhist *stupas* or the Hindu and Jain temples. Nor did they force conversions; instead they gave protection to non-Muslims in lieu of a tax. The voluntary conversions that followed were from lower-caste Hindus who wanted to acquire equality in social and religious status. Centuries later, Malcolm X and his followers would convert to Islam for the same reason. As for the upper class Hindus (the Brahmins of those days), the Arabs benefited by learning certain concepts of mathematics from them. After all, it was under the early Muslim Califs in Baghdad, in the early eighth century, that mathematics and other sciences from around the world were collected and preserved.

Three centuries after the conquest of Sindh, Islam spread to other areas of India. That era began with the looting of the Hindu temple of Somnath; it is the story of imperialism, which is always written in blood. Sindh was spared such destruction. Even in the early sixteenth century, when Babar laid the foundations of the Moghul Empire in India, Sindh continued to remain independent. It was during the time of the later Moghuls that Sindh was obliged to pay taxes to the Moghul governors, but it remained very marginal to the Moghul Empire. It continued to be ruled by its indigenous rulers and lived in splendid isolation until the British conquest in 1843.

My village is in the Tharparkar district of Sindh. This district still retains its pre-Islamic remnants and is proud to be home to the largest Hindu population in Pakistan. The land is dotted with Buddhist *stupas* and Jain and Hindu temples. These remnants suggest that Islam in Sindh harmoniously coexisted with the local religions. Describing the "popular" Islam in India and Pakistan, Annemarie Schimmel (1982) states that the common people tended to a more mystical and sometimes superstitious faith. Their religion often incorporated the religious and social customs of their Hindu ancestors. Their faith in the saints (*pir* or *sayyid*) sustained them in the hardships of life, and Muslims and Hindus sometimes shared the veneration of the same spiritual guide. Schimmel focuses on Sindh to illustrate the mutual exchange of religion and culture between Muslims and Hindus:

A strange fact—more visible in Sind than in the Punjab—is the way Hindus shared the Muslim orders. Some saints were claimed by both communities, like Shaikh Tahir, who was called Lal Udero by the Hindus . . . Hindu writers wrote mystical poems in honor of the Prophet and even wrote Ta'ziya for the Muharram mourning of the Shia community of Sind; or they devoted ballads to the fate of famous Sufi martyrs. They played a prominent part in the study of Sufism as well, though they usually lacked a true understanding of the Koran and the foundations of Muslim faith and tried to explain everything in the light of Hindu philosophy. (Schimmel 1975, 6)

It is this spiritual face of Islam, expressed by the Sufi tradition, that has survived in Sindh. Saints, dead and alive, are worshipped here as the intermediaries between God and man. Every fifth village has its own saint. The largest necropolis of the world, containing millions of graves, is in Sindh; 125,000 of these graves are of saints. It is said that at some point Persian influence of Sufi Islam entered Sindh and, due to its semblance to the Hindu concept of *Bhakti* (devotion to God), got mixed with the Hindu religion and gave birth to the Sufi tradition in Sindh. It may be true that Sufism has pre-Islamic and non-Islamic traits, but it cannot be ruled out that Islam in its pure form has the capability of developing the mysticism of the Sufi tradition.

As with its many concepts, the history of Islam also has been subjected to distortions. *Jihad,* for instance, according to the Sufi version, is a battle with one's own heart as it struggles to rid itself of the baser instincts. But *jihad* according to a mullah is an offensive battle against all non-Muslims. Islam stands for enlightenment, not vandalism; it is a battle against ignorance. When the Taliban bombed the Buddha statues carved into the cliffs of Bamiyan, Afghan Islam proved its own ignorance.

It will not be out of place to mention here that the mystic spirit of Islam as seen in Sindh also is prevalent in other parts of Pakistan, though somewhat diluted. The source of this spirit is sometimes traced to pre-Partition Northern India, to the town of Bareilly, where a Muslim scholar put forward the theory that there was no contradiction between practicing Islam and drawing on the sub-continent's ancient religious practices. "The Barelvis offer prayers to holy men or *pirs,*" writes one Western author. "To this day, many Pakistanis believe that *pirs* and their direct descendants have supernatural powers; each year, millions visit shrines of the *pirs* so that they can participate in ceremonies replete with lavish supplies of cannabis and music" (Jones 2002, 10).

To explain the prevalence of "moderate Islam" in Pakistan, Jones emphasizes: "It is nonetheless important to remember that most Pakistanis are loyal to the Barelvi tradition. That fact has had an important bearing on the nature of the Pakistani state" (Jones 2002, 11).

The Barelvi tradition[4] succeeded in Pakistan and prospered further with the coming of Indian immigrants in 1947, but part of its success was the prevalence of an ancient Barelvi-like tradition in the Indus region. Most people in rural Sindh and Punjab do not know what the Barelvi tradition is; they simply continue following their indigenous religious practices, which happen to bear some semblance to the more recent Barelvi traditions.

It is also important to mention the Taliban brand of Islam that has been born in Pakistani *madrassas.* As opposed to the moderate Barelvi tradition, Taliban's Islam is derived from the orthodox Deobandi school of Islam. The history of this school can be traced back to 1867, when the first *madrassa* was established in Deoband, at a distance of about 100 miles from Delhi. The teachers and students of the *madrassa* believed in an austere interpretation of Islam and were bitterly opposed to the British rule.

Strangely, a generation later, when the idea of a separate Muslim country was becoming popular among Indian Muslims, this group did not support the creation of Pakistan, though some of them migrated to the new country. A small percentage of the Pakistani population became followers of their orthodox and militant teachings. This group became popular only after the Soviet occupation of Afghanistan, when the Pakistani government—with the aid of the United States and Saudi Arabia—began to encourage militant Islamists to combat Soviet troops. The militants were trained in the Deobandi *madrassas* that cropped up overnight along the Pakistan-Afghanistan borders. It was the overexposure of this border territory (during the Taliban period) in the Western media that overshadowed the majority of moderate Muslims in Pakistan. Hence, very little is known about the more popular mystic Islam of Pakistan. In America, Sufism is best known for the dance of whirling dervishes; many Americans associate Sufism with Rumi. The general idea is that Sufis hold secret knowledge and, at best, Sufism is described as the synthesis of the Persian civilization and Indo-Islamic traditions.

If my description of Sufism gives the impression that I am preaching Sufism, that conclusion would be wrong. My parents were not followers of any *pir;* in fact, they were disillusioned by the degeneration of Sufi tradition that had given birth to many charlatans. My journey to "seek Paradise" was as skeptical as that of Zia Sardar in *Desperately Seeking Paradise: Journeys of a Skeptical Muslim,* and like him, I, too, say, "Where contemporary Sufi Masters of various kinds led, I was not about to follow" (Sardar 2004, 9).

However, I am a product of the moderate religious environment that dominates Sindh. It had broadened my parents' outlook—and mine. They strived to be good human beings and were progressive in the Pakistani context. Western education was very important to them and educating their daughters was absolutely vital. I was enrolled in the nearest convent school. I was the only Muslim among the Christian and Hindu girls in my class. My exposure to those peers and my own upbringing has shaped my psyche. The outlook I developed through my family held strong during the part of my life that I spent in Karachi, far from the rural province of Sindh. Pakistan, in any event, was a tolerant country during the early 1970s. Although Pakistan was created in the name of Islam, its citizens had a secular attitude in their daily lives and minorities were never under any attack. It was only after the Soviet occupation of Afghanistan in 1979 that Pakistan began to create and recruit a force of *mujahideens* to combat communism. The North West Frontier Province of Pakistan became a breeding ground for the *mullahs* and their *taliban* (students) who later took over Afghanistan. As recent history shows, wars in neighboring countries have spilled over and shaped politics and religion in Pakistan.

It is important to clarify here that Taliban do not represent Afghanistan. According to Ahmed Rashid:

> The Taliban leaders were all from the poorest, most conservative, and least literate southern Pashtun province of Afghanistan . . . For a time, some aid agencies claimed that this was the Afghan cultural tradition which had to be respected. But in a country so diverse in its ethnicity and levels of development, there was no universal standard of tradition and culture for women's role in society. Nor had any Afghan ruler before the Taliban ever insisted on such dress codes as compulsory beards for men and the burkha . . . The rest of Afghanistan was not even remotely like the south. (Rashid 2001, 10)

The Afghan families of Herat in the West were highly westernized, as they continued to emulate the lifestyles of Iranians under the rule of Reza Shah Pehlavi. The Pashtuns in the East were heavily influenced by Pakistani Pashtuns and educated their girls. Many of them continued to do so even under the Taliban, by sending their families to Pakistan. Nasim Wali Khan, daughter-in-law of Khan Abdul Ghaffar Khan, the Frontier Gandhi, is an example of an educated and politically charged Pakistani Pashtun woman.

Once the *madrassa* culture developed in Pakistan, the Pakistani government's policy to Islamize the country encouraged it further. The Shariat courts that were established in Pakistan inflicted Islamic punishments. Women become vulnerable to these changes. Cases of gang rape such as Mukhtaran Mai's did happen in the past, but the rapists were thrown in prison. It was with the sanction of *distorted* Islamic laws that criminals, like the ones who assaulted Mukhtaran, became licentious. By using certain loopholes and by bribing the police, they would gain advantage over their victim's defense. It also is a mockery of the Islamic laws that a fraction of the public has picked the trivialities of Islam, such as the growing of beards. Urban women began to cover their heads and their attendance in the mosques became conspicuous. Women's attendance in the mosques itself was a new phenomenon as, until then, Pakistani women performed their prayers in their homes. (Having grown up in an environment of home-based prayers, I still feel uncomfortable with the communal prayers held in the mosques.) Furthermore, Pakistani urban women wore sleeveless shirts and Western attire, slacks, and jeans, and even bathing suits in exclusive clubs. It was only in the 1980s that the veils and *hijabs* became conspicuous as they spread from other countries to Pakistan. This was the period when the Pakistani public began to feel the pinch of fundamentalism. Demonstrations against Islamic laws became common; women protested on the streets. This was precisely the time that I made a quiet exit to the United States.

What Lies Ahead

I landed in the peace of Ithaca in the United States. My children grew up here in safety, and my days were spent at the Olin Library at Cornell, deciphering the "pre-Islamic" symbols engraved on ancient Indus seals. Yet, the peace of my world is not something I can take for granted. It remains contingent on the continuing power of knowledgeable moderates of all religions.

Notes

1. After 9/11, Valarie Kaur, a Sikh American junior at Stanford University, traveled to several American cities to document many stories of prejudice, hate, and fear. Her documentary depicts hate crimes committed against people who "looked Arab" and how this has affected Sikhs, Muslims, and Arabs in the United States.

2. In 2002, Mukhtaran Mai was gang-raped on the orders of the village council after her 12-year-old brother allegedly had offended the honor of a powerful clan by befriending a woman from their tribe. The barbaric form of punishment stems from tribal customs perpetuated by feudalism, which predate Islam.

3. Former Wall Street reporter Asra Nomani, a Muslim left-leaning feminist, has been leading the fight to stop the current practice of segregating men and women during prayer and allowing women to enter the mosque only by the back door instead of the main entrance. She claims women have the right to pray beside men in the mosque, and the practice of the physical separation

of genders is only because few dare to oppose conservative backers of this practice.

4. Founded to defend the existing beliefs of the Muslims of South Asia, Barelvi is a Sufi movement started by Ahmed Raza Khan of Bareilly, India.

5

At the Crossroads of Religions: The Experiences of a Newar Woman in Nepal and the United States

Bidya Ranjeet

I have lived in the United States for 23 years, and my experience of living my religion can be summed up as a process of ongoing adjustment and change. I was raised in the ancient city of Kathmandu, where Hinduism and Buddhism have collided and merged. As a Newar woman, I claim both Buddhism *and* Hinduism as my (one) religion. Being raised as a Newar in Kathmandu also meant that practicing our religion was a community affair, celebrated with members of Newari *guthis* (community organizations). In the United States, where there are few Nepalis and even fewer Newars, maintaining some of our customs is difficult. Other challenges arise from how little other people know about our religion and how this leads to cultural gaps.

The theme of this chapter is about religious boundaries: Sharp boundaries that impede religious practices and separate people, and blurred boundaries that bring people together. I begin this chapter with a description of the challenges we face being Newars in the United States. I then present a description of the customs I was raised with in Nepal, showing both the blurred boundaries between religions and the embedded boundaries within the groups. In the concluding section, I return to life in the United States to show how we try to uphold the principles of our religion even when we cannot maintain all our customs.

Religious Customs in a Time of Sorrow

Issues of religion assume great importance when loved ones pass away. We are socialized to mourn in specific ways, and we engage in sets of rituals that express how our religion has taught us to think about existence. In times of joy, such as weddings, it is easier to introduce new and innovative ways to express our feelings. Death in the family brings on a very different set of social, cultural, and political challenges.

This year, I went through a very difficult period in my life. My mother, who had just returned to Nepal after visiting me, and my brother, who had been living in the United States for about six years, passed away within a few weeks of each other. I went back to Nepal and was able to complete my mother's last rites in a manner befitting a woman who had lived a full life and was widely respected for her wisdom and achievements. The *Si Guthi* (community organization) of my Newar community was there to help me with the arrangements—the rituals, the priests, and informing people—and to provide solace. We performed all the rituals according to our religion, and I finally experienced a sense of closure.

When my brother died of throat cancer, we had to try to recreate many customs to adapt to conditions in the United States and in the absence of the *Si Guthi*. We had no hopes of finding a priest who would be knowledgeable about our Newari customs; we considered ourselves lucky to find a Tibetan monk who could speak a little Nepali. Even though he could not say the prayers in Nepali, the Buddhist chanting created a peaceful atmosphere to which we could relate. Normally, the oldest son or a close male relative lights the funeral pyre to the accompaniment of prayers for the departed. We had to do without such rituals because there was no appropriate setup for performing these rites.

Upon reflection, I realize that part of the reason why we could not recreate some of the rituals is because we don't have sufficient family members here or a sufficiently large community to support priests who are knowledgeable about our customs. There also are other embedded restrictions. Even if any of the family members from Nepal wanted (and could afford) to come for the funeral, it is very unlikely that they would have gotten visas to come. In this post-9/11 era, visa applications require very detailed and elaborate paperwork and background checks, which is much too time-consuming. Similarly, it is difficult for us to recreate community or-ganizations like *guthis* because of how family is defined when workplaces assess family leave. Even with time off from work, there is little cultural space for us to carry out certain rituals that we would like to perform.

Generally, following a death, we believe the spirit wanders back to its home on the seventh day, and a feast is prepared for the dead and hung out of the window in a bamboo basket during the night. We could not follow this ritual because we feared the reactions of our neighbors. Instead, we offered a small-scale feast on a plate next to my brother's picture. During this time of mourning, we just could not face several rounds of explanations of what we were doing and why.

On the tenth day, as in Nepal, my nephew and sister-in-law, dressed in white and accompanied by other relatives, went to the ocean to complete a ritual bath. In Nepal, neither of them would be expected to attend to any work or chores outside the home; the community would take care of it. Here, my nephew had to leave the house during this mourning period. In Nepal, he would have been greeted with sympathy by strangers and acquaintances who would know what his shaved head and white clothes symbolized. Here, he was an object of curiosity. While this curiosity is not ill meant, it is an additional burden to deal with a lot of questions about culture during this period of mourning. It certainly added to a feeling of being foreign through this difficult period.

We had a Brahmin priest perform the thirteenth day prayers in place of a Newari priest. At the end of the rituals, the family was reintroduced to eating nonvegetarian food and resuming their prayers. (Until that day the family is considered impure and does not perform *pujas;* they eat a very restricted diet as a ritualized form of mourning.) The priest performed the *hom,* a ceremony sacrific-ing different kinds of grains to the fire to purify the family in mourn-ing and the house. However, at the end of the ceremonies, we did not know what to do with the *puja* offerings of flowers, sweets, and rice. In Nepal, we would throw it into the river. We discussed taking it to the ocean or a river near our house, but we were worried that, in a post-9/11 environment, people might get suspicious. In the end, we poured everything out in our backyard. My brother's ashes remain in my nephew's car, waiting to go home when one of the family members is able to travel to Nepal.

The lack of prior cultural understanding of our customs introduced some other interesting situations. During the time I was in Nepal attending to my mother's funeral rites, my colleagues brought food for my family in the United States. My husband was very appreciative of their thoughtfulness, but he didn't know what to do with the food, since most of it was nonvegetarian. In Nepal during periods of mourning, people drop by informally and take care of everyday needs so the grieving family can cut themselves off completely from the daily routine. After my brother's death, people kept asking me what they could do to help out. Others asked about the arrangements for the funeral service. Though I recognized their good intentions, it forced me to get involved in such day-to-day arrangements. We don't lead the kind of community lives where people can just stop by the house and take over daily tasks such as cleaning, cooking, or shopping for everyday provisions. People started giving us money in envelopes instead of food so that we could use it however we needed it.

Although we tried to recreate some rituals we would have followed in Nepal, and people visited, I still felt some kind of void in my soul. In Nepal after a person's passing, a *saradha* is done every month, and one on the forty-fifth day, followed by once-a-year ceremonies. The mourning family invites other family and community members, especially all those who took care of the funeral arrangements, for a meal on the 45th day, and then for the other follow-up occasions. In order to accommodate our non-Nepali friends, as well as reach some closure ourselves, I created a mixed ceremony. I decided to host an event to celebrate the lives of my mother and brother, and I invited all my friends, family, and colleagues. I tried to uphold the principle of coming together at a sorrowful time and remembering those who passed away, if not through the religious rituals, then through an event that at least brought people together to reflect on the lives of my mother and brother.

Overall, this phase of my life has made me realize that we are in the process of forming a new culture of religion in the United States. We retain some of the values from back home and are creating some new ones that are feasible and acceptable in this country.

No Clear Boundaries

As I was growing up in Kathmandu, I did not consciously know to what religion my family and I belonged. I was raised in a place where every street led to a courtyard or a square, where one could not miss the presence of some religious monument: a pagoda, a serene *stupa*, a shrine, or a temple. The trays of ritual offerings, flowers and incense sticks, the smell of the butter lamps, the creaking sound of the prayer wheel, and the crowds around the temples every morning and evening made us feel as if we were living among gods and goddesses. Both Hinduism and Buddhism have developed detailed, ritualized ways of living, although both emphasize connectedness to others and the duties and responsibilities each individual is supposed to fulfill to enact this connectedness. Thus, the religion I was raised with—the mix of Hinduism and Buddhism— was a part of the cultural fabric of Kathmandu.

The religious symbols scattered over the area reflected this blurring of boundaries between Hinduism and Buddhism. Our year was filled with various religious events that kept everyone, particularly the young and the old, very engaged in festivities. I remember celebrating *Shri Panchami* as a child by visiting the Swyambhu temple at the beginning of spring to worship the goddess Saraswoti (goddess of learning). Swyambhu is a place where Buddhism and Hinduism come together. The Swyambhu houses the Hindu deities Saraswoti and Harati Mata (goddess Durga) along with Gautama Buddha. As a youngster, I was unaware of the various facets of Swyambhu. We simply paid our homage to each of the gods and goddesses along the path, without knowing the distinction between Hindu and Buddhist gods. We would worship at the temples of Saraswoti, Harati Mata, and Gautama Buddha, then go to the monasteries and turn the giant wheels of prayer, and then participate in the ritual circling of the Buddha *stupa*. On the same trip, we would stop to worship Ajima (another form of Durga literally meaning "grandmother god"), praying for *shakti* (power) to build tolerance.

Reflecting on Swyambhu now, I can see multiple aspects of life woven into these visits. People go there for religious purposes, but it is also a form of disciplined morning exercise to climb that hill, so the secular and sacred are melded into each day. On special occasions, such as *gulan,* one man from each household would go to Swyambhu accompanied by a band of community musicians (*dhime baja*). After the ritual visit, they assembled at the *sa* (a place where edible oil used to be pressed) for morning tea. At this point, the community members took attendance; if a family failed to send someone for this ritual, they were fined. Very often, bereaved families take turns to serve breakfast to this group. As a female member of my family, I have served breakfast (tea and sweets) to the group a few times. As an adult, I am fascinated by some of these traditions that have a built-in system of community support and public opportunities to process grief by symbolically reconnecting with the larger community.

Kathmandu is also unique because, along with the coexistence of deities and symbols of different religions, we find different groups meeting to worship in the same places while maintaining their cultural diversities. There are temples where the Newars, Tibetans, and Indians all gather. The Indians and Newars worship the Mahankal deity as Shani Dev (god of Saturn) and the Tibetans worship the deity as Khotan Gunjo. Another intriguing feature of the temples are the Hindu idols that have the Buddha on their foreheads, such as the Buddha Nilkantha (form of Bishnu). My memory of the idols—symbolizing two religions and festooned with flowers—has begun to wane, but these carvings indicate a longer history of religious coexistence in Nepal.

In order to understand this coexistence, we must understand the long history of this region, situated as it is at the crossroads of Asia, between contemporary India and China. Gautama Buddha was born in Lumbini, now a part of Nepal. By 300 C.E., Emperor Ashoka, who gave up all forms of violence, built several pillars to commemorate Buddhist messages throughout Kathmandu valley. The kings of Kathmandu sent emissaries to Tibet, where the king and the kingdom soon adopted Buddhism. While the practices associated with Hinduism were evident from at least 800 C.E., Hinduism became the royal religion under the Malla kings who ruled from the twelfth to eighteenth centuries C.E. The palace of the living goddess, Kumari (described below), was built during this period. But the intermingling of politics and religion also is clear in recent times because there have been some attempts to separate Buddhism and Hinduism in order to establish Nepal as the world's only Hindu kingdom.

The most prominent symbol of the mingling of the religions is reflected in the living goddess Kumari. According to what has been relayed in Newar families over the generations, at the time when Nepal was just the Kathmandu valley, the King of Nepal used *mantra, tantra,* and *yantra* (a comingling of Hindu, Buddhist, and tantric rites) to summon the goddess Taleju (goddess Durga/Shakti) so he could consult her on certain issues. She would appear before him with a curtain separating them. One day, the king wanted to see the goddess directly and moved the curtain; she had appeared in the form of a beautiful woman, and the King desired her. Goddess Taleju was furious and said that he would no longer be able to consult her directly, but he would have to seek her through a Kumari (a child virgin). The Kumari then became the living goddess.[1]

The people of Nepal, including the King, worship the symbol of the Hindu kingdom, Kumari, the living goddess. But the paradox is that Kumari is selected from a Shakya family (who mainly practice Buddhism) when she is around 4 or 5 years old, and then is worshipped as a goddess until she reaches puberty. When a Kumari is selected, she goes through numerous secret rituals. She faces a series of tests that a normal 5-year-old girl would not be able to withstand; these rituals determine whether she possesses the necessary 32 *lachan* (qualities) of god. Once she passes these tests, she goes to live at the Kumari House, where the people of Nepal come to worship her. Crowds of people gather for her daily appearances. And, to this day, the King of Nepal comes to the Kumari House to seek blessings from the living goddess.

Overall, the year-round celebrations and daily and weekly rituals that were a part of my youth emphasized collective gatherings and traditions. There was little separation of Hindu and Buddhist temples and rituals. These were all simply part of our lives.

The Newars: Community and Religion

Just as my religious experiences as a Newar straddle Buddhism and Hinduism, my religious experiences are hard to separate from cultural experiences. Much of our family and community celebrations involved visits to Hindu and Buddhist temples, but these were woven in with specific sets of family practices.

The Newars

The Newars are indigenous people of Kathmandu valley whose native tongue is the Nepal *Bhasa*, also known as *Newari*, which is one of the Tibeto-Burman languages (though since the 1980s, the need grew to speak Nepali, the national language, and also use English for higher education purposes). The Newars' love for their community and their family is proven by the way their residences are situated. Kathmandu overflows with adjoined houses and courtyards known as *baha*. Each community has its own Ganesh temple. Newari life revolves around a unique institution: cooperatives/trusts that are known as *guthis*, which are mainly run by representatives of various male members of the community. A key *guthi* is the *Si Guthi* composed of male family members. When a death occurs within a family of this community, the *Si Guthi* makes all the arrangements for the funeral and uses its funds for the cremation and last rites so that grieving family members do not have to think about mundane matters for some time. This is the support I sorely missed this year.

Guthis perform a very supportive role, but they also exert a great deal of control over people's lives, such as upholding caste boundaries.[2] When I chose to marry outside my caste, my brother told me that I would encounter difficulties because my spouse's *guthi*, the Ranjitkars, believe that they are of higher status than the Manandhars. (Of course my group, the Manandhars, feel that they are higher than the Ranjitkars.) Many Newars have faced social ostracism imposed by *guthis, for life,* for marrying lower-caste Dalits. Thus, *guthis* are very supportive, but they also create and uphold social boundaries that can be devastating to people who are not considered insiders.

Female-centered Rituals

Like most women in Nepal—Hindu or Newar—I was raised with a series of female-centered religiocultural rituals. These events place women at the center of religiocultural events. While they are often ritualized opportunities for fun, leisure, and female bonding, some of them establish the differences between men and women and age-based status hierarchies.

Most girls grow up with the ideology of powerful female goddesses, whom they are surrounded by in everyday life: Sarswoti, the goddesses of learning; Durga, the goddess of power; and Laxmi, the goddess of wealth. In some households, girls are ritually worshiped as kumaris every day as part of the daily *puja,* until they reach puberty. My US-born daughters always were flattered when they visited Kathmandu, because their grandfather and uncles would come and lower their heads on the girls' feet and seek their blessings each morning. (They tried, in vain, to convince their father of the value of continuing this custom in Connecticut.) These customs of worship and the sense of being all-powerful make it especially difficult when the women get married and are no longer cosseted and worshiped in this way. Then they experience the subordinated position of being the newest outsider in the family. However, when they become mothers, they are again venerated as goddesses. Sons, at all ages, are expected to touch their mother's (and grandmothers') feet with their heads and seek their blessings as part of their daily routine. Thus, with age, the women are reestablished as the centers of power in the households.

Three religiocultural rituals, *ihi, barha,* and *junko,* that have been part of our family illustrate the intersections of age and women's position. These events ritually establish an individual's ties with the community.

Ihi

I remember sitting on my father's lap when I was eight during my marriage ceremony. I got married, not to a human, but to a *bel* (a kind of fruit). *Bel* symbolizes the god Bishnu, and during the *ihi* ceremony (or *bel bibaha,* in Nepali), I was married to the god Bishnu. My father performed the *kanya dan* (giving away the virgin bride).[3]

Barha

The next rite of passage for a Newar girl is the *barha* (*gufa,* in Nepali).[4] *Barha* is a rite of passage for girls who have not reached puberty, and is a time for bonding with the older women in the family. During my *barha* ceremony, I was placed in seclusion for 11 days, away from the sunlight and all men. As the central figure in this ceremony, I had a wonderful time. I still cherish the time I got to spend exclusively with my grandmothers, aunts, and friends. My friends and girls from the community came to play with me every day. I still feel very blessed to have had this rite of passage because of the multigenerational bonding experience.

By the twelfth day, the *barha* girl has great skin from the *kon buliu* (facials) she receives during this time and from being sheltered from the sun's rays. It is, in some respects, like spending a few days at a spa. On the twelfth day, my mother and aunts, after the customary *pujas,* covered my head with a large piece of cloth and took me to the balcony to offer my prayers to the sun god. Afterwards, I was taken to pay my respects at the local Ganesh temple. All the community members came to their windows or verandahs, and the people on the streets stopped to watch the procession.

Junko

A few years back, we were fortunate enough to be able to celebrate my mother's *junko* when she turned 77 years, 7 months, and 7 days old. This ceremony lasts for two days, with a lot of tantric rituals performed by the priest. My mother was acknowledged as having a third eye (denoting complete wisdom) during this occasion. A silver-and-gold eye was placed on the forehead, symbolizing that she had risen to the level of a goddess.[5] On the second day of the ceremonies, relatives and community members placed my mother on a chariot and took her, as a goddess, on an elaborate parade. A white carpet was laid on the path of the chariot, and her arrival announced by a band and local *dhime baja* (of *guthi* members). Relatives and community members followed. That evening, 1,400 people came over for a *bhoye* (feast).

It is very difficult to describe these traditions to Westerners. Many of these customs make sense within specific contexts. Customs like *ihi* and *barha* are meant to celebrate certain aspects of female lives; they also are social occasions for female gatherings and bonding. Even though scholars who are less familiar with the *lived* meanings of these events point to such ceremonies as upholding the separation of women and men (and consequently sustaining patriarchy); in practice, however, these are affirmative, joyful events where women are dominant. *Junko* is another rite of passage. It is a celebration of an older person's wisdom, and the person's sex is no longer relevant. Collectively, each of these customs provides many ways to celebrate women's roles and women who otherwise would remain isolated individuals weighed down by family work and responsibilities.

Recreating Religion in the United States

Compared to the world of Kathmandu, where we rarely thought about separating the sacred and the secular or even clearly distinguishing between religions, the context in which I practice religion in the United States is very different. If the descriptions in this section seem to emphasize personal feelings and reactions, it is because that is an accurate reflection of how I live my religion here in the absence of the environment of Kathmandu.

My husband and I have tried to recreate some of the things that we practiced back home, though hardly in the same way. I have tried to emulate a bit of Kathmandu in my home. I have Buddha and Tara statues, as well as models of *stupas* and Shiva *lingas*. On a kitchen counter is the *sukanda,* an oil lamp with a Ganesh on the top, which is primarily used by the Newars. I have few *thankas*

(Tibeto-Nepali paintings of Buddha) on my wall. I still look at the Nepali and the Newar calendar and reminisce about the upcoming holidays and the related celebrations. But as soon as I step outside my house, I know I no longer have the ability to recreate this aspect of my life. Most people don't understand the kind of customs or organization of religion I was used to. The institutional, social, and cultural space does not exist in the same way. Here, "religion" has to be practiced outside work hours and on weekends.

A major adjustment I have made is that, in my public life in the United States, I have learned to think of Hinduism and Buddhism as different religions. While I lived in Nepal, no one asked me to what religion I belonged. But when people in the United States find out I am from Nepal, I am often prompted with, "Oh, so you are Hindu?" I say, "Yes, I am Hindu, but Buddhist as well." I explain how people in Kathmandu practice both religions side by side, and do so in distinctive ways depending on their family and ethnic traditions. But I cannot easily recreate that syncretism, which reflects centuries of Nepali tradition. In the United States, there are expectations that immigrants will assimilate, but these ideas of assimilation have been imagined in terms of Christian immigrants who are likely to move to mainstream churches and follow services in English. For Newars, there is a different set of challenges. For us, religious "assimilation" can happen only by fitting in with other immigrant groups who practice Hinduism or Buddhism rather than the mainstream. During my life in the United States, I have gone to Hindu temples built by Indian Americans and Buddhist pagodas built by Japanese- and/or Cambodian-Americans. These demographically larger groups have set up institutions that reflect *their* religious customs and languages. I cannot go to the equivalent of Swyambhu, where Buddha and Harati Mata (goddess Durga) coexist. The Nepali community has been able to build small temples, within houses, in the Washington D.C. and New York City areas, where Shiva and Buddha are placed side by side. But the distance is a hindrance for me. Recently our *guruju* (religious guide) told me that we practiced *Bajrayana* Buddhism; this is why we worship Buddha and Hindu gods and embrace *tantra*. But such "border crossings" among religions cannot be easily expressed in the United States, where institutions and practices are based on clearly separate, identifiable religions that are linked with specific nationalities or ethnic groups.

As Nepalis in the United States, we have been able to celebrate only *Dashain* and *bhai tika* ceremonies each year. Occasionally we celebrate *mha puja* (the worship of oneself), which also is the Newar New Year. In the United States, I have never asserted myself to take the time off for these festivals. I work at a university, so I can take a few days off, but the rest of the community members are not so fortunate. They cannot take time off from school or work. There are always deadlines, exams, and other demands that pay no attention to our religious calendar. People who work in blue-collar jobs or in marginal occupations certainly cannot afford to lose a day's wages because there is no official recognition of a holiday. I am personally not so deeply invested in many of the rituals that I exert myself to recreate some version, even in the absence of a community to share it with.

We do celebrate some modified events. We celebrate *bhai-puja* on the weekend closest to the actual day. We do not draw the *mandalas*, which are a key part of the ceremony along with the *yantra* (the part of the tantric practices for summoning gods and goddesses for the blessings), because the houses, with their carpeted floors, do not accommodate such practices. We also don't burn much incense or light the oil lamps because of the fire alarms in the homes. But even without the sights, smells, and ceremonies, we invite our brothers or "adopted brothers" to join us to mark this auspicious event.

The same can be said about the *Dashain* festival. In the United States, we celebrate this two-week-long festival over a weekend. While *Dashain* is a family affair in Nepal; in the United States it has become a community affair for Nepali people to keep their culture alive through performance. The religious content cannot be recreated with images, music, flowers, pujas, and *homs*, but we try to keep the spiritual principle of collective celebration alive. We try to have food just the way it is prepared in Nepal, and we receive the *tika* (a dot on the forehead) and *jamara* (sprig of grain) from our elders as blessings.

My children were raised in a mixed cultural environment, having celebrated Christmas and Thanksgiving holidays. We have assimilated the major events for complex reasons. When my children were young, we celebrated Christmas so that they wouldn't feel left out at school. As they grew older, it already was a tradition in our home. Thanksgiving, of course, is a nondenominational holiday, so it is easy to celebrate a gathering of families. At the same time, I arranged for each of my three daughters to go through the *Ihi* ceremony. Like many others, I consider it to be a part of my *karma* as a Newar householder to pass on our traditions and create occasions to celebrate as a family and community.

Conclusion: Reflections on Religion

Religion, for me, has been a process of celebrating the young and the old, men and women, ourselves, and our teachers, brothers, sisters, parents, friends, and all living beings. I remember my grandmother saying every day, "Sakal prani lai namaskar" ("I worship all living things"). While I was growing up, I gained a lot of "religious" knowledge and information from grandparents and elders. For each aspect of life, they had a saying or a story with a moral. I can see myself doing the same thing. A lesson I cherish is: "You have to welcome your guests as gods, especially the ones who come in the evening—feed them even if you don't eat that day." This seems to embody the principle that you do your duty regardless of the goodness or wickedness of the other person. We perform these duties regardless of circumstances. I think we have been trying to keep to these values even though we have not been able to keep up our customs and rituals in the United States.

Like most Newars, I do not really understand the reasons behind many rituals and traditions that I follow. But I still follow some customs and traditions because I see some positive aspects in each of them. As a child, I did not notice the Newars' unique syncretic Hindu and Buddhist culture, but I now see how fortunate I was being raised in an environment that maintained religious harmony. As I became aware of the embedded boundaries that also are part of these practices—for instance, the caste-based restrictions—it has been easy for me to reject those and keep to the positive principles that blur boundaries instead of sustaining them. I now understand religion as a part of living and breathing. It is what we do in every aspect of our lives, from birth to death. I don't have a separate religion; I have a culture of day-to-day living with my family and community. This upbringing definitely has helped me to see the good in everything. I mentioned earlier that living in Kathmandu felt like I was living among the gods and goddesses. Although I am not physically in Kathmandu, I have been fortunate to come to know a lot of friends who I feel have most of the *lachan* (qualities) of god. And so, while I miss the air of Kathmandu, I also have been able to live my life here in the United States with Kathmandu in my heart.

Notes

1. There is another version of this story that I read in a Nepali newspaper. In this version, Malla kings summoned the Taleju Bhavani by using the Sri Yantra, a tantric device. However, one day during Trailokya Malla's reign, the Sri Yantra was opened by his daughter. The goddess was furious and told King Trailokya that she would consult with him only through a Kumari. From then on, the Malla kings consulted the Taleju Bhavani via the Kumari. During the rule of Jaya Prakash Malla, the last Malla king, Kathmandu was under constant attack by the Shaha King. One day, Jaya Prakash Malla dreamed that his reign over Nepal was to end, but he could prolong it by maintaining the Kumari House and starting the Kumari Chariot procession. By the order of Jaya Prakash Malla, in 1756 the foundation of the Kumari Residence was laid and completed within six months. The Kumari Chariot procession also commenced, and Jaya Prakash Malla ruled for 12 additional years (Sharma 2001).

2. Newars have a caste system much the same as Hindus. The Hindu caste system is based on an originary myth of the creation of humans, but the Newar's caste system is heavily based on their occupation. The belief in the Hindu religion is that Brahmins came out of the head; the Chetris came from the arms; the Baisyas from the body (chest and stomach); and the Shudras came out of the feet of a divine being. So even though all humans came out of Brahma, the interpretation has been that the Shudras and some castes of Baisyas have been designated as "untouchables." During the Malla regime,

Jayasthithi Malla (1354–1395) established the caste system, borrowing heavily from Hinduism (Rotto 2000), as he saw a dire need for a division of labor. The Newars' occupation was passed from one generation to another. The caste system was applied to both Buddhist and Hindus (The Rising Nepal 2001). Although the beginnings of the caste system had the good intentions of the welfare of the country, the caste system has taken the form of a class system. People have arranged castes in a hierarchical order that has created discrimination—including untouchability. On August 17, 1963 (Mulki Ain New Civil Code of Nepal, Bhadra 1, 2020 B.S.) caste discrimination was legally abolished, but the discrimination is still deeply rooted in the daily lives of people. As the ruling Ranas of Nepal deprived citizens of education because they feared that educated citizens would be able to overthrow their rule of Nepal, in the absence of formal education, the caste system has kept the Newars rich, and the artisans and craftsmanship alive. However, this does not in any way justify the deprivation of the educational opportunity and the discriminations the lower caste Newars have had to face.

3. I have heard different explanations as to why Newars follow this ceremony, most of which center around providing a young girl with social protection. After the *Ihi*, girls are allowed to wear *sindur* (a vermillion powder) on their heads as a symbol of their married status. The girls who go through this ceremony are given some protection from men who are more likely to stay clear of a god's wife. Other explanations that have been given center on preventing widowhood. Even if a Newar girl's husband dies, she can continue to wear *sindur* because, in principle, she is still married to the god. A few years ago, one of my aunts told me that Newars started the ritual in order to protect their daughters from committing *sati,* a Hindu ritual especially prevalent in the nineteenth century, where the wife ritually died on her husband's funeral pyre (Gellener 1991).

4. There are many scholarly debates about the sources (tribal or Hindu) and purpose of this ceremony: Ritual confinement of women to emulate customs of Hindu Brahmans or ritual freedom granted to females *not* to follow Brahmanic traditions of confinement during menarche (Gellener 1991).

5. If both husband and wife are alive, the *junko* ceremony is performed based on the husband's age. During the ceremony, relatives shower the immediate family with rice, grain, and clothes. Men receive long pieces of white cloth to wrap around their heads, signifying their state of blessedness to have a parent live that long. The priest receives several items on the assumption the *junko* would use these in their afterlife.

6

Color of God:
Resplendent Clay of Hindu Images
as the Glow of the Ineffable

Neela Bhattacharya Saxena

Into the World of Color

In January of 2006, I was visiting my parents in a remote town in eastern India called Dharmanagar and was struck by the rows and rows of half-made clay effigies, not yet recognizable as Saraswati, in an image maker's shed. Perhaps my gaze was a result of my sojourn in the United States, for if I had stayed in India, such a scene would have been taken for granted and not been the sight of wonder. As a US-based scholar who has written about the Divine Feminine in her many aspects within the Indic milieu, I was keenly aware how such images create a seamless spiritual landscape that provides continual sustenance to people and structures their lives around multiple images of the Great Goddess. Such images seep into the depth of the unconscious and begin to sow seeds in the human mind in ways unreachable by simple ratiocination. They create culture, and they create a gynocentric sensibility—a spirituality focused on the Divine Feminine—which I have described later and which coexists with patriarchal social modes.

Headless and simple forms of clay and straw, those figures were harbingers of spring; my mother and I knew these would be transformed into resplendent images of the white goddess within a few days as Basant Panchami, an early spring festival in February, was just around the corner. But my mother and I were returning from a visit to the Shmashan Kali (Kali of the cremation ground) temple—the black goddess, perhaps the other end of the spectrum of color that numerous symbols of the Divine in Hinduism inhabit. I had gazed at the dark and fierce image of the Great Goddess who captivated me. In the courtyard of the temple, I also saw images of the flamboyantly colored Lakshmi, and a rare image of white Kali, that had been left to the elements and were in various stages of decay. Strewn around the courtyard were other crumbling and moldering images, unrecognizable and ready to vanish into the earth. The Divine essence was invoked in them during the special ceremonies and then were bid farewell as the spirit interfused back into the atmosphere. A short distance away, a meandering little stream with intimations of burning dead bodies on her shores that I could not see but imagine were stark reminders of the ephemerality of all.

I was filled with a strange joy that was mixed with apprehensions, as I was about to leave my aging parents to return to my family in the United States. Such pendulous journeys between two worlds that I have taken many times since coming to the United States in 1986 have helped shape my intellectual and spiritual being. I was privileged enough to return to the site of my birth and be regenerated by its ancient wisdom and complex history. This in turn would enrich my American self, both as a teacher and a scholar, who had to come to terms with the racialized and gendered identity thrust upon her. My intellectual quests were guided by the superbly female figure of Saraswati. Now recollecting my emotions in relative tranquility to write this essay, I find myself transported into another time when I was a child, perhaps in 1968, and recall a vivid scene.

An art teacher from a vocational school in a small town in Uttar Pradesh cleans his brush, picks up color from the palate, and begins to clothe the clay Saraswati in exquisite lines. His eyes close in rapt attention or in meditation in the ancient tradition of visualizing the form of the god before sculpting the image. The eyes of the goddess of learning are being drawn now as small children watch the form take shape and become a pratima. She is serene and her eyes too, like her image maker's, are half-closed in meditation; her ears elongated like the Buddha; and she wears a garland of flowers whose fragrance mixed with burning incense would soon turn the artistic exercise of the *shilpi* into the ritual of worship. The swan at her feet looks on at the *veena* she plays soundlessly—perhaps to call us to the unheard sound of the Divine vibration, the seed sound of beginnings and endings—to awaken us from the torpor of unconsciousness of our everyday reality.

As students whose only job was to learn, Saraswati was the center of our ritual life. No studying was allowed that day. The rationalists would question: Why no studying on that special day of learning? Who cared why; we just had fun. Now I can speculate as this adult has a tendency to try to "understand" the rituals. Perhaps because it was the day to be aware of the Devi and focus on her form as the all-pervasive sound who presides over all learning, both exoteric and esoteric. I recognize how those resplendent deities I encountered as a child in India introduced me to a divinely colorful world that later helped me theorize that world as essentially gynocentric (Saxena 2004), which is suffused with the Feminine Divine and her many manifestations of a joyous religiosity that initiates one into the ananda element of the triadic *sat, chit,* and *ananda* (truth, consciousness, and bliss), qualities that the supreme Brahman is supposed to inhabit. That is a scholarly mask that I will not put on in this chapter; I will simply introduce the colorful deities that saturated and shaped my world.

My world was not simply inhabited by female goddesses. My paternal grandmother, whose unconditional love catered to my every whim, introduced a new ritual of Satya Narayan puja. This is a curious new deity who appeared rather late in India's history and has close connections with a Sufi figure called Satya Pir. My father seemed surprised when I pointed out that at the end of the story people utter "amin, amin," the Muslim form of Amen. Such is the malleable border of folk religiosity in India that different religions and their festivities interpenetrate without conflict or contradiction, a fact often neglected by communalists and scholars alike.

An incarnation of Vishnu, Satya Narayan appears as a fakir or Sufi saint in the story told during his puja. At our home, Narayan puja punctuated the month halfway on full moon nights, whereas my father's visit to the Kali temple every new moon night marked the other half. I do not remember ever missing that visit even during a big flood when we went to the Kali temple by boat. Kali, who shatters all illusions of little identities, enveloped the dark side of the month, and a Fakir Narayana illuminated the brighter side. No wonder I later became enamored with Kali and imaginatively visited the Sufi Arab world of such *shaikhs* as Ibn Arabi.

Our lives spanned Islam and Hinduism as well as castes. I witnessed a Brahmin teacher making the image of Saraswati in a leather school where cowhides were a constant presence. Our household included workers of different religions and castes. The constant interaction and copresence made all simple notions about caste restrictions appear rather quaint, or was it that perhaps my experiences were aberrant. I also remembered the schools we went to where morning prayers meant singing a song that Gandhi loved: "Raghupati Raghav Raja Ram, patiapavan Sitaram; Ishwar Allah tero nam sabko sanmati de Bhagvan." This can be roughly translated as a recitation of the many names of Lord Ram, who is called both Ishwar and Allah, and we pray that he may give good sense to all—a prayer much needed in a more communally divided world today.

My sister tells me that in some places in Canada, the word Allah has been removed from the song. This is the legacy of a recently imagined, exclusivist Hindutva identity that was rarely a part of India's history. And, South Asian Islam historically appeared quite malleable and saturated with Sufi visions, as Parveen's, Elora's, and Selina's chapters point out, until more Talibanized versions of Islam began to take hold of its moorings. These recent exclusivist and often highly androcentric religiosities are threatening to tear apart the very fabric of spiritual lives in many parts of the world.

I recall visiting my Muslim friends in the city during Muharram and watching the brightly colored *tajias* that Shia Muslims would take out in great fanfare. We were raised in a world that was the face of a curious secularism, quite unique to India's history of pluralism. Eating *siwai* brought by Muslims was a matter of course in our home, and Christmas was celebrated as *Bara din* or long day to celebrate the winter solstice. My mother would bake cakes and puddings during this festival. Later I would eat fruitcakes at our Christian friends' homes. Lisha and I once walked into the beautiful cathedral in Kolkata during one of our visits, and my curiosity to see the rituals up close had brought us to the line of communion takers. Both of us took the communion wafer and wine quite devoutly, although some of my Christian friends later objected to our behavior.

I intensely relived my connection with the Divine Feminine during my first visit to the Kamakhya temple after living in the United States for 20 years. I was there with my sister-in-law and her young daughter, and I imagined a sacred triad of three women visiting the most famous Yoni pitha in the world. My friends Julia Jean and Frederique Apfel-Marglin have done extraordinary work about the yearly Ambubachi festival at Kamakhya.[1] Julia, an initiated tantric *sadhika,* had asked me to visit various Mahavidya shrines strewn around those ancient Nilgiri hills. Having been under the spell of Chinnamasta (Saxena forthcoming), one of the most complex great knowledge forms of Kali, I made sure to visit her shrine.

It was completely deserted as I walked down the steep stairs into the darkened shrine. There was no image in the dark chamber as I reached the bottom, only a flat, uneven, and moist rock. The two little snakes, whether of rock or clay, faced each other; in the dim light of an earthen lamp they appeared amazingly alive, reminding me of the serpent power of the Kundalini lying dormant within the human body. They say if awakened consciously or unconsciously, Kundalini could plunge one into the depths of the maddening universe of the goddess. If one is fortunate enough to get a glimpse of the other universe beholding darkly through that momentous gap between consciousness and the unconscious, one is never the same, as all illusory borders we build around our little identities are smashed to pieces. No wonder the tantric universe is fraught with dangers not to be dabbled with in idle curiosity. I walked back up the stairs and out of the reverie and into the daylight. My head still smeared with red vermillion and a marigold garland around my neck, I felt an affinity with the goats sacrificed at all Shakta shrines.

As a child I had watched many such sacrifices during Kali worship that my father participated in when we visited Dharmanagar.

I find the ritual hard to watch now in spite of my "understanding" the deeper tantric meaning, but as a child it was quite a taken-for-granted scene, and I wonder how such an experience might have affected me. In India, where death and life events happen in the open and without too much sentimentality, perhaps one is initiated automatically into an intricately balanced universe of arrivals and departures as simple rest stops on a long journey. Again, a rationalist would find such practices primitive and a mark of degenerate religiosities as most orientalist Europeans did during colonial periods, and even many Indians still do, but most of the same rationalists would have no qualms eating an enormous amount of meat bought at supermarkets—of animals raised and killed, often in horrific and mechanized environments, hidden away from the delicate eyes of the consumer.

Today, most *bali* rituals have been replaced with symbolic offerings of a fruit or vegetable as "modernity" has overtaken even the Shakta Hindu mind except for a few stubborn Kali worshippers. Like the Native American who would pray to the animal he killed for food, I find it much more honest to offer the animal as a sacred being to the deity and face its death before consuming its flesh. Although the objections of the vegetarians are more compelling, Indians mostly eat vegetarian food anyway since meat is expensive, and the habits of the nonvegetarians there hardly endanger the environment or their health with excessive consumption of meat. As a meat-eating and Shakti-worshipping woman, I found it interesting to tell people in the United States that I am not a religious vegetarian, which is assumed Hindus generally are. When I would tell them that vegetarianism for a Shakta is rather inauspicious, I would realize how enormously complex and diverse the so-called Hindu world is.

Kali puja night for the Bengali is the night of Diwali in most of India. It is the festival of lights when we would decorate our homes with little lamps to ward off all darkness from all corners of the house. But for most children, the sparkling displays of fireworks were a special attraction. We also would buy clay images of red Lakshmi and golden Ganesh who are specially worshipped at that time in UP. Markets would be full of little white animals and toy images made with sugar cane that were the special festive foods of the region.

Diwali is one of a whole series of autumn festivities. The goddess is worshipped in many forms in different parts of India. For the Bengalis, Durga puja, which Bandana and Monoswita describe in their chapters, is of central importance. The *Garba* dance of the *Gujaratis* during *Navratri,* or nine nights of the Devi—which is much celebrated in films and even in the streets of New York—is a *Garbha* or the womb festival. The last day of Durga puja is celebrated as *Dusshera* in many states. We watched *Ramlila* in our neighborhoods when the epic Ramayana is enacted with fanfare for 10 days. Sita's cries as she was being abducted by Ravan, and the valiant fight of the bird Jatayu against the demon, were crowd-pleasers. One of my first rebellions against the Ramayana morality came in 1975, the UN year of the woman. The issue was whether women should cross the *Lakshman Rekha* (the magic line drawn by Sita's brother-in-law as protection and not to be crossed, which of course she did), and I wrote my first debate piece that said: Yes, they should cross the line, and won the contest.

Closer to home, I became aware of gender hierarchies through the discontent in my mother's eyes. My educated mother, displaced by the partition of India and Pakistan, had married late and had left her elementary school teaching job in Assam to join my father in UP; she always regretted not finishing her BA. Although a product of her times, my mother also had seen her own widowed mother arrange a wedding for another young widow in her charge. She recalls my grandmother putting gold bangles on the wrists of this woman. Perhaps such memories and her personal discontent created a personality that I have come to love so deeply. It is extraordinary that now she openly voices her rebellion against television shows that depict submissive Indian women and finds the ascetic ways of my widowed aunts problematic. My mother has encouraged her own widowed sister-in-law to eat meat and wear whatever she wants.

A more subdued and centered goddess mainly at Bengali homes is the Lakshmi puja that I fondly recall because she is my mother's deity. Another form of *Shakti,* depicted in pink or red, and also known as Kamala in tantric forms, she comes closer to the idealized image of Hindu women. She is the goddess of prosperity and peace, and mothers give their daughters an image of Lakshmi, the consort of Vishnu, when they marry. Iconography shows her sitting at the feet of her husband and devoutly massaging his feet, a reason why I never found her particularly appealing. But I now recognize her calming effect on the psyche, and the peace that comes with prosperity as an important aspect of life. Since the Vedic period, considerable importance has been placed on women's auspicious presence in the home, the center of ritual and spiritual life in India. Women have found—though within their limited sphere—self-fulfillment in their association with the beauty and grace of the goddess Sri Lakshmi. For me, the image of my mother making beautiful *alpana* or floor decorations with ground rice is an indelible memory.

As the season transformed into cooler nights, smaller festivals would continue to enliven the life of a child. One of special fun for us was the *Paush* or pitha Sankranti. I was happy to be with my family in Dharmanagar recently after many years, and I could enjoy eating those sweet specialties called *pithas*. Although it was difficult for my octogenarian mother to make them, she still made one of her specialties called *patishapta,* a kind of pancake filled with candied coconut or dried milk.

In Allahabad, this particular time was of special importance because a month-long festival called *Magh Mela* would bring thousands of people to the city where three rivers—Ganga, Yamuna, and the vanished Saraswati—meet and create an especially auspicious point of spiritual intensity. The central event of the entire festival is a dip in the Ganga early in the morning, and the earlier the better. Having lived in Allahabad for years, I had many such shivering occasions of auspicious bathing that I will not dare repeat now.

Spring, right after Saraswati puja arrived, ushered in the most colorful of all festivals: *Holi.* This is a fun event and truly a festival of colors that celebrates Krishna, the blue god's playful *Raslila* with his beloved *Radha* and other *gopis.* But *Holi* celebrates the transgression inherent in the Krishna myths. This can be a rowdy festival and one truly carnivalesque in India. Once again, the markets would fill with special foods, and rows of multicolored *abeer*—colored powder—would be heaped on the streets. The Color of God denotes "One Becoming Many" in a sublime dance of creation in its full diversity, and *Holi* seems to literally celebrate this profusion of color in the universe of Devi's play.

Moving Away from Color

The description above is partial and regional, being primarily a tiny picture of the life of a Bengali Hindu girl in UP. The magnificent traditions of Southern India are not even mentioned as they were beyond my experience. I left this colorful India in 1986. My entry into the United States was marked by a partial and temporary psychological break since I had married against my parents' wishes and crossed caste, culture, age, language, and even national boundaries. I did not realize then that I carried in my blood an India that was as old as the rivers. When I landed in the United States, it seemed absolutely different from the one I seemingly left behind. I struggled to make sense of a new world and my new life where my past identity as a university professor had little value.

After a year of working for minimum wage in a bookstore, I found part-time teaching jobs in a couple of universities—a cog in the skillfully created and maintained unequal and underpaid system of adjunct teachers who support the base of the big pyramid called academia. I would go to academic conferences eager to present my knowledge and find myself floating in spaces that did not recognize me as a scholar. I began to learn of overt and subtle discrimination.

Recently globalization forces dramatically have changed the image of Indians of my class position. In the 1980s, I still bore the mark of the poor Third World immigrant. It soon began to dawn on me from stray comments from students, strangers, and colleagues about my great luck to have escaped the Third World. I was perplexed by the astounding ignorance of the average American about the rest of the world and the taken-for-granted ethnocentric truisms about non-Western traditions. Since I have worked at the very bottom of the academic pyramid, I have the curious good fortune of learning about the average American youth and their self-enclosed worlds. While I deeply admired the hardworking young people who tried to balance their busy lives with academic demands, I also found they have little knowledge, less time to explore, and the least interest in other worlds. They live in a constructed world of "multi-culturalism" but far from global realities. Only now, forced by the economic logic of capitalism in search of the cheapest skilled labor in a globalizing world, is there a glimmer of recognition about the larger world.

As far as Hinduism was concerned, it was the least understood tradition within American popular culture. Looking back, I realize it was a comment here and a remark there that made me quite slowly but deliberately externalize the inner world of the Kali spirit. During a social gathering, a colleague was casually chatting about my background. When I mentioned Kali, she exclaimed—referring to another esteemed colleague's description of this deity—that this was something like devil worship. I was quite astounded by this revelation. The colleague who gave her the informed opinion happened to be of Indian origin, although not a Hindu. I made some effort to give my side of the story but was not sure if I was getting through. Such episodes combined with Hollywood Kali of Indiana Jones fame, the devouring goddess of barbaric Indians that Indian actors themselves were enacting with jollity, made me aware of how important it was for me to speak my truth.

I also discovered that my students could not even imagine God as female or Mother. This was quite extraordinary that even atheists were denying the existence of a Father God; the image of a Mother God was beyond the pale of their psyches. She could not be denied if she could not be conceived. I was baffled to hear once a fellow panelist at a conference telling me that India is this dark world whereas the United States is all about light. I wrote a paper about the goddess figures I grew up with that were summarily dismissed by a colleague as of no importance since all Indian women were thoroughly oppressed. I was forced to look at my identity; my racialized and gendered self was practically thrown at me, although I had no interest in identity politics. I could have tried to explain that my psychospiritual identity as a woman was deeply shaped by the towering figure of the Mother God, a symbol of the ultimate power in the universe. But to many of my peers, I bore the mark of the oppressed woman who did not even know that she was oppressed. So what I said also did not matter since I did not have the "authority" to say so; after all, no matter how aggressive people may be when it comes to talking about victims, a victim is a victim because she is mute. Talking victims are a bore because you can't quite pity them, and they seem to throw people off their complacent certainties about the world.

Somewhere around this time as I began to question prevalent and sometimes firmly held ideologies about gender and global realities, I began to externalize my deeply personal spiritual journey. I began to write more about India, even though I continued to teach British and American literature and struggled to teach American students how to write coherent essays. My personal research into Kali, which I had begun during my days in Allahabad, opened up an incredible universe. As I relentlessly searched for an explanation for my curious waking and dreaming experiences, I began to tell the stories in spite of myself.

As far as keeping the traditions I grew up with alive, in the beginning I continued some of the rituals, especially the weekly Lakshmi ritual that my mother had ordained me to continue as a married woman. Absence of a cultural landscape steeped in mythic grandeur of stories, temples, and festivals and a lack of holidays that we took for granted in India ushered in a drift away from these rituals in the United States. It contributed to my moving away from external and ritual expression of my religiosity into a deeper realm of my being. It was a curious reversal of sorts. In India, I lived the religion and kept quiet about my deeper questions, even while searching for Kali beyond the image and rituals. In some ways moving to the United States made my spiritual quest more intense, and my rituals turned to a deeply internalized visualization and were transformed into what is known as *manas puja* or mental worship. But the world outside forced me to vocalize that inner reality, which might not have happened in India. I have come to realize that women's religiosities always have been different from the power-wielding world of men.

When in 1996, I walked into a Kali conference in New York, it marked a turning point in my life. The walls of this room at a well-known college were plastered with huge and myriad images of Kali. Important Kali scholars from all around the world were bustling about, and expert opinions were being exchanged about the nature of this violent and sexually voracious deity. Although I was merely an observer, I found myself asking one question after another. Somewhere around those hallowed grounds, I discovered my voice and thought that I might have something to say, especially since among the experts there was only one other Indian woman present.

I wondered why many more women who actually live by the goddess weren't speaking. I was quite naïve about all the hierarchical intricacies of the religion departments. The realm of discourse about Indic traditions was squarely within the Western academia by an imperial and convenient logic of objectivity. The theory goes that only those who do not live by it really know what it is all about. It seemed then that Western men with all their "scientific" tools were best suited to understand, evaluate, and proclaim the meaning of all these primitive cultures. There were a number of Western women who had embarked on this journey, but until recently they were following the same male logic and its methodologies to pass judgments on traditions that are utterly different from the one with which they are familiar. Indian women were way down on the totem pole; after all, it already had been decided they are all mute victims of Kali who is meant to serve men and their patriarchal power.

I also discovered an entire tantric industry of both the academic and commercial kind in the United States. Tantra is a body of texts, a philosophy, and a set of meditative practices that help the practitioner realize or "make real" for oneself the non-dual philosophy of the Indic tradition. Literally the word means "that which extends knowledge," but it has many undertones depending on the particular tantric tradition. Every branch of the Indic spiritual tradition, Buddhist, Jain, or Hindu in all their myriad variations, has its own tantras. Tibetan Buddhism, currently the most well known in the United States, is a tantric tradition called Vajrayana or the diamond vehicle. Since this is not necessarily a dogma, one can practice tantric visualization and meditation skills without giving up one's particular religious affiliations.

The most extraordinary aspect of all the tantric tradition is that it gives supreme importance to the Feminine Principle. The Shakta tradition that I belong to is centered on Shakti, which is variously translated as energy, force, and power and is considered feminine. The Indic tradition is the only one in the world where the active force of the universe is described as feminine and the masculine is a principle of quiescence and inactivity. Although highly misunderstood even among sections of people in India, especially because it is centered on women and their generative power, I consider this tradition the most extraordinary philosophical development in a long line of speculation about the relationship between the ultimate reality and the phenomenal world. It is world affirming and deeply satisfying to a woman's sense of herself. It is also the very source of Indian art and the colorful tradition of festivals that celebrate the Great Goddess's immense creativity and diversity. The part that made it a target of both fascination and revulsion, especially in its Western incarnations, is that it employs sexual imagery to denote the ultimate unity of the dancing dualities of the male and female principles, imaged in the figure of Shakti and Shiva.

Spurred by my experiences both internal and external, I began to explore the textual Kali as I turned inward to figure out who I was within an academic and social world of this powerful civilization and my new adoptive country. When my two sons arrived on our domestic scene, once again I would agonize over the question of their identity in a world where they would face a similar question: What are you? And they surely do. I recognized the radical difference between the world I was raised in and the one they inhabit, a fast globalizing world where plural identities are a real possibility if exclusivist religions would give it a chance. My older son, Harsha, jokes and tells me he changes his religion depending on the holiday and simply follows what's convenient. It is fine for him to pretend to be Jewish when that particular holiday gives him a reprieve from homework.

I constantly move from image to image and from one mode of worship to another. In India, different paths and images are meant to accommodate differences between people, even when they imagine an ultimate unity. Not only are there myriad faces of the Divine to pick and choose from, but there are different ways of approaching the deity, too—*jnana* yoga, *karma* yoga, *bhakti* yoga, and so forth. Designed for particular personalities, I doubt there's only one way for a person. One day I wake up in the *bhakti* mode. Another day, I'm more in the *jnana* yoga mode. In terms of religion, maybe early in the morning I am a Hindu, a little later a Buddhist, then a Muslim, then I imagine a Christian path, and late at night I become perhaps an Iroquois. But I have become increasingly aware that in a so called "faith-based" society where beliefs and loyalty to one faith rather than ways of knowing are paramount, such easy movement from mode to mode and from image to image is not an easy one to make, at least not in any public expression of it.

I do often wonder if my children were deprived of all those festivals that make a religion a living one, but I know these are different times and they are growing up in a different universe. I could never replicate the environment here, so I never tried. I do make an effort to celebrate *Diwali* and *Holi* when we light candles and throw colorful confetti at each other. This is a trick I invented when our daycare provider and a good friend, Yvonne, wanted to involve the children in the festivals native to my old country so that my kids would feel connected. I greatly appreciated the suggestion as that was when our little *Holi* party and confetti playing event was born.

When they were younger, my children would accompany me to Durga festivals; now they prefer to stay home. While I am glad to talk about stories and traditions I was raised with, I decided to stay with my paternal grandfather's tradition and not impose anything on my children. But looking around in the strife-ridden religious world today, I am almost more comfortable with their Big Bang atheism and shudder at the narrow identities that are thrown around these days in the name of religions that appear completely alien to me. Any effort to talk about a one, true, and authentic Hinduism is an exercise not only in futility, but also in serious distortion if my little story has any meaning. Living religions operate in a living human environment of interconnectedness and interdependence; theorizing them always captures only a fraction that should not be taken to be the truth.

As I travel around the world and see famous sculptures and paintings of my beloved deities in museums from Amsterdam to London to here in the Asia Society in New York, I feel a strangely comfortable distance. Perhaps these museumized deities of bronze and marble evoke the scholarly desire to understand the meaning of their *mudras* and their expressions as they sit in crisp and clean environments. They are so far away from the messy and noisy India, where temples are still muddy and wet and full of torn flowers and sticky sweets even though a new energy has been sweeping the old land.

I am fortunate that I can fly to that messy India every now and then and watch my mother run barefoot to our home temple every evening and light the earthen lamp and hear my father recite the *Gita* and the *Chandi* as I sit quietly on the temple verandah. I am fortunate that I hear their voices on the phone every week and catch sounds of that noisy world that keeps creating new deities. The staggering diversity of images that the Hindu imagination continues to create is a reminder of a wisdom acquired ages ago that there is no access to the formless without form, but the name and form given to the nameless one cannot be uniform. The Hindu world gave each of us the freedom to put the favorite form of our *Ishta devata*—be it man, woman, animal, or plant—in the frame that is ultimately empty. There is a strange equality among all creatures as all can claim to inhabit the Color of God.

There is a sacredness flowing through the body of that land that is filled with a deep sensuality of *rupa, rasa,* and *gandha:* form, fluidity, and fragrance that I never tire of talking about. In these two decades, new images have appeared on the altar my parents have built; old images of gods from our childhood are still there. The colorful sheets my parents used to make the bed of the deities were familiar for a long time; now I see new colorful sheets as the old familiar and faded ones turned into rags. Everything gets recycled in that ancient land, *murtis* becomes clay and clay becomes *murtis* in a wondrously cyclical temporality that we, too, are a part of. However far the formless and ineffable Brahman of the *shastras* may be, ordinary people catch her glorious glow in the color of their imagined gods.

Those of us who have spilled out of its malleable borders continue to search for our identities amid powerful, yet fascinating other lands. When I had finished writing my book *In the Begin-ning Is Desire: Tracing Kali's Footprints in Indian Literature,* I had answered the question of identity to myself: I am nobody. An ex-cursion into Kali, whom I called "pregnant nothingness," opens up a vastly expansive and radically expanding universe where ques-tions about little identities and tiny egos are mere masks to be played with and discarded. I also recognized that below the patri-archal world of the Indic traditions, there is a powerful gynocentric layering that has tremendous potential for both women and men as they search for liberation.

So how do we, women, find a source of strength in a spiritual tradition? I would argue that if we wish to think about Hindu fem-inism, we need to think of gynocentrism with a capital G. We need to move away from reductive feminism that is a result of a particu-lar history, a modernist feminism that in its third stage has been co-opted by consumer feminism. Because it is a result of a particu-lar history, it cannot be universalized to the world.

In an increasingly violent global world of mainly androcentric and agonistic religious fundamentalisms—and all of these are in some ways either antiwomen or regressive in their view of women and their roles in a new millennium—I will dare to pose the tantric tradition as an alternative that can provide a spiritual mode of being that asserts women's power, not as an oppressive but as a lib-erating force. Going back to gynocentric Indic traditions, I find nu-ances within male hegemony that are not uniform. The masculinity of Shiva is not a reflection of the hypermasculine. And looking at society I find, just below the patriarchal superstructure, a gyno-centric matrix that continues to create a very different history and different texts as other sources of liberation.

Note

1. Ambubachi is a special festival to mark the time of the earth's men-struation. As children we were taught not to hurt the earth with any digging or tilling during this special time. I wondered later: What great homology

between human women and the Great Goddess, who is also known as Kamakhya, whose name is Desire. The same goddess who takes all back into her bosom at death also lights the first spark of desire, the creative impulse both human and divine.

7

I Am Muslim First

Salma Kamal

My mother says that those babies born into Islam are some of the luckiest in the world, for they have been put on the right path before they even open their eyes. I was born into a devout family where religion was the foundation for existence. Islam was introduced to me just a few hours after my birth when my father recited the *Azan* into my right ear. Said before every prayer fives times a day, the *Azan* is a way to call Muslims to prayer. I was just a few hours old when the role of Allah was whispered into my ear, words that would eventually echo in my mind for the rest of my life.

> Allah is Most Great. I bear witness that there is none worthy of worship except Allah. I bear witness that Muhammad (pbuh) is the messenger of Allah. Come to Prayer. Come to Success. Allah is Most Great. There is none worthy of worship except Allah.

I was born in New Jersey and spent a faineant childhood in a middle-class neighborhood, where houses looked similar and children played tag in each other's yards. If a stranger walked into our home, he instantly would realize that this was a Muslim household; on the walls in each room were vibrant pictures of Islam's holiest sites in Saudi Arabia. There were posters and plaques hanging in each room illustrating excerpts from the Quran written in beautiful calligraphy to remind you that Allah's words are always close. Closets were full of vibrantly colored *janimaz* (prayer mats) and several copies of the Quran, should there ever be more than one person who desired to read it. Each bed in every bedroom was set in a way that a sleeping person's feet would never point toward the east, a direction in which we pray. A large heap of shoes by the front door greeted you when you walked in—not so we wouldn't dirty the carpet, but because walking across the floor on which we pray is disrespectful. Sometimes, in our haste to pick up forgotten keys or a sweater, my sister and I would hurriedly sneak across the living room carpet in our sneakers, but never to any avail—we would always be caught by our mother and admonished, "Yanh Namaz puhrthee hoon! Joo-thow keh saath kaisa chalthe!" (I pray on this carpet. How you dare walk across it with your dirty shoes!)

Praying fives times a day is one of the five tenets of Islam, an act of reverence toward Allah believed to be so important, it is un-equalled by any other act of worship. Many Muslims, such as my mother, wake up at dawn to pray *Fajir,* the first prayer; others take time out of their work and school schedules to pray *Zuhur* and *Asar,* the afternoon prayers. As a child, I would pray every night with my mother before I went to sleep. While the rest of the world was watching sitcoms, I happily stood next to my mother and mim-icked her as she expertly bowed down in prayer, her mouth mov-ing silently as she recited *surrahs* (readings from the Quran). Each night, my mother would help me memorize *surrahs* from the Quran. She would recite each line, and I would repeat it until it was virtually engraved into my mind.

I was taught how to read the Quran when I was seven years old, a difficult task my mother decided to tackle herself. Every night after the dishes were washed and leftovers stored away, she and I would sit at our kitchen table and I would read the Arabic out loud, stopping only to rectify my pronunciation after every few sentences. The entire Quran was divided into 30 books, and I would read sev-eral pages each night, diligently marking my last read word with a yellow highlighter, so as to easily find my place the next evening. After each chapter in the Quran was read correctly and put away, my mother would reward me with five or six Hershey Kisses, which she would pull from a stash she wisely hid, mainly because I had a fanatic tendency at that age to eat an entire bag in one sitting.

Some Muslim children spend years training to memorize the en-tire Quran, but I never did that. At the age of seven, I had not grasped the profound intricacies of the words written in the holy Quran or even begun to fathom what impact those words have on Islam. I faithfully read out loud in Arabic, a language I neither spoke nor understood. It was not until adolescence that I received an English translation of the Quran and was able to comprehend how significant and meaningful the text was to my religion.

I was told that the Quran is quite literally the written and definitive word of Allah, passages he kindly decreed for every Muslim to live their life in accordance with Islam. At age eight, I recall thinking that Allah himself had somehow hand delivered the Quran to our house or perhaps Fed-Ex'd it so that our family would have a copy to read. For hours when no one was looking, I would intently gaze at the printed Arabic calligraphy in wonder and imagine that it was actually Allah's very own handwriting.

Every Sunday while in elementary school, I attended Sunday school at the local mosque. There, I was taught the basic tenets of Islam and heard fascinating and ancient stories of Islam. Through practice, I also learned to appropriately perform *wudu* (cleansing before prayer), and learned about the significance of Muslim holidays like Eid.

In public school, however, I learned the hard way that there was no national celebration for Eid, which is celebrated after the month of Ramadan. There were no days off from school, and no time spent in class making Eid decorations. None of my classmates had ever even heard of Eid. Instead, in school I learned that the ubiquitous Santa Claus was keen to drop off toys if you had behaved. My parents had to explain gently that we did not celebrate this American holiday after I excitedly told them about the prospect of new toys dropping down our chimney in the middle of the night. Still, for years I thought the reason why Santa Claus didn't make a stop at our house was because we didn't have a decorated tree or hang any lights outside. On several nights, I would kneel by the French windows in our living room and try to spot his sleigh flying through the air, as if to wave him down and make him aware that he was skipping a house.

The month of Ramadan is my favorite tradition of Islam—the month in which all Muslims fast from dawn until dusk; a task when performed with the right intentions leads to spiritual growth. At the end of the month, Eid is celebrated with massive commemoration and feasts with friends and family. When I was growing up, Ramadan was very sacred to our family. Every evening, we would break our fast together with juicy dates and my mother's homemade *pajiyeh* (yogurt snack) and pray together as a family. During the evenings, we would go to the mosque, which would be filled to capacity with followers who had come to pray well into the night. On Eid, we would drive to a local park or mosque where the entire Muslim community would be clad in their newest clothes to pray together. Afterwards, hours would be spent while each person hugged, and gleeful shouts of "Eid Mubarak!" (Happy Eid) would be heard all day. Similar to how some children get presents on Christmas morning, Muslim children would get *Eidi* (money) from their elders. Somewhere along the line, I realized that smiling cutely was the way to get the most cash. A week later the money would be gone, frivolously squandered on Chiclets and ice cream.

When Eid fell on a weekday, my parents predictably would take a personal day, and my sister and I inevitably would take the day off from school; although our teachers understood, we still were required to make up the missed work in a timely fashion. During college, I made it home only for one Eid during my four years. I suppose I found it selfishly arduous to make the four-hour trek home and miss one or two day's worth of lectures and labs. There was no immense Eid celebration while I was in college as there was back at home and, except for an occasional event sponsored by the Muslim Students Association, the month would pass by without any tangible acknowledgment on my part. In college it was easy to forget what Ramadan symbolized and, because I did not surround myself with fellow Muslims, there was no recognition of the fasting or praying. For every Eid that I missed, my mother would phone at night and sadly declare that "Bacho keh bagar Eid nahin bunthee" (Without my children with me, it's hard to enjoy Eid).

Growing up, I knew that Islam was an innate part of me, a distinctive trait that differentiated me from my American friends. Throughout my life, my religion is the one thing that has remained familiar and constant. I am by no means a religious scholar nor am

I particularly religious, yet there are some things that I do or say that specifically characterize me as Muslim. It is reflected in the way I carefully say and type "peace be upon him" after I whisper or type the Prophet's name, or instinctively say "Al-hamdullilah" (Praise be to Allah) after I sneeze. It is revealed when I recite the *Ayat-al-kursi* (a verse in the Quran) before I go to sleep or start the car, vigilantly turning off the radio in order to recite it in complete silence. "Allah hoo lahilaha illa-hual, hyum kyum . . ." (There is no deity save Him, the Ever-Living, the Self Subsistent . . .); I have recited this passage continuously throughout my life. I am eternally grateful to my mother for having made me memorize it during those nights so many years ago.

Although I never battled with the meaning of Islam while I was growing up, I did constantly struggle with a sense of identity and often forced myself to choose between being Indian–Muslim or American. At home, it seemed I was complacently Indian—eating Indian food, wearing Indian clothes, speaking Urdu, and watching Indian movies with my parents. Yet, when I stepped out of the house and into my American surroundings, I felt I was an entirely different person, almost leading two distinctive lives.

Growing up, I was a typical nerd—a lanky, studious, and intensely shy girl who wore her hair in two tight braids down her back. Every morning until the ninth grade, my mother would comb out the knots that had developed overnight, rub a generous amount of coconut oil into my hair, and tightly plait two braids, tying the ends with a colorful ribbon. "Luhrkee ki kubsoorat uski lumbeh baalow meh hain" (An Indian girl's beauty lies in her long hair) she would tell me as I grimaced. "Humare Muzhub meh hain," (It is part of our culture) she would assure me when I threatened to cut my braids off. I quietly endured children at school who derided me as Pippi Longstocking because of the solitary hairstyle I sported for a solid decade.

By the time I started high school, teenage rebellion had found its way to me. While most of my friends rebelled by staying out late or drinking alcohol, I did so by trimming my hair. Cutting it was out of the question, according to my parents; it was an inherent part of my culture—my long hair was what made me Indian.

At the salon, I told the stylist I wanted it cut to my shoulders. I remember the look in my father's eyes as he furiously fought against this idea, as if he had never heard of a length so absurd, and insisted I cut it only a few inches before finally stalking off in distress. By the time I left the salon, my hair was a mere 2 inches shorter, and my father was half a cigarette pack lighter. Two inches may not be much, but it was a revolutionary change for me and another twist in my struggle for identity between what is considered Indian and what my parents believed was too American. That haircut did not guide me to experiment with new "American" hairstyles; I wore my hair in a giant bun for the next four years. And when I went home to show off my new length, my mother did not speak to me for a solid week.

My mother used to try to teach me to be more domestic, although she has given up on the notion now. It would be her dream for me to learn to cook Indian food, clean swiftly, and perhaps even sew. Much to her aggravation, I made sure to be inept at all three. At 14, I was fiercely determined not to become what I believed a typical Indian girl did when she wasn't studying or watching television: Cooking, cleaning, and sewing on missing buttons. "Who will marry you if you can't tell the difference between *dhaniya* (coriander seed) and *dalchini* (cinnamon)?" my mother wondered.

My mother was fiercely determined to preserve a semblance of Indian culture in her children. To this day, she allows me to speak to her only in Urdu—no English—though she can speak and understand both. The outcome has been that I too speak both languages with a smooth fluency I never knew I was capable of.

My adolescence was spent grappling between my Indian identity, of which religion played a large role, and my American one. It was a struggle my parents ceased to understand. Struggling to define myself as either American or Indian and not some distinct creation of both, I often forced myself to alienate one side while I reveled in the other. At home I was as Indian and Muslim as could be, promptly changing out of my jeans and polo shirt after school into *salwar-kameez*, eating Indian food including the *bhaji* (spinach) my mother would stuff into pita bread and cram into my lunchbox. I hurriedly would eat the sandwich before the others were able to distinguish the green filling from their own peanut butter and jelly or ham and cheese sandwiches. At home I continued to pray beside my mother, practiced reading the Quran, and effortlessly conversed with my parents in Urdu as if I had learned the language back in India.

It was outside of my house that I constantly tried to shed my Indian image in order to relate to my American identity. I listened to American music when my parents weren't around, wore the latest but conservative American clothing when in school, and spoke solid English in which the only accent detectable was a New Jersey one. I had American friends and tried to pretend to eat a fish fillet at McDonald's with the same vigor that my friends ate their Big Mac and Chicken McNuggets. I had to explain that I was unable to eat meat because it wasn't *halal*. "It's like the Muslim version of kosher meat," I would swiftly explain with the rehearsed line. As American as I attempted to act, I was always the Indian girl in the group.

I spent a summer in high school backpacking through Italy with friends. After reaching our first destination, Milan, our group filed into the small but airy airport where we were greeted by an overtly jovial man whose job was to inspect our passports before pointing us to baggage claim. As we each handed him our passports, he decided to engage us in a game of "guessing" our nationalities. "American!" he declared as blonde-haired Lindsey trailed through the metal detector. "American!" he confidently guessed as black-haired Jack ducked through. "You're American, too!" he confirmed as Venezuelan native Emily went through. Finally it was my turn. I handed him my American passport and waited for what seemed like half a nanosecond. "Indian!" he declared without even glancing so much at my picture and shooed me through the detectors. Even in Italy, I was no more American than I was in my own native country.

Like most teenagers, I often believed that the expectations my parents had of me were completely void of the expectations accepted in America. There were typical arguments about going out with friends and wasting life on idle activities versus staying home, studying, and succeeding in life, or so my parents tried to explain the difference to me. When faced with my teenage needs, like desperately wanting to subscribe to *Seventeen*, my parents would throw up their hands in despair, convinced that the un-Islamic American culture was seeping into my brain, for why else would I want to read about such distasteful topics like "How to Find and Keep the Perfect Boyfriend" or "Do-It-Yourself Miniskirts!" When it got too much for them, my parents would instantly begin reminiscing about their own childhood in India, in which they were sure to remind me that they rarely gave their parents any unwarranted trouble. They would talk about India's warmth, both temperature and personality wise; the way one could pick mangos from the trees in front of the house; or the close-knit community that was always available to lend a hand. Yet India remained a huge enigma to me; a country I was neither born in nor remembered visiting and to which I felt virtually no connection. At least this was the case until my parents declared that we would be moving to India for several weeks for my sister's impending arranged marriage.

Traveling to India by plane is no easy feat and, back then at least, Air India was not all it promised to be in its advertisements. The journey that would take me to the land where my parents were born, the place where my grandparents and ancestors had borne their own identities, began with me becoming airsick and homesick before we even crossed the Atlantic.

Hyderabad was everything I imagined it would be. It was unbearably hot in the afternoons and, although the wedding was scheduled for November, the sun beat down on the back of my already sunburned shoulders. It was dusty enough that I had to cover my nose with a handkerchief when going to the bazaar to pick up my tailored clothes. India also had an endless swarm of mosquitoes, and I had to sleep inside of a mosquito net, something that at first had seemed rather trendy, but soon lost its novelty when my claustrophobia set in. There also were hoards of people on the roads that seemed to lack basic traffic laws. We had arrived at Hyderabad airport and were received by a throng of never-seen-before aunts, uncles, and cousins. Garlands of flowers were placed around all of our necks and, in the chaos of hugs and introductions, I witnessed an uninhibited joy in the eyes of my parents. They were home.

In India, it was easy for me to embrace the culture and the ideals. I dressed in Indian clothes at all times of the day, never taking out the pair of Levi's I had carefully packed in the back of my suitcase. I watched Indian cartoons, was driven to the cinema on the back of a scooter, learned to play cricket in my bare feet, and prayed together with the entire extended family. It seemed that the world would stop five times a day, and there would be nothing left to do but pray with my cousins before getting back to the cricket game we had put on hold.

I could have fooled anyone into believing I had been born in India all along, at least until I opened my mouth and busted out some English-accented Urdu. Then some may have believed that I was just an "American" playing dress-up in Indian clothes, one who could never grasp the intricacies of Indian culture and tradition. Yet India with all its heat, dust, and mosquitoes almost began to feel like home, a place where Islam and my Indian identity became interlocked, and a place where my American identity was left far behind and no reconciliation between the two was necessary.

I often would ask my sister what it feels like to be a part of an arranged marriage, a custom still widely practiced and accepted in my family. "How can you marry someone whose facial features you haven't memorized, whose voice you've never even heard?" I would try to fathom. I wanted to know if it was really worth it not to impede or break the cycle that had consumed generations before us. "Yes," she would tell me. "It *is* worth it, but only you know if it will work for you. You trust in Allah, and you just believe," she still reassures me.

Eventually, the time came for me to attend college, and choosing one that was a four-hour hike gave me enough assurance that it was far enough to prevent any surprise visits from my parents but close enough for those home-cooked meals. It wasn't until I came to college that people began to express an earnest interest in my Indian-ness and my religion. When I was growing up, it seemed popularity had been measured by the blonde hue of a girl's hair or the intensity of blue in a boy's eyes, but in college I was suddenly startled to realize that being Muslim had become intriguing and being Indian had become beautiful.

I knew there was an active Muslim Students Association (MSA) on campus, but never made any attempts to become a part of it. My father would telephone and encourage me to become a member or at least take part in its weekly prayers or religious activities, but I never did, though I occasionally would drop in on a guest lecture or group picnic. I did not look outwardly Muslim like some of the girls I saw on campus who wore *hijab*. I wore my tank tops and capris to class and made no attempt to cover my hair. Rather, while I was settling into campus life, I focused on doing the things I was unable to do at home. During those first few weeks, I freely wore the knee-length dresses and cut-offs I proudly had picked out from a clearance rack in Sears, fully aware that if my conservative parents caught a glimpse of me, they would recoil in shock. When food in the dining hall became dull, I would order takeout, pushing qualms of *halal* meat to the back of my mind to wolf down steaks, hamburgers, and chicken wings without so much as a blink of an eye. And when I wasn't trying to figure out elliptic integrals in calculus or write papers for political science in the library, I was learning the difference between a screwdriver and a fuzzy navel with my fellow dorm mates. Sure, I knew in the back of my mind that I was a Muslim and originally would have balked at what I would have considered "sins" a few years ago, but right now all I was interested in was squeezing out everything college had to offer. It was the farthest I had ever strayed from Islam.

Up until this point, I had struggled with my Indian and American identities, often trying to fit Islam into both, until I simply learned to connect all three. Right when things were beginning to make sense and I had just begun to settle in, the unimaginable happened, something so horrific it would change the way people saw Islam forever.

I was a freshman in college when 9/11 occurred. On that sunny, crisp Tuesday morning (one of the few I remember in such minute detail), I was studying for my chemistry lab in a quiet dorm room. My roommate rushed into our room and told me a plane had crashed into the World Trade Center. We turned on the television to see the first tower on fire with a gaping hole in it. While we were shocked at the sight and the chaos unfolding, we believed it was a terrible accident. It was only then that we spotted another plane soaring toward the second tower, each moment turning to dread until it finally crashed into a ball of fire, leaving us stunned beyond belief.

It was at that point that the television anchors declared this to be an act of terrorism, a word I was neither familiar with nor whose true meaning I clearly grasped. I only knew that the World Trade Center, a place my own sister had worked just a few months prior to finding a new job, now lay in ruins. Several days later, new details would emerge about the terrorist attacks, the most profound being that they were carried out by Muslim nationals, acting in the name of Allah but doing nothing more than blaspheming it. I had no idea that Islam was about to be thrust into the hostile glare of public opinion and international spotlight.

Following the attacks, Islam was everywhere. Specials on *60 Minutes* and *20/20* about the history of Islam and bold headlines printed across every national newspaper were a constant reminder that Muslims had been responsible for the attacks. CNN and PBS had exclusive documentaries where anchors traveled to an Islamic country in the Middle East and reported on the "backwardness" of Afghanistan or Saudi Arabia. It embarrassed me to see this, to see people linking the atrocious acts of some deplorable radicals with the general population of Muslims. The endless debates on *Fox News* over the true meaning of Islam made it clear to me that Islam and terrorism were becoming synonymous.

Across the United States, there were reports of Muslims being harassed or accused of outright calumny. In a sudden outpouring of patriotism shortly after the attacks, it seemed that Americans had forgotten what this country once stood for; the freedom of religion and culture was lost in a whirlwind of emotion. At home, afraid our Muslim family would be subjected to harassment, my father tied the American flag to the antenna on the back of our car. It was to be a symbol to explain we were just as American and patriotic as everyone else, and that just because a few foolish men who called themselves Muslims had tainted the peacefulness of our religion to forward their own sordid agendas, we were not a part of that.

At college, for the first time in my life, I hesitated to tell people I was Muslim for fear they would believe I was a quisling and part of some grand terrorist network. In retrospect, I should have taken the time to explain what Islam was really about. Instead, I cowered away, believing it was easier to hide behind a veil of ignorance. Yet,

I felt as if the true meaning of Islam was being stripped away as misconceived notions were penetrating through the world. The images that were constantly reflected on television to show what America had labeled the "backwardness of Islam" had come to haunt my own Islamic identity.

After 9/11, the West suddenly began to scrutinize the lack of democracy and women's rights in the Islamic world. The United States has called upon Saudi Arabia and other Middle Eastern governments to address women's rights as it begins to expand social, economic, and political rights.

It is inaccurate to define any woman who wears the veil as oppressed. For many women, this is a symbol of their own modesty. I do not believe the idea of veiling is repressive. If, in fact, it serves the purpose of being modest, which is required in the Quran, it is nothing more than a gratifying, cultural custom. However, the problem with veiling arises when women are forced to do so.

Human rights under international standards, including women's rights and Islam, are reconcilable. In order to come to this reconciliation, Muslim states will have to stop vacillating between actual religious beliefs and perceived cultural norms. Author Eve Ensler once wrote, "In order for the human race to continue, women must be safe and empowered." Indeed, this is a simple idea, but one that will take time and persistence.

I rarely find myself in the struggle of Indian vs. American anymore. I have accepted that I am both Indian and American, and Islam is an essential part of both. When having to use a label, I describe myself as a "Muslim Indian American." Still, there are times when I am suddenly reminded of my conflict. There is a common stereotype, for instance, that all Indians are born with an intrinsic ability to devour the spiciest food known to man. For me, the inkling of anything spicy is enough to make my eyes water and my nose start to instantly run. Recently, I was home eating dinner with my parents when my mother asked me how the food tasted. I was too busy drowning myself in two glasses of ice water to answer, but I did manage to scream out, "*Mirchi!*" (Spicy!) between large gulps. My father looked up from his plate, shook his head, and commented, "All that American food has rendered your Indian taste buds useless."

I recall another similar incident at an Indian restaurant in New York with friends. I had specifically whispered, "make it mild" to the waiter when I ordered my *Tandoori* chicken and Goat *Vindaloo*, much to the amusement of my Indian friends. When the food arrived, I mistakenly sampled some of my friend's explicitly spicy *chutney*, which caused me to spend the next half hour blowing my nose. He looked over at me and shook his head in astonishment, "God, you are so white-washed!" he laughed. And although his voice was at all times jocular, I couldn't help but feel a small sense of agitation. It was as if my entire Indian identity was dependent on and measured by the number of chili peppers I could tolerate eating.

I can't remember the last time I prayed properly or read the Quran. And although I haven't fasted regularly during Ramadan in several years and am a frequent customer of "Outback Steakhouse," where I don't think they've yet heard of *halal* meat, I still consider myself to be a practicing Muslim because of the underlying spiritual faith I carry within me. I guess what it boils down to is that you can choose to practice religiously, not practice at all, or find a compromising medium between the two. I feel that my journey with Islam has been a concatenation of events in which I chose my own path while reconciling the values of my culture with what I confronted.

My father once told me to remember that I am Muslim first. "Nothing else," he would say, "is germane." One day, I hope to tell my own children the same thing. "You are Muslim first," I will say. "That is your path. How you eventually walk down that path is up to you."

8

Red, Bulls, and Tea:
Cultural Hashing of a 1.5er
(A.K.A. Second-generation Reflections)

Monoswita Saha

It's a reflex, almost innate repetition: the quick touch of index and middle fingers to my forehead and to my heart in contrition if ever I graze a book, paper, pen, pencil, or person with my feet. This swift movement is a minuscule distraction in the midst of a conversation, lounging, or a walk. The gesture is a remnant from my earliest childhood, an emblem of my Indian-ness other than my name, I suppose, and my brown skin and the fact that I look Indian. As a second-generation Hindu Bengali girl in the United States, I find that Wikipedia explanations, PBS and Link TV documentaries (as convenient as they are) on Hinduism fall short. It's impossible to make generalizations about people. So I will describe one strand of being Hindu, albeit a strand that is based on my life as an American Hindu of immigrant parents.

I spent my elementary and middle school years where white picket fences existed only in storybooks. High school was spent in a white-picket-fenced Caucasian suburbia. Both environments insist upon harsh exoskeletons if one is to have any type of social success in school. My comments on Hinduism reflect these different worlds.

My world of Hinduism in America is structured by the opportunities and challenges first-generation immigrant families place on their children. My parents' generation came from a world of intense competition for academic excellence, and they had similar expectations of us. My friends happily drowned themselves in summertime morning cartoons while I spent two hours every morning sitting cross-legged on my parents' bed practicing long division and completing dictations in Bengali and English. I went through my Bangla reading and writing exercises with dread and pleasure. The Bangla alphabet has over 50 characters, and consonants such as "S" and "T," among many others—so simple in English—have multiple forms in Bengali for soft, nasal, and sharp sounds. I constantly used the wrong characters and accents. To this day, picking the right "S" is largely guesswork. Beyond the annoyances of spelling and grammar, my mornings were colored with poetry, ancient epics, forests, and fantasies. My grandfather in India copied poems in his letters to my mother: "Ey kobita guli amar Rusha-Diddon ke sheekiye thebe" (Teach these poems to my *Diddon*). When it rained we sang, "Jal pore, pata nore / Pagla hatir matha nore" (Water falls, leaves stir / The mad elephant nods its head). Or, if I felt fanciful, "Kaat-berrali, Kaat-berrali peyara tumi kao? / Gur muri kao? / Doodth bhath kao?" (Wood cat, Wood cat, what will you eat? / How about date-sugar, puffed rice? / How about milk-rice?). Separated from every relative by thousands of miles, I became most familiar with Dadu's[1] voice through his letters.

Bangla, this language of nuances, lilting humor, irony, melancholy, beauty, and implication was a private world, one I could not share or translate. What little I heard and read of Tagore's poetry opened me to the humor, tragedy, longing, irony, and poignancies of life. Kalidasa's *Shakuntala,* with its forests and enchantments, engaged me longer than the mandatory two hours for lessons. My illustrated copies of the *Ramayana* and the *Mahabharata* became frayed and tattered by constant thumbing. Close my eyes, find a corner, and open the *Mahabharata*. Whitewashed walls, ceilings, and dull brown carpets fade into a world where miracles occur every day; where gods are embroiled in intrigue and the politics of the material world. Beyond the pull of burnt milk and rice offerings to the fire god, *rishi*s with superhuman yogic powers and tempers, diabolical kings and flying monkeys, and beyond the romance, each reading posed the inklings of philosophical problems, triggering questions. How can the model son and king abandon his wife? What is duty and to whom do we owe it? Is it really necessary to obliterate an entire people through war to bring a new peace? Must we destroy to create? Why does Draupadi[2] make it to heaven last? Why do the women in India's great Hindu fairytales get gypped after every gargantuan war (it's not the way it plays out in Grimm's)? Of course, I didn't exactly explore these issues in any great detail in second grade. However, my exposure to Bengali literature and Hindu epics seeped into my subconsciousness as I imbibed the core maxim: the human condition is in constant flux. Amelia Bedelia, Beverly Cleary's *Ramona*, the Babysitter's Club, Nancy Drew, the Hardy Boys, books on sharks, dinosaurs, lighting, and other miscellaneous topics occupied their fair share of my reading list as well.

I have changed schools nine times and lived in four different states; however, going to middle school in New Jersey sparked the awareness of my identity as a Bengali Hindu Indian. Despite being surrounded by brown people, African-Americans, Hispanics, and Puerto Ricans, spending Friday and Saturday evenings at Bengali get-togethers, smelling curry leaves down the hall, and watching sari-clad grandmothers taking evening strolls every day, I never knew how Indian I was until my middle-school peers thoughtfully pointed it out.

My peers assumed several traits that characterize Indians: (1) we are annoyingly adroit with grades (the tacit commandment), (2) we are unfailingly polite to teachers, even the worst ones, (3) we are meek, that is, perpetual pacifists, (4) every fifth Indian is a Patel, (5) we are all vegetarians, (6) we worship cows, hence we all must be vegetarians, (7) we perform sacrifices to the gods (courtesy of *Indiana Jones, Temple of Doom*), (8) we are cheap, (9) in New Jersey, at least, the turban tribe Indians have taken over gas stations through clandestine and underhanded means, and (10) we all speak "Indian."

I'm sure that I missed a few items. In lieu of all this, if you would like to fit in with the "American" crowd, the first thing to do is to learn as many *good* Desi[3]/FOB[4] jokes, learn to mimic a heavy Indian accent, and be sure to do impressions and crack jokes in front of all your non-Indian friends. You might as well resign yourself to the fact the substitute teacher will skip your name and see who is left. You can always get back at him or her later by making the teacher try to pronounce your name for a few painful moments before you mercifully enunciate it for them and throw in a pet name for future reference. It's nothing personal. And so the first step to establishing an Indian identity is realizing how irksome it is to people in my adolescent world. Parents are not only embarrassing because they don't know what they are doing, but because they are Indian and inept at maneuvering accented tongues around the English language. Where do your loyalties lie? Are they to your friends the "American culture" or to your parents and their culture? Do you laugh along at the quickie mart, turbaned gas station jokes? After all, your father is a computer analyst. He wears a suit to work and is Bengali, not the Punjabi or Sikh the joke is aimed at. Technically, they are not your people. Except that you share the same country and, even to this pre-teen mind, "the same country" intimates a vague sense of solidarity. The desire to blend in with the crowd often overpowers the inklings of solidarity. Thankfully, Indian youths—and youths of all minorities and majorities for that matter—also bring peanut-butter-and-jelly sandwiches or buy whatever it is the Food and Drug Administration approves as food for lunch, bond over crappy teachers who can be safely cursed outside the classroom, and bemoan the dismal state of students affairs with white, black, brown, and purple-polka-dotted cohorts.

As a child, the most vivid and interesting part of being Bengali centered on religious observations, events, and festivities. Those aspects were the most visible differences between us and everyone else. The shrine holding pictures of framed saints, gods, goddesses, and deceased elders, perfumed with incense and decorated with flowers and offerings, marked the difference between my home and my friends'. The only times I absolutely needed to dress differently from my friends—in Indian clothes (saris and salwar kameezes)—was on religious occasions. I used religion and culture interchangeably. Most importantly, my first trip back to India at the age of nine was for *Durga Puja.*[5] The very shock of the experience temporarily ensconced itself as the embodiment of Bengali culture. I was plucked from staid whitewashed walls, asphalt roads, Eggo waffles, and crucifixes and thrust in front of a magnificent 10-foot, 10-armed goddess, Durga, riding a roaring lion and plunging her trident into the heart of a demon.

All Are Welcome: The Poetics of Public Worship

The city of Kolkata dances during *Durga Puja*. The streets teem with crowds unimagined in the craziest of Christmas shopping sprees. The air crackles with the anticipation of Christmas and Hanukah sprinkled with the solemnity of Palm Sunday. I have a special entry into the world of *Durga Pujas*. My paternal grand-father is one of four brothers. For more than a century they have been taking turns hosting *Durga Puja*, so every four years this fes-tival is held at our Kolkata house. Our place is filled with guests pouring in and out of our home; the bedrooms are full of women lounging on beds, catching up on months of gossip. For five days, all the floors of our stone house are teeming with friends and fam-ily. Children eat seated in lines on the floor of our stone hallways, which are strewn with stairs and an endless supply of sweet tea and biscuits. The goddess and her children are in the courtyard, earthen figures suffused with divinity. Drummers (*dhakis*) sleep under mos-quito nets outside. The house is garlanded with tiny gold lights, and the open roof transformed into a pink-and-saffron pavilion dining area where guests eat in shifts of 75 for the *Prasad* or *Bhog*.[6] For five days the household wakes to drums and burning coconut husks at sunrise and falls asleep to drums, gongs, and conch calls. The atmosphere is never still, always flowing from solemn prayers to laughter, gossip, and dance. There are the inevitable arguments over how many kilos of sugar, how many liters of milk today, where to buy the fresh lotuses, etc. . . . but the irritation is fleeting. Every-one is welcome. Crowds, villagers, neighbors, relatives, and friends pray, eat, chatter, and dance. Beggars leave with full stomachs. On the fifth night, the whole village follows in a procession to send the goddess back. She is borne along like a queen, accompanied by the constant beating of drums and dancing on the way to the patch of sand by the pond. Not even a fluorescent street lamp, only the moon, lanterns, and torches cast light. The moody mother from next door breaks into tearful smiles—tears for the departing goddess and smiles for the drums and dancing boys who tease her in their midst. The wives have streaked each other with red vermillion as a mark of auspicious blessings for a happy family life. Seven men from our family take the goddess on their shoulders, spin her seven times, and plunge into the pond with her. On one occasion, my brother screamed, thinking my father had drowned in the black water. All seven surfaced, sputtering and laughing. My 19-year-old cousin burst out of the water laughing and tossed his wet T-shirt to me. In the dead of the night we all walk back, touch the feet of our elders in respect, and they place their hands on our heads in blessing—*ashirbadh*. Men hug each other as brothers, touching opposite shoulders. It's over. The air is heavy with joy and sadness; mother Durga has left, but it has been an auspicious day.

Such rites and sacred days that were a way of life for our parents are still the way of life in India, but they must be penciled into our lives here. Like appointments, they can be inconvenient and annoying. Days that are suffused with joy and excitement laced with astute solemnity in India are dull and almost inconsequential by comparison in the United States. *Durga Puja* is an occasion that warrants public celebration for Bengalis. Goddess Durga (*Devi*) is the protector, daughter, mother, wife, and warrior. She is love, warmth, tenderness, and ferocity. In the United States, she is the embodiment of nostalgia.

In order to recreate some semblance of *Durga Puja* in the United States around the time of the real holiday, families arrive at the designated high school on a Saturday from midday to late afternoon. Children are deposited and discarded until after midnight. It's a tremendous show of community spirit. Children, always slightly disgruntled at the sudden break in their weekend routine, are compelled to enjoy themselves with an empty high school at their disposal and no parental supervision. The dull roar of gossip stops at *anjali*.[7] Everyone congregates around the priest as he recites the chants. Trays of flowers surface and everyone takes a flower, but instead of throwing the flowers at the goddess's feet as an offering, we put them back on the tray to reuse for each time the chants are repeated. (Flowers are expensive, and we must keep the rented places clean. We cannot actually bestow the flowers on the goddess's feet, for fear a stray petal would signal our presence). The crowds are vast and come in shifts. One is never sure of having enough flowers. Very carefully, the tray holding a small flame is passed around so that everyone may receive the goddess's blessings. There is always a function lasting from evening into the night, with singing, dancing, and plays. The traditional five-day celebration is scattered over a few available Saturdays. Had I not been in India during a *Durga Puja* season, I never would have known the difference.

Infected with the exhilaration of the authentic *Durga Puja* in Kolkata, I understand why my parents cling to those few Saturdays packed into a high school gym and auditorium as a stand-in for *Durga Puja*. Paltry as makeshift *pujas* seem in comparison to the grandeur in India, the gym is both a vent and a chamber for all the reminiscing. At the very least Bengalis need to feel the hectic crowd associated with *puja* times.

Blood-red vermillion smeared into the hair and streaked over faces like Amazon warrior paint, ruthless kohl-rimmed eyes, the throbbing of the drums from dawn into night, the call of the conch, coconut husks smoking in red clay pots clogging and stinging the eyes, silver trays heavy with offerings, 108 blooming lotuses, and teeming bodies redolent of sweat and incense are seared into my brain. I will never forget the real *Durga Puja*. On the surface, this is my culture. These are the images and traditions I associate with my people. This is what finally gave me a tangible origin, an identity, a flavor. Going deeper, I see the intricacy, detail, devotion, and sweat poured into the preparation and the passionate splendor of the presentation as a symbol of India's spiritual energy. The intensity and the awesome sense of importance compelled me to be respectful of my parents' religious observations and perceive Hinduism as something worth looking into. I can understand how this exotic aura and the conspicuousness of religious practices in India foster the skewed Western perception of her as primarily a land of mysticism and spirituality.

Beyond the Idols: Hinduism and Vedanta

My neighbors used to bring us palm leaves during Easter. We went to church for the baptism of their daughter and the confirmation of their son. We stood up and kneeled with the crowd; we were duly solemn and contemplative. In the middle of the service, our neighbor leaned over and whispered, "You can only receive the wafer if you are baptized. You guys need to stay seated." All the pews emptied, and four bodies remained sitting. I felt very Indian—not in the warm and fuzzy sense. The first and only midnight Mass we attended on Christmas Eve, Papa joined the line to take the wafer, despite my fiercest whispers. My skin burned. I was sure the priest could tell. The priest would refuse him in front of the entire congregation. Fear, and the shame of fear, scorched the inside of my chest. I realized that the most important essence of Hinduism, of *Durga Puja,* or of any religious occasion lies in the fact that no one is turned away from receiving sacrament (*prasad* or *bhog*). The idols, incense, flowers, and pageantry are gift-wrap. My father took the wafer. We left the church.

The ritual is embedded in my mind. The sanctified air is comforting and peaceful. The daily *puja,* the gestures, are an undemanding reassurance of my uniqueness and reinsertion into the familiar. At home, it is a routine. After showering, my mother sits with her worn book of Sanskrit hymns. She lights the incense and offers a fresh hibiscus. Lotus incense sticks release smoke tendrils in sensuous hypnotizing patterns. The offerings of crystallized sugar, raisins, cashews, or sweets are to be eaten later. One summer the offerings kept disappearing. We caught the culprits one morning. My neighbor's children crept upstairs during their morning visits and picked them off the altar. My family was amused and delighted.

The all-encompassing, all-accepting view of humanity is typical of Vedanta. Vedanta is a highly respected ideology within Hinduism (Bhaskarananda 1994). Hinduism accepts that there are multiple paths toward divinity; therefore it has no difficulty accepting Christianity, Jesus, Islam, Allah, Buddhism, Buddha, Judaism, Yahweh, Zoroastrianism, Jainism, etc. Within Hinduism, divinity takes on different guises, thus the pantheon of deities; people choose their favored deities depending on their personalities, capabilities, and preferences. Ultimately it boils down to pragmatism at an individual and group level, which allows for human growth and change. In a country of a diverse array of cultures, mutual acceptance of untold numbers of religious practices avoids conflict. The stance of acknowledgment and acceptance is more respectful than tolerance.

I am wary of using the word "spirituality" to describe my experiences since it has developed suggestions of airiness, a hermit-like existence, and a sort of exemption from society, which are all false. As the Nobel laureate Amartya Sen points out in his discussion of India, "This home of endless spirituality has perhaps the largest atheistic and materialist literature of all the ancient civilizations" (Sen 2005, 168). Vedanta develops the concept of human unity and equity further. Activism is the core of Vedantic, Indian spirituality (Vivekananda 2003). The point is to live life in the most proactive, enthusiastic sense. This concept is closely aligned to the Western mentality.

My active adult involvement in Hinduism began inconspicuously. In the United States, interactions with monks of the Ramakrishna Order,[8] as part of my family interactions, invoked my initial respect and appreciation for Indian philosophy. Initially, I was not excited about being dragged by my parents to spend a few days at a monastery, Belur Math[9] near Kolkata. I'm from the generation of "Sex, Drugs, and Cocoa Puffs" (Klosterman 2003). Watching a snake ripple the letter S across the pond at Belur Math was not enlightening. But I outwardly conformed to the rhythm of the place. The meditations, songs, and prayers starting at dawn, blended naturally with the huge group meals served to devotees and visitors, and with the official, social, and domestic work conducted throughout the day. Devotees of every religion and color flocked to the compound. I have since wondered what intrinsic element draws this motley crowd. Harmony between modern day life and "spirituality" was fascinating. The languid tempo is an illusion. The order I was visiting, the Ramakrishna Order, emphasizes that there are multiple paths to the ultimate realization. They (and the "sister" organization, Sarada Math) emphasize service to people over rituals. The monks don't sit still; action was a form of regular meditation. They are required to complete higher education (master's and PhDs) before joining the order. These monks stand shoulder-to-shoulder with the rickshaw pullers and street vendors. They are at the forefront of disaster relief in every corner of the country. They are educators and, most of all, social barrier breakers. Strangely I still do not find this atmosphere of monks masculine. Everywhere I look, I see women working on par among themselves and with men.

Belur Math was a short visit. I wanted to see more of the practical application of spirituality at the source. Being raised in the nation of rags-to-riches tales, the advocator of individualism, and the trademark do-it-yourself attitude makes it difficult to surrender to an unknown power. Despite my appreciation of Indic spiritual philosophy, it still begs the question: How do you apply it to the masses? My life is not extremely taxing, and I lose my temper over who has the TV remote. How can people living beneath the poverty threshold stay serene? Born in the generation of fabulously fabricated resumes, we rely on ourselves to fill in the blanks. Faith is a seldom-used safety net. I trust faith a bit more than I trust the government, but I have come to trust Vedic philosophy. Vedanta uses logic as its core, which puts cynics, atheists, and me at ease. It transcends consumerism and defies ethnocentric boxes.

Five years later, supported by a grant from my university, I spent 10 days at the Sri Aurobindo Institute of Culture to explore spirituality with a different religiocultural institution. The Sri Aurobindo Institute functions under the same essential concept of activism and service as the Ramakrishna Mission, but the people devoted to this cause are not monks. Spirituality does not extract you from *samsara;* it improves the quality of life. Spirituality promises no miracles, only what you make of it, which is digestible for me.

It rained the whole way to the Ashram. Men going to work rolled trousers above their knees; some held shoes in one hand and briefcases in another as they waded through murky water. Sitting in a flooded alley for a good half-hour, not even 2 kilometers away from the institute, I wondered what the hell I was doing there. Inside the Ashram gates the traffic noise, shouting, and incessant bleating of horns muted into the background. I had to concentrate to hear outside the noise. The statement on their brochure captures it precisely:

A spiritual ideal has always been the characteristic idea and aspiration of India. But the progress of time and the need of humanity demand a new orientation and another form of that ideal . . . An outer activity as well as inner change is needed, and it must be at once spiritual, cultural, educational, social, and economical.

With these words as the nucleus, the institute has five branches: a school (pre-school through grade 12), a cultural unit, a research unit, a women's empowerment unit, and a medical unit. Each day ushered in visitors, artists, playwrights, professors, and personnel related to the arts and cultural industry of India. In the midst of running five different units, strictly observed tea and meal times impressed me. My world is of on-the-go lunches and timed caffeine injections. The environment brimmed with incessant activity unmarred by a hint of stress. I was told that, as agents of a higher entity, the administration has no cause for anxiety. Administrators and workers at the institute possess multitasking capabilities that soccer moms dream of. Outside the gates, the city carried on as usual: autos, trucks, taxis, cars, buses, stray animals, and people kicked up dust, smog, and traffic. Inside the compound I remained oblivious to the din.

My caretakers put me in the guest room adjacent to the shrine and meditation chamber. Each morning I watched workers create intricate designs around the white marble meditation chamber with fresh flowers. As the largest and noisiest structure on the premises, the school is the most visible branch of the institute. Students are not required to come to the meditation area, but many stopped by before classes. The essence of spiritual teaching here is that no belief system is imposed on anyone.

The institute's women's empowerment center is in a town named Boral. A botanical jungle under hot white sunlight envelops the house. Trees, shrubs, or flowers shout in wild greens, yellows, and forbidding maroons. It's a relief to enter the dim coolness of sprawling stone-and-cement corridors and airy rooms to escape the cacophony of color. The first room one enters is the meditation room. The walls are a sober blue and the floor is slate gray. Two large pictures of the Mother and Sri Aurobindo sit on a wooden box covered with a silky orange cloth and flowers. Women come every morning to dust the pictures and arrange flowers. Interviews with a few of the underprivileged women working at Boral proved to be the defining aspect of my visit. One of the women, Monju-Di, explained to me,

> The days that I cannot come, how does it feel? My mind feels no peace unless I come. Sitting in this room, near the Mother, I need to come. How to say it? Like a shadow it came, still now it creeps up like a shadow. I meditate here *ar nirobhhoy jay.* That is how the attachment to this place came, how I came to love it. This lessens my householder's pain. I cannot be working at other places, not for more money.

Monju-Di's account represents many women at the center. These women take spirituality beyond metaphysics and ephemeral characteristics, and ground the concept with activity. Spirituality does not cloister. Impoverished women would rather come to Boral instead of taking jobs that pay more money. Nothing mystical about it; something about sanctity works.

Tug of War: Philosophy and Culture Quarrels

I don't want to give the wrong impression. I devote barely a sliver of my life to prayer, meditation, and religious functions. Appreciation doesn't necessarily mean application. I emphasize my trips to India because they help cultivate an understanding of my Indian-ness and solidarity, which is necessary to mediate the cultural divides. During one's adolescent years, the alchemy for the comfortable middle path remains hidden. Tripping over cow dung actually helped establish a more appealing identity. Any culture that throws a five-day party for a goddess where the whole town—good citizens and hobos—is welcome cannot be cheap. Of course, I don't know if my friends will sit, waiting for me to explain the multiple appendages, the demon, the lion, the third eye (and the rest of it) appropriately. And, while in India, the monkeys outside my window are cooler than the squirrels here, although I do miss the States; it's a trade-off. There's a scale and the balances are always shifting, but somewhere in this process my Indian Bengali Hindu-ness has changed from a struggle to becoming intrinsic. I am an Indian, Bengali, Hindu American.

Women: Enough Said

In a culture where the only word for strength (*Shakti*) is feminine, the woman's world is bizarre. Watching women haggle over egg-plants, fish, and ornaments in the market, hail down autos, stake out seats on jammed trains, "timid" and "sheltered" are not the adjectives that come to mind. Thinking of female doctors, teachers, business owners, and the like, "restricted" is not the word that comes to mind. The tick, the drop of resentment and distrust to-ward Indian culture, stems from the fact that these Indian women have secure reputations through marriage. They are going to go home and make *daal*—lentil soup—for their families.

Successful, well-behaved single Bengali women are respected social pariahs. *Sex and the City* is not an accurate reflection of life, but to a follower of the sitcom, Indian society's prescription of women detracts from the overall luster and fragrance of its philos-ophy and warmth. The thriving spinster can expect wary appreci-ation and bemusement. Devi Durga can sweep the floor with demon ass, but when it comes to *Charlie's Angels*, Bengali men con-tinue to look at the silver screen with disbelieving eyes. My cousin explained to me, "Be serious. In real life, girls can't beat boys. It just doesn't happen," as he sat enthralled by a Hindi movie fight scene complete with a three-second delay between the sound effect and the actual punch, and the finale where the hero survives a hail of 25 bullets to the chest to give a 15-minute eulogy.

I see the ferocious female goddess Durga plunging her trident into the demon, *shakti*—strength incarnate—the deity commanding the most expensive, ostentatious public displays of devotion. I see the goddess Kali, garlanded with skulls and human appendages. She is the goddess of time and devourer of evil, the primordial feminine. The intensity of the goddess fills me with awe and confidence. The widow shrouded in a white sari, condemned to a sexless existence haunts me. The widower never proclaims his loss through attire, diet, or behavior. That tick won't die.

To my child eyes, my great-grandmother was a phantom-like figure. No blouse, a white sari wrapped around her wrinkled skin, and loose white hair; my brother and I would avoid her. Despite all the stories of how attached I was to her as a toddler, as an adolescent I avoided the eerie, ghost-like figure without even the barest red trim on her white sari. My brother never embraced her unless instructed to do so. As a widow, this woman single-handedly smuggled my entire family out of Bangladesh after the partition of India and managed the family estate after the death of her husband. She stayed behind and continued to manage the estate by herself during the riots. Her activism was completely geared to the welfare of the family with no attention to personal desires. As the second wife, she denied herself the right to bear any children of her own so that she could devote herself to my grandfather and his brothers. The stories about her are told with such fierce love, pride, and admiration that I can scarcely connect them to the silent woman cloaked in white. The flesh-and-blood woman takes up the role of the all-powerful, fiery Devi Durga, Kali, and Draupadi during the moments of crisis for the sake of her family, and then she retreats to a silent place during "normal" times. I don't get it.

Clad in miniskirts or business suits, playing the role of the artless teenager in their quirky 20s or established 30s, the Western female image is independent, forward, candid, and pro-choice. Compared to the immaculate, sexy, suave vixens, the proper Indian housewife appears as an oppressed, boring, drab woman. You may not want the person on TV for a mother; nonetheless you would rather be the person on TV than be your mother. Married woman are defined by the degree of devotion poured into their roles as mothers and wives. Regular home-cooked meals and the constant availability and concern are taken for granted. The Indian American wife spoils her family with care. Her children turn up their noses in disdain at cafeteria food. Her husband has zero tolerance for bad restaurants. I look at the person who saw to my comfort and say that she deserved more. Indian culture is warm, generous, and hospitable. But there are stringent rules. Women are not to be forward, scantily dressed, loud, and provocative. If they are to break out into careers, it should be something along the lines of education, medicine, or law; something with enough prestige and money to justify breaking the housewife norm. Preferably the woman should be demure, even if she is opinionated. In the Indian community people don't date; they get engaged and then they marry, or so they tell us. If parents shudder at the word "dating," they wither away in shame at the idea of live-in relationships. Upon reading Jhumpa Lahiri's "Namesake," my mother frantically made me promise never to behave like Mousumi, a girl who grows out of her demure Indian cocoon into a woman who relishes many lovers but settles for a traditional Indian marriage to placate her family. Dissatisfied in her marriage, her romantic indiscretions propel her to a divorce. My mother, while empathizing with Mousumi's discontent, ultimately took her behavior (her many lovers) as a betrayal to family, friends, and culture. Family is everything. In gearing your actions to fulfill familial duty, you automatically fulfill yourself. In the Western culture, family is important, but one's actions are geared to one's self first and others next.

Indian culture allures one with its warmth. Sabita Mashi, the housekeeper at the Sri Aurobindo Institute, insisted on combing my hair. A few times a day she asked if I had enough bottled water, reminded me not to bathe in cold water—and most touching of all, offered to stay in the room if I was afraid to sleep alone at night. Our parents grew up in extended families. I need my solitude. We learned to share in kindergarten, but some of us still haven't grasped the concept. No one taught our parents to share; it was a given. Despite all the inconveniences (too many eyes) of the extended family, no one is obliged to feel alone. Pleasing my parents is at times annoying but not restrictive. It's intimidating, the magnitude of culture you feel you not only have to live up to but carry. There is much to praise in the country and the culture, and there is much you would like to ignore. A dual upbringing opened me to universal empathy.

No Longer a Tourist

Identity crisis staved, I now explore those nooks and crannies closed to tourists. In the summer of 2007, I traveled to Pune, Bangalore, Pondicherry, Kolkata, and Shantiniketan to interview people from all walks of life to study the impact of globalization. I spent my winter break in West Bengal visiting the Sunderbans and villages near Shantiniketan to research sustainable living initiatives. I walked in the Sunderbans at dawn—the river glistened gold over slate blue ripples to my right, and the jungle screamed green and tiger-striped orange to my left. I spoke with mothers and ex-poachers at sunrise. I ate in the villages near Shantiniketan—the oxen chewed straw next to me, and ducks and chickens ran over my feet, while someone slapped fresh cow dung patties on the wall behind me. Santhal women smelling of coconut oil, with flowers in their hair, took me into their midst, and we danced through their village into the clearing. The sun sank behind us. For the first time I woke to, lived in, and fell asleep to beauty—ferocious, dignified, and fragile. My idealism, drive, and inspiration stems from jungles, waterways, dark deities, earth, drums, and narrow roads toward villages and tribes. My experience took place in India. It could have happened anywhere.

Born in India and raised in New England, technically I fall into the 1.5 generational block. Luckily I have not found a niche for a Hindu woman in the United States outside of the ethnic community. Boundaries limit, and I have been—and always will be—a liminal being.

Notes

1. Dadu: grandfather
2. Draupadi: one of the main female characters in the *Mahabharata*.
3. Desi: Slang for a person of Indian origin.
4. FOB: Fresh Off the Boat.
5. Durga Puja: An annual celebration of the warrior mother goddess coming to spend five days at her paternal home; the entire journey is 10 days. The first five days cover her descent from the Himalayas, the heavenly abode. The remaining five days celebrate her presence on earth among her devotees. On the fifth day, clay statues of the goddess are cast into large bodies of water. This is symbolic of her return to the Himalayas. As the supreme mother goddess, she has 10 arms extending in 10 directions symbolizing her presence and availability to devotees at all times and everywhere.

6. Prasad or Bhog: The offerings to the goddess, blessed with the essence of the deity, equivalent to Holy Communion.

7. Anjali: A chanting of adulations toward the goddess. The crowd repeats the chants after the priest. Everyone throws flowers at the goddess's feet. In return, each person receives the blessings of the goddess by placing their hands over a sacred fire and then over their heads. Usually cotton dipped in clarified butter is burned.

8. Ramakrishna Mission: Belur Math in Kolkata, India. Headquarters of the Ramakrishna Math and Mission 2006. For more information, see www.ramakrishna.org/rmk_ordr.htm.

9. The Belur Math Mission, located in Kolkata, India, was founded in 1938 at the urging of many monks and Swami Vivekananda (1863–1902) and named after his mentor, Shri Ramakrishna (1836–1886), and is a part of the Ramakrishna Mission. The Ramakrishna Mission is world-renowned for its missionary work.

9

Interpretive Intervention: Religion, Gender, and Boundaries

Bandana Purkayastha

> Where the world has not been broken up into fragments by narrow
> domestic walls. . . . (Tagore 1913b)

The preceding chapters, and the ones following this interpretive intervention, provide detailed discussions about Hinduism and Islam in South Asia and the United States. The authors describe their beliefs and practices, the kinds of opportunities they have had to practice their religions, and the boundaries—especially the social and ideological boundaries—they have encountered. In this chapter we link some of the descriptions in the essays to discussions in academic literature on religion, and gender and religion. We focus primarily on social and ideological boundaries, examining the notions about dual spheres and the conceptual boundaries that make it difficult to study religion in more holistic, inclusive ways. We use the idea of "boundaries as complex structures—physical, social, ideological, and psychological   which establish differences and commonalties between men and women, among women, and among men" (Gerson and Peiss 1985, 317). We do not provide an exhaustive review of these debates, simply some indication of the ways in which the views of the authors (in this book) contribute to supporting or challenging existing knowledge.

One of our key theoretical arguments in the introduction was about the definition of religion. We argued that most definitions take Christianity as the norm and this affects how gender and religion are

147

studied. In this book, what emerged from the chapters was a picture of religion that is " nonmonolithic and operationally plural" (Nandy 1999, 322). Neither the older functionalist idea of religion, which emphasizes shared values and rituals that lead to group cohesion, or religious activities that explicitly draw on the notion of the supernatural source of values (Wilson 1979), or the idea that religions are accompanied by powerful institutions that attempt to spread their influence (Mitchell 2006), are able to capture what is being described here. Nor does Gans' (1979) concept of "symbolic religiosity," which refers to a religious culture that does not involve regular participation in its rituals or organization, or Demerath's cultural religion, which means "an identification with a religious heritage without any religious participation or a sense of personal involvement per se" (2001, 59) capture the descriptions in these chapters. The authors describe religion as a way of life, a "confederation of a number of ways of life," linked by shared values and de-linked from institutions seeking to spread their influence (and to draw boundaries between the groups that belong and those that do not). The authors describe fluid and heterogeneous practices that keep the boundaries between religions blurred, emphasizing connections between people instead of ways of fragmenting them into distinctive groups.

In the accounts by Bandana Purkayastha, Selina Jamil, Bidya Ranjeet, Neela Bhattacharya Saxena, Parveen Talpur, Salma Kamal, and Monoswita Saha, religion spills out of the boundaries of "religion," "symbolic religion," and "cultural religion" so that it becomes difficult, in the conventional sense, to separate culture from religion, and religion from spirituality. Many authors acknowledge drawing from more than one religious tradition. Neela Bhattacharya Saxena presents a "conventional" Hindu puja that ends with a call to Amin, an invocation of an Islamic pir, showing how blurred boundaries can coexist with the formally acknowledged religious "differences." Bidya Ranjeet points out that she is both Hindu and Buddhist, so it is a constant challenge for her to identify herself in one category. Trying to fit these religious beliefs and practices into narrow compartments contribute to the racialization and gendering of the spirit (Ahmed 2002).

Much of the discussion on religion is based on the idea that religions are separate from public worlds in secular societies (Bhargava 1999; Bush 2007). The chapters in this book show that the two spheres intersect. Indeed, the authors point out the lack of holidays or space for religiocultural events (e.g., Bandana Purkayastha, Bidya Ranjeet, and Salma Kamal) and racial profiling (e.g., Parveen Talpur, also Aysha Saeed and Rafia Zakaria in the next section) as examples of institutionalized ways of ascribing boundaries on minority religions. The authors discuss the ways in which the stereotypes about their religions carry over to other aspects of their lives. Neela Bhattacharya Saxena and Selina Jamil, and in the next section Elora Halim Chowdhury, show how their authority as academics are constantly challenged (and co-opted) by their colleagues; their knowledge and expertise is marginalized as "ethnic knowledge" in academic enterprises. The accounts by Salma Kamal and Monoswita Saha depict their struggles to overcome the boundaries that exclude them from full membership into the category "American" because of their phenotypes and their religion. Regardless of the actual difference of their religious beliefs from mainstream beliefs, the politicization of religious boundaries by the mainstream lead to unequal freedom for them to practice their religion. The chapters by Parveen Talpur in this section, and Aysha Saeed and Rafia Zakaria in the next section, illustrate the overlap between the sacred and secular spheres as well.

Just as there is an ongoing belief about the separateness of the secular and sacred spheres, a private-public binary has been used, historically, to relegate women to the private sphere. This ideology is vigorously challenged by feminist scholars who have shown how it negatively affects women's freedoms, citizenship status, ability to travel, work, claim just wages, access healthcare, own property, marry whom they choose, and other aspects of their lives. But, as we pointed out in the introduction, much of the "W"estern feminist discussions assume ethnic women are mostly shaped (subordinated) by their religions, so that despite the scholarship that insists on getting beyond dual spheres, ethnic women are only seen as victims of their religions and cultures within the private, nonsecular sphere. Indeed, in arguing that multiculturalism is bad for women, Okin states, "[minority women] *might* be better off if the cultures into which they were born were either to become extinct (so that its members would become integrated into the less sexist surrounding culture) or be encouraged to alter itself so as to reinforce the equality of women—at least to the degree to which this value is upheld in majority society" (1999, 22–23). The authors show that, contrary to such "W"estern feminist arguments, some of the most significant boundaries they encounter arise out of *mainstream* institutional and ideological structures that restrict their lives as minority women.

A great deal of feminist scholarship has described how women are ideologically excluded from religions. Much of this scholarship has been based on notions of Adam and Eve, the concept of original sin, and the need for the priest to resemble Christ. Such ideological barriers have been translated into organizational practice in Christianity, and despite the attempts of a few groups like the Shakers to break away from such gendered organizational forms, women typically have been second-class participants in church hierarchy. Christian women have, therefore, engaged in a range of organized effort to create a space for themselves in church (e.g., Katzenstein 1996). In contrast, Saxena (along with Bandana Purkayastha, Monoswita Saha, Shobha Hamal Gurung, and Anjana Narayan) discusses the continuing importance of the feminine (gynocentric) principle in Hinduism. In fact, Bandana Purkayastha and Neela Bhattacharya Saxena (and later Anjana Narayan) point out that the concept of ardhanariswara does not create gender hierarchies in the ways that the Adam and Eve stories do. Many authors in this book indicate that the feminist discussions about the need to develop feminist frames to challenge male-dominated ideologies in religions effectively silences the centuries-long, ongoing importance of the female—Durga, Kali, Sarawati, and Lakshmi—and feminine principles in religions like Hinduism. Similarly, Talpur and Jamil (and later, Elora Halim Chowdhury and Aysha Saeed) point out that Islam offers many humane, gender-neutral paths of religious practice that are not mediated by a male priestly hierarchy. But these views are often silenced because there is a predetermined framework of religion and gender-subordination that is used to discuss minority religions. While many Western scholars claim that feminism has contributed to "new" perspectives inspired by feminist spirituality and theology, the authors here, especially Saxena, show that these are not "new" perspectives. Bidya Ranjeet and Shobha Hamal Gurung's descriptions of women's roles in home-based rituals, even when these sustain gender-segregated activity, serve as an important acknowledged role in family and community life that differ in ways that women are excluded from churches. The roles of these mothers and grandmothers are acknowledged in almost reverential terms (also see Monoswita Saha's account of her grandmother).

The authors point out that there is no linear progression from tradition to modernity in the sense of a move toward a more progressive position. Instead, the pressure to give up decentralized forms of practice in the United States reinscribes new gendered boundaries. As Purkayastha describes, a series of laws that require centralized authority structures and unitary memberships in congregations invariably marginalize women. Practicing religion in a variety of spaces and settings provides much more opportunity to blur religious boundaries and uphold women's central role in religions (e.g., Bidya Ranjeet and Shobha Hamal Gurung). So the gendered boundaries the authors describe are a reflection of sets of intersecting mainstream and ethnic-community factors that contribute to the altered organization of these religions.

While none of the first-generation authors—Bandana Purkayastha, Selina Jamil, Parveen Talpur, and Neela Bhattacharya Saxena—are deeply invested in any congregation, they all describe within-group boundaries that disadvantage women. In spite of describing various ways in which their lives have been enriched by gender-neutral symbolism, religious coexistence, and blurring of religious boundaries through everyday practice, the authors do not romanticize the lives of women. They strongly criticize fundamentalists of their ethnic communities, and offer strong conceptual challenges to the fundamentalist reconstructions of history and religious interpretations. And as Anjana Narayan, Rafia Zakaria, Shanthi Rao, and Aysha Saeed show in the next section, the authors also identify the complicity of a larger group of people who appear to be persuaded by the fundamentalists' ethnocentric ideologies.

In effect, these narratives offer a new way of thinking about religion/spirituality that take these women's understanding and experiences as central to understanding the endeavor of living religions.

PART II

Religion, Practices,
Resistances

10

The Many Facets of Hinduism

Anjana Narayan

Reflecting on my life through the lens of religion is a challenging task. For the most part, I am not used to thinking of myself primarily as a *Hindu* woman. As Amartya Sen (2006) states in his book on identity and violence, I am many things: a scholar, an immigrant, an Indian, an Indian American, a self-taught singer and artist, and an activist. I belong to many webs of relationships that span various parts of India and the United States: my families, close friends who have become "fictive" kin, and professional and activist networks. Each of these networks shapes an aspect of my identity. Yet, I am also the person defined by others who see me through their ideological lens: as an immigrant from the Third World, a woman of color, and a Hindu (read subordinated) woman in the United States. My religious values help me to tie these different facets of myself together, just as the social and political circumstances in which I am located shape specific ways in which I compose my life.

My account of being a Hindu from India is grounded in a very long history of religious encounters in India. I have been influenced by the principles of folk religions in Kerala, South India, as well as the more secular forms of religiocultures in India's commercial capital, Mumbai. I am also affected by the religiocultural history-in-the-making in contemporary America, where "new" religions, Islam and Hinduism, are attempting to carve their space in a largely Christian country.

My lived religion is not composed of ritualized attendance in places of worship, participating in congregational prayers, or believing in a set of tenets. Rather, it is a set of spiritual principles based on my understanding of my connections with others and of my self-as-a-part-of-a-larger-universe, and a sense of respect for other religions. It is not a religion in the sense of a formal membership in a faith-based congregation; instead, it consists of a set of spiritual values that animate all aspects of my life.

Reflections on Hinduism in the United States

Unlike India, where Christianity and Hinduism have coexisted since 50 C.E., Hinduism is a "new" religion in the United States. During the nineteenth and early twentieth centuries, public discourses on Hinduism often depicted "Hindoos" as savage heathens with exotic—often horrifying—rituals (Burke 1983). Although Indian philosophers like Vivekananda tried to correct this negative stereotype by portraying Hinduism as a global religion of tolerance, Hinduism remained shrouded in a number of stereotypes (Prashad 2000b).

The large-scale Hindu migration to the United States began with the Immigration Act of 1965. The post-1965 period brought the first wave of Indian graduate students and highly educated professionals who found ready employment in managerial positions, followed by the highly skilled guest workers (H1-B visa holders) in the 1980s. As this period coincided with increasing openness toward multiculturalism in America, Hindu Indian migrants were able to claim *some* space for practicing their religion (such as building temples and organized sects practicing their own version of Hinduism), but these outward signs of religious presence have been hard won. Indians continue to face racial discrimination in public spaces based on reactions to observable characteristics and the perception of their religions as "foreign" (Joshi 2006; Purkayastha 2005).

I have lived on the East Coast, the West Coast, and the Midwest, and my experiences as a Hindu in the United States have been largely associated with three groups of people. The first group (that I do not interact with on a daily level) consists of the right-wing Hindu organizations that have been very active in the United States, seeking to establish their hegemonic version of Hinduism. Their zeal is partially a response to the racial discrimination they experienced from fundamentalists of other religions and the orientalist mindsets of otherwise liberal people (Joshi 2006). However, they also have seized the opportunities available in multicultural America to assert a version of religiocultural nationalism that *fits* the US majority group's expectation of religion. Their version asserts one set of practices, key books, temple-based rituals, and a complementary (read subordinated) role for women. While these Hindutva groups are attempting to transform Hinduism to fit the structures in the United States, they are also using the religion to construct sharper boundaries between Hinduism, Christianity, and Islam. These organizations, with their ideology of Hindu nationalism, have been very active on the Internet, asserting a homogenous centralized form of Hinduism and vigorously reaching out to student groups on college campuses to persuade more people to join their cause. The pluralistic, decentralized forms of Hinduism that I will describe later in this chapter are in the process of being simplified and standardized to create a global Hinduism. However, this Hinduism is not so much a religion as a transterritorial dimension of the Hindu nationalist movement (Hindutva) that attempts to popularize a uniform, scripture-based Hinduism, intended to appeal to the upwardly mobile sections of the diaspora. I encounter this group each time I try to look up anything on Hinduism on the Internet, and I am forced to react to their many outrageous public claims on behalf of "Hindus" (Lal 2002; Narayan 2006; Kurien 2007). Their discourse shapes how non-Hindus learn about my religion in the United States. More importantly, I hear echoes of their discourse among the second group, the more secular Indians.

The second group is a section of urbanized, professional, middle-class Indians in the United States who have no affiliations with Hindutva organizations. Yet, this group appears to display an alarming susceptibility to a resurgent Hinduism that they see as a means to remotivate Hindu sentiment among the diaspora in the United States.

The final group consists of people I have met in the United States and who have contributed greatly to my own thinking about religion. This group of South Asian women continues to shape my reactions and fuel my motivation. I have been able to consciously think about and practice what I always have valued as a humane Hinduism, as I will describe later.

I came to the United States as a student at a university on the East Coast, located in a small rural township. As the majority of the student body was white Caucasian, I instinctively gravitated toward the Indian community. Within weeks of my arrival, I found myself exposed to aspects of Hinduism I had not directly encountered back in India and did not expect to see in this country.

My first encounter was with an Indian graduate student who introduced herself to me as a Hindu Brahmin who performed daily *pujas* and visited the temple every weekend. As an orthodox Hindu, she laid great stress on the concepts of purity and pollution. I also discovered she had run a "background check" on every Indian student who was from her region in India, by closely questioning them about their religion and caste status. As she found them lacking in the good breeding and sophistication of her own background, and speaking only regional dialects of her own "pure" language, she preferred her own company to theirs. As I got to know more Indian graduate students, I found echoes of the same negative appraisal, as these students attempted to create self-privilege through their caste/region exclusivist lenses. For instance, I often heard variations of: "Oh, she may not be a Brahmin, but at least she behaves like one" or "We Brahmins use completely different ingredients for this recipe." As a social scientist, I explain these attempts to revive caste privileges—the worst aspect of Hinduism—as mechanisms to cope with the deep invisibility and marginality that foreign students encounter in US academic settings. Yet, as a member of this group, I was placed in the difficult position of remaining a part of the group while distancing myself from these ideologies.

Looking for some evidence of solidarity across caste, religious, and ethnic lines, I began engaging with the South Asian Student Association, composed of students from India, Pakistan, Nepal, Bangladesh, and Sri Lanka. Sadly, the situation there was no better. The association had a predominantly Indian membership. The very year I joined the university, the leading committee members of the association made radical changes to its constitution, so that the

"South Asian Student Association" became the "Indian Student Association." Despite protests, the new amendments effectively blocked students from Nepal, Pakistan, Bangladesh, and Sri Lanka from having a voice in any important decisions. And, despite the name "Indian," the organization became overtly "Hindu." Nobody paid much attention to my protests that the association was intended to be a South Asian cultural organization meant to promote the interests of all the South Asian communities, not a Hindu religious body. Even today, the association celebrates only *Diwali* or *Holi* each year, blatantly disregarding some of the most important festivals of Nepal, Pakistan, Bangladesh, and Sri Lanka, as well as some of India's best-loved non-Hindu festivals, like Christmas and Eid. Besides, while the essence of *Diwali* in India is lighting lamps and exploding firecrackers, the association has reversed the significance. A *Diwali* program I attended consisted of Hindu *bhajans* (devotional songs), Vedic chanting, and a formal discourse by a keynote speaker on how Brahmins celebrate the festival. All in all, I was inclined to agree with several of my non-Hindu friends and fellow students—who justifiably felt marginalized—that an Indian organization had essentially come to mean a Hindu organization.

I have progressively discovered that Hinduism, as I knew it in India, has mutated into a new form in the United States. Over the last seven years, my social network has grown to include many decent, liberal-minded, and educated professionals, who have well-paying jobs and a promising future in this country. Yet, when we get together for a meal or an informal gathering and the conversation turns to India, particularly the Hindu-Muslim clashes in Gujarat, the response is something like: "Of course, it's sad this happened. But they [Muslims] deserved it." I've heard the same sentiment expressed time and again, even by strangers whom I talk to during a flight, or people I meet elsewhere. There is a persistent refrain of irreconcilable differences between Hindus and Muslims—a divide that is gloatingly justified after the 9/11 World Trade Center terrorist attacks and the much-flouted "war on terror" in Iraq.

Such parochial views are being applied to other events. As a case in point, the incident of the bomb blasts in Mumbai, dubbed 7/11, was a grotesque tragedy with a toll of 200 dead and more than 700 injured, which included both Hindus and Muslims. Yet, the reaction of these Hindus ranged from "How does this affect the Sensex [the Indian Stock Exchange]?" or "Will this affect the Indian BPO industry?" to declarations like: "These terrorists aren't going to succeed" or "We won't take this lying down any longer." Likewise, the Internet has been clogged with hate mail against the Muslim community. Typical remarks are: "Finally somebody's doing something about these Muslims attacking innocent Hindus" and "We cannot let these Muslims get away with murder; we have to retaliate." There is no acknowledgment that the 7/11 incident in Mumbai was a purely random attack that did not target any one community. Nor is it reported anywhere that it was Mumbai's Muslim slum-dwellers who first rushed to help the victims of the blasts.

It seems that no opportunity is lost to feed racial and religious bigotry in the inexorable construction of a Hindu-Muslim communal divide, in particular, and the promotion of Hindu supremacy over all religions in general. Even natural calamities have been exploited to this end. Take the case of the December 2004 tsunami. A popular Indian news portal carried an article implying that the very timing of the disaster indicates retribution for the Christian community because of its role in undermining Hinduism. A blogger on another popular portal emphasized the hand of a Hindu god, claiming that while the tsunami lashed the church at Velankani, a Hindu temple on the beachfront was left unscarred. Again, there was no mention of how people did their utmost to offer help and succor to the victims, regardless of religion and community.

What I find most intriguing is that these strong communal sentiments are expressed by educated moderates, many of them scholars and eminent personalities, who divide their professional lives between the United States and India. The popular Indian portals hosting these views are US-based, and the pages that are most visited are written by Hindus living in the United States. These are individuals who are evidently not part of organized religious groups or supporters of Hindu nationalist movements. And yet, their views undeniably lean toward covert and overt sentiments that support ethnocentric nationalism. Two intersecting reasons could account for this trend. As assimilated Americans (in terms of education, jobs, and residences), these Indians are participating in acts of distancing themselves from Muslims, much like the sentiments pervasive among larger swaths of US society. Or, it could be similar to how Chinese Americans distanced themselves from Japanese Americans during internment, a futile way to escape racist backlashes. But these also are acts of narrow ethnonationalisms, contrary to some of the lived practices of Hinduism.

Formative Influences in India

My rejection of various forms of boundary-making ideologies on communal or ethnocentric lines is based on my experiences with lived religious practices in India. I trace my formative influences to the variegated mosaic of mythologies, rituals, and gods, which, down the ages, enriched Hindu culture with a unique ability to absorb, incorporate, and synthesize other cultures. In fact, while I was in India, I did not have to consciously think of myself as a Hindu who had to draw boundaries around her religion. As a sociologist, I realize that my ability to live without a consciousness of boundaries was partly based on my social location as a member of the majority religious group in India. But it was not a fact of structural position alone; the religio*cultural* practices that I absorbed unconsciously also shaped my understanding about multiple, coexisting religions where people have the right to practice their religiocultures. The observation that it is a challenge to reflect on my lived practices of Hinduism arises from my discomfort in trying to identify exactly what are exclusively Hindu practices. The folk traditions that influence my thinking emphasize broad zones of overlap between religions, rather than sharp boundaries of difference. At the same time, these folk forms of religions have helped me develop an irreverent attitude toward entrenched hierarchies and the practices that promote them.

I value having been brought up in India, with its rich religious tapestry of Hinduism, Islam, Buddhism, Jainism, Sikhism, Christianity, Judaism, Baha'ism, Zoroastrianism, and other faiths. Most people recognize the centuries-old roots of Hinduism in India, but

Buddhism and Jainism were founded there, too. Christianity was introduced into the country by St. Thomas in by the middle of the first century C.E. and had gained some ground in India even before it was embraced in Europe. The Muslim influence began in the twelfth century C.E., and we see many forms of Islam in India. Kings and emperors frequently have been at the forefront of promoting forward-thinking religiocultural values. In the third century B.C.E., the Hindu emperor Ashoka eschewed war and spent his life promoting the central Buddhist principle of non-injury to all life forms. In the sixteenth century C.E., the Muslim emperor Akbar set up *Din-Ilahi* to promote the value of all religions. These efforts to nurture religious diversity at the state level are matched by syncretic religiocultural practices at the grassroots level. For instance, the Ahmediyas are a religious sect that follows the teachings of the Koran, but also practices the essentially Hindu ritual of idol worship (Das 2006). The *Bhakti* movement of the fourteenth to seventeenth centuries included saints like Kabir, who was of Muslim origin, and Meerabai, who was of Hindu origin. Bhakti saints believed God was beyond the exclusive claims of established religions, and many Hindus continue to seamlessly visit places of pilgrimage of various religions. Hinduism, which traces its roots to at least the third century B.C.E., has grown out of encounters with all these religions and has gone through several phases of quiescence and reform movements. Without a book or one iconic figure, it is an amalgam of varied practices, customs, beliefs, and organizations. Its extremely varied forms reflect regional cultures and histories, and family forms, as well as class position, caste status, sex, and age of the individual who practices it. Hinduism is, at any given time, practiced in thousands of different ways.

Kerala, where my family originates, offers a microcosm of a variety of religiocultural influences. The earlier Dravidian inhabitants of Kerala followed primitive animism and spirit worship to propitiate the gods. With the arrival of Aryans from the north, other religious practices evolved into Hinduism. Kerala's commercial ties to the Middle East began in the seventh century C.E. The Middle Easterners of the pre-Islamic and Islamic periods were among the pioneers of the spice trade with Kerala and later settled into the coastal regions. The Syrian Christians of Kerala—belonging to one of the oldest Christian sects in the world—were peaceably converted by St. Thomas. Jews have a ten-century-old history with Kerala, where they found refuge and acceptance when fleeing from Roman persecution. This history has allowed a spirit of coexistence to flourish (Tharoor 1998).

I was well into my late teens before I even began to identify myself as a Hindu. Throughout my childhood and early adolescence, I identified myself with Christianity rather than Hinduism, because my exposure to religion was mainly through the missionary schools I attended. Our family did not practice any Hindu rituals at home, and our celebrations of major Malayali festivals, such as *Onam* and *Vishu*, were social community gatherings, not religious observances. Nor did this lack of traditional religious practices seem strange or unusual in the cosmopolitan cities of Mumbai and Delhi where I was raised.

As a city-bred child, my acquaintance and subsequent familiarization with Hindu gods and goddesses came about during our annual visits to Kerala, where we would spend the long summer vacation at my parents' ancestral homes in their native village. A native village surrounded by dense forest is a far cry from the placid ideal of swaying coconut palms, plantain groves, tranquil backwaters, and lush greenery of tourist-centric locations. As in any location deep within the countryside, darkness enfolds the village at night. When there is a power outage (a frequent occurrence), the pitch-dark night magnifies the rustle of plants, the scuttle of nocturnal animals—and can be quite sinister for a child used to the city. At such times, my grandmother and granduncles would light the oil lamp and tell us stories from folklore—amazing tales about gods and goddesses, demons, and vampires.

When I look back, I realize that much of my knowledge and understanding about Hinduism, and the way I apply its precepts, comes from these fascinating stories and the innuendos and elaborations woven into the telling. These tales often diverge widely from the literary forms: the epics, the *shastras* (scriptures), and *puranas* (mythology) that are the ancient Hindu writings. The oral stories gleefully recount how the mighty have fallen, mock the priesthood and the caste system, and are indifferent to the "high sanctity" of the upper-caste religions (Lal 1991).

Another aspect of lived religious practice has always captivated me. Kerala has a long history of nature worship, and even today vegetation and plants are venerated as externalizations of divine beings, with trees, plants, and forests often protected in sacred groves dedicated to local deities or ancestral spirits. Most people live in their own private forests, where a typical home is built in the middle of a large, open tract of land, with coconut palms forming a natural protective canopy over the homestead to bear the brunt of the tropical sun. Divine beings are said to inhabit the vegetation, from the benign deities residing in trees to the rather malevolent lesser gods who live in flowering shrubs and bewitch the women who pluck the flowers for their hair. There is a rich abundance of such imagery in Kerala's folk songs and folklore. I now realize that the essential lesson, the sense of sacredness that imbues all life forms, has become a part of me. Priests, sects, conflicts, and clashes are not part of such lived religions. It is indeed India's common people who are the true guardians and promoters of Hinduism.

According to the popular press and even academic literature, Kerala is singularly noted for its progress through communal peace and harmony, and is portrayed as an exemplar of good governance. Statistics are quoted to underline the direct link between communal and religious tolerance and progress; a distinction that the inhabitants are quick to point out to any casual visitor to Kerala. Nonetheless, in recent times, there have been attempts to breach this oasis of communal tolerance and racial harmony. Kerala's political machinery is (and has been) marked by repeated instances of violence that are motivated by the hunger for political, economic, and ethnoreligious control. Over the last few years, Hindu communal forces have been attacking and threatening this cultural pluralism to establish their own power coterie in the state. However, most of these ploys have failed to gain a stronghold, and I believe this is due to the "folk values" I have described.

I would argue that the cultural conflicts that fuel extremism in other parts of India and other countries are often arrested because of the lived practices of ordinary people in Kerala. For instance, it is in the normal course of events for the Hindu priest at the temple to hold off his amplified incantations until the muezzin has finished summoning the faithful to prayer at the mosque. It is a tacit understanding based on mutual respect, human decency, and communal coexistence.

Dempsey (2001) writes about an interesting display of communal solidarity in the face of politically motivated incitement. The district of Kannur has a long-standing practice that considers St. Sebastian and the goddess Kali brother and sister, so the doors of the goddess's temple remain open during the annual St. Sebastian church parade. Some years ago, political members of a Hindu fundamentalist party declared this Hindu-Christian bonding unacceptable, and persuaded the temple to close its doors during the parade. However, the following year brought much misfortune to the Hindu community. They reasoned that Kali's forced estrangement from her brother during his annual parade had enraged the goddess, and the temple resumed its earlier practice. Such anecdotes strengthen my belief that, despite extreme provocation from factions of Hindus, Muslims, and Christians, the day-to-day lives of people have the quiet but immeasurably powerful capacity to lay and enforce a foundation strong enough to challenge the threat of extremists and fundamentalists.

Yet, my exposure to these forms of interconnections also is tinged with memories of an interesting juxtaposition of the centrality of female deities and the restrictions on public forms of worship by certain groups of women. Kerala's reigning Hindu deity is the goddess Bhagavati. As part of their daily obeisance, Hindu Malayalis flock to the thousands of temples dedicated to Bhagavati that are scattered throughout Kerala. My mother's village has one such temple. The goddess is perceived as the embodiment of life itself and, through the numerous prescribed rituals of faith, devotion, and invocations, devotees may invite, embody, and experience her divine presence within the physical shell of their own bodies. One such entity is the *velichapaadu* (divine oracle), who is an obligatory presence in any temple dedicated to Bhagavati and who acts as a medium between the goddess and her devotees. Though he is "attached" to his temple, he is also the goddess's vehicle to mingle with her devotees by visiting local households.

During one of my childhood visits to my mother's village, I witnessed the events preceding the oracle's arrival. It was a sweltering summer day, which made me wonder why all the womenfolk of the household were confined indoors. I was told that the oracle was due to arrive that day to make prophetic pronouncements under Bhagavati's divine dispensation, and that the presence of a woman—even a little girl—outside the house would anger the goddess. While the women waited indoors, the men outside busied themselves with all the necessary arrangements for the event. The oracle came, announced his prophecy, and left. I did not get to see a thing, though I had been able to hear the steady beat of the drums accompanying the oracle's frenzied moans and sinister incantations.

I was terrified by the experience and avoided any mention of it for several years. Sometime later, my granduncle explained why women were barred from the oracle's presence. The goddess Bhagavati is a powerful and fearsome entity. She is often depicted wearing a necklace of human skulls, with her tongue protruding threateningly. According to legend, the demon Darikan, after undergoing arduous penance for his misdeeds, requested Brahma (the Creator of the Universe) to make him an omnipotent male entity, unbeatable by men or gods. Brahma asked Darikan if that invincibility should also extend to female entities, a suggestion Darikan scoffed at dismissively. After being granted the blessing, the demon reverted to type and unleashed terror and mayhem on an unprecedented scale. Helpless and powerless against Darikan's invincibility, the gods implored Shiva (the Destroyer) to save all creation from the demon's malevolence. Shiva harnessed his formidable psychic energy to create a powerful and fierce six-armed female deity, Bhagavati. She confronted Darikan in a dramatic battle and hacked off his head.

In another story recounted to me, the fearsome Bhagavati disguises herself as a pitiful beggar and goes to an upper-class Nair household in the village to plead for alms, only to be shunned. She then goes into the forest and asks the tribals there for something to eat and drink. They cordially welcome her into their homes and show her due hospitality. Gratified, Bhagavati returns to her original form and blesses the tribals. As a mark of her anger toward the Nair women who treated her shabbily, she withholds her blessing from all the women of that particular village. Thus, while women everywhere in Kerala are allowed to be present when the oracle visits their homes, it is only in my mother's village that the women are barred from participating in the ritual, or even being present.

Another story that fascinated me was the legend of the *yakshi* who is believed to be an evil tree spirit, hell-bent on enticing and destroying men. My mother later explained that the *yakshi*'s murderous deeds are often the result of her being ill-treated or abused during her earthly life as a human.

While these stories of formidable women could be very inspiring for Hindu women in Kerala, there are equally obvious indications of the gaps between the goddess and the living-breathing women (Caldwell 2001). In Kerala, both the terms *bhadrakali* and *yakshi* continue to retain connotations of shrewish, unseemly, or unwomanly behavior, used to describe a bad-tempered loudmouth given to unseemly emotional outbursts—the very things a respectable Malayali woman should *not* be. I have to wonder whether this negative association explains why hardly any middle-class women—and certainly none in my immediate or extended family—feel a sense of empathy with the goddess.

Yet another example of this segregation is evident in the worship of Lord Ayappan. I remember an incident when my cousin insisted on accompanying her brother on the annual pilgrimage to Sabarimala, the hugely popular temple dedicated to the bachelor god Ayappan, one of South India's most revered deities. The Sabarimala temple, picturesquely located atop a hill in Kerala, holds the rather dubious distinction of being the only Hindu temple in India where women between 10 and 50 years of age are not allowed. Consequently, my cousin's "perverse" demand was promptly vetoed under a spate of arguments. First, the sight of a woman would seriously threaten Lord Ayappan's bachelorhood. Second, the arduous trek to the temple was to be preceded by 41 days of strict penance that required the discipline of a saint—quite beyond a woman's capabilities. Third, the men would be distracted by a woman's presence, as she would provoke wanton desires that would destroy their hard-won penance. Fourth, allowing a woman into the temple would seriously disrupt religious protocol. And so on . . .

Back then, I did not quite get the point my cousin was trying to make. It was only over time that I noticed the male-dominant nature of the pilgrimage, which clarified her argument. Lord Ayappan is believed to be conceived by two male gods, Shiva and Vishnu—the kind of binary-sex transcending symbolism that Ahmed (2002) and Vanita (2002) document—and is worshipped for his celibate status. He is a *brahmacharya* (celibate student) whose tremendous powers arise from his sexual abstinence, a practice emulated by his devotees during the penance and pilgrimage. Women of childbearing age could lure Ayappan away from his holy shrine and are thus barred not only from the temple, but also from the forest around Sabarimala. And so, while my aunts who were daily temple-goers, who assiduously lit the sacred brass lamps each evening at sunset, and who regularly fasted to invoke the blessings of the gods on their families and homes were not allowed at Sabarimala.

In fact, the ideological underpinning of the pilgrimage asserts that the men who undertake the all-male pilgrimage are the true motivators for their womenfolk's continued piety and devotion (Osella and Osella 2003). Thus, it was supposedly my uncles who had won lasting prosperity and comfort for their households by undertaking the 41 days of penance and the pilgrimage, thereby invoking Ayappan's blessings. To all intents and purposes, this one much-lauded act of ritualistic male bonding overshadows and effectively effaces the women's quiet and patient daily devotions and painstaking religious adherence for their families' welfare (Osella and Osella 2003). But it is the women's ongoing tasks, such as the folk practices, that weave the day-to-day connections between people.

In Mumbai, where I was raised amid amazing extremes of affluence and poverty, I encountered other forms of religious and gendered inclusions and exclusions. Muslims, who are emphatically opposed to idol worship, were an enthusiastic part of the festive crowds celebrating the Ganapathi festival, a tribute to one of Hinduism's most popular gods. Hindus absorbed Sai Baba (a prophet who dedicated himself to the cause of Hindu-Muslim unity) into their galaxy of gods, as demonstrated by shrines across the city and pictures of the saint gracing the rear windows of cabs. Each day, the daily routines seamlessly bring Muslims, Hindus, and other religionists together. The Bollywood idols whose faces dominate the billboards are Muslims and Hindus; the "street foods" are prepared by people of different religions; the journey on commuter trains crush people of different religions into the closest physical proximity: and merchants doing brisk business in stores are of all different faiths. Multiple identities kept religious identities from becoming dominant.

But this pattern of interreligious interaction has been punctured by the rising tide of ethnonationalism engendered by Hindu nationalists. Mumbai's honored status as the cosmopolitan center of India was ineradicably marred by a protracted period of unrest following the sporadic Hindu-Muslim riots of 1992 and the more widespread riots the following year, culminating in a choreographed series of bomb blasts that transformed the city's landscape and disfigured its very spirit. In the aftermath of this appalling violence, Mumbai went through an intense period of self-evaluation. Prior to these aggressive displays of communal conflict, there had been isolated pockets of Hindu or Muslim neighborhoods, but the scale of the 1992 rioting established a new order. More than a decade later, Muslims have every reason to live in safe proximity. The existence of these communal islands was a shocking eye-opener.

Sadly, the 1992 incidents were only the beginning. My college years were marked by a sequence of incidents, which only underscored the growing communal and gendered divide fueled by violent cultural nationalism. One such incident was the raging controversy over the Indian movie *Fire*, where the female protagonists are involved in a sexual relationship. Infuriated Hindu fundamentalists banned the movie and were vociferous in trying to prove that lesbianism has its origin and source in Islam.

As a college student, I found myself wondering why a sensitive and genuine portrayal of women's issues and an exploration of women's sexuality should draw political gunfire. Where does Hinduism prescribe a sexual identity as a mark of sanctity? On the contrary, numerous symbols of androgyny (Ruth 2002) abound in Hindu folklore, in tales about manly goddesses and effeminate gods, of the sexual transformation from men to women and women to men, kings "being with child," and male protagonists who don women's garb for years. From epics to folk songs, India's folklore seems to hold a fluid concept of maleness-femaleness, sexuality, and every theme of gender transfer or same-sex partners. Several people of Indian origin, when confronted with their sexual preferences— whether homosexual, bisexual, or transgender—have found an empathic precedent in these tales. Yet, sexuality, like faith, was being targeted as a divisive tactic by some political parties to gain attention and power.

Even as power-hungry groups were creating these divisions, the other layers of Hinduism survived. All through college, I had heard a litany of derogatory reports about certain "godmen" and "gurus" who had amassed fortunes by preying on the gullible. While these reports could well be true, I preferred to reserve my opinion. So, when Mata Amritanandamayi,[1] (Amma) was scheduled for a visit to the city, I joined the large gathering of several thousands. It is common knowledge that Amma never turns away anyone in need of her hug.

The evening began with Amma, draped in her familiar white sari, and her entourage singing *bhajans*, followed by group meditation and chanting, after which she was ready for the *darshan* (contact). When I reached her, Amma drew me toward her and embraced me warmly, murmuring into my ears in her native Malayalam, "*Amma Kutti*" ("Mother's child"). The hugs and blessings continued all night, and it was morning before the last devotee left her embrace. Her ministrations affected people differently; some wept, others laughed, and still others went into a deep spiritual trance. Several observers, like me, merely watched her, trying to understand her spirit.

I find Amma extraordinary for the way she has positioned herself in the pantheon of Hindu spiritual leaders. She has deployed the legend of the goddess Bhagavati for her own empowerment, and effectively breached the male-dominated bastion in Kerala. She is widely accepted as the embodiment of the spirit of Bhagavati, and several devotees believe she is an incarnation of the goddess. Amma has managed to take Kerala's tradition of Bhagavati worship and adapt it to attain her own spiritual objectives, all the while building on her reputation as a world leader in promoting benevolent spiritual healing (Caldwell 2001). In this presentation, Bhagavati is no longer a representative of untrammeled power, but embodies healing and benevolence.

The experience of my *darshan* with Amma revealed another salient feature of Hinduism: Hindu deities are not remote divine beings in heaven, but a throbbing everyday reality in most people's lives. There is no demarcation placing the gods on one side and humans on the other, but a fluid interchange, best discerned in the idolization of powerful or charismatic public figures, in the kind of veneration that is tantamount to deifying them.[2]

This fundamental adaptability extends to sacred rituals as well, a phenomenon I witnessed after my father's unexpected death. The shock of this untimely event traumatized my mother, sister, and me. While our relatives were keen on a big funeral, my mother and I felt that the immediate disposal of my father's body was a fitting tribute to a man who was not one to observe spun-out ceremonial rites. My mother, however, seemed to need the comfort of age-old purification rituals that are necessary for the soul to rest in peace. Since my sister and brother-in-law had to return to their jobs in the United States, we had to restrict the traditional ceremony, which extends 16 days, to just 5 days. Three days after his death, my father's remains, handed over to us in an earthen pot, had to return to the elements. We took the ashes to Panchavati, located on the banks of the Godavari.[3] Here, we carried out the final ritual; my brother-in-law, as the eldest scion of the family, waded into the water to scatter the ashes. The final day of the rituals, the *Sanchayan,* is a grand feast for all close and extended family members. Again, we made a family decision to replace this repast with a donation of food to a children's home in the neighborhood.

The official mourning period depends largely on individual tradition,[4] but the Hindu scriptures do not recommend excessive mourning, because they see death as a joyous release. While a family is in mourning, the departed soul is obliged to be receptive to emotional currents from those left behind. Prolonged grieving, say the scriptures, inhibits the soul's release.

These religious rites, though only symbolic, were crucial in comforting my mother and helping her to come to terms with her crippling loss. These rituals were a gentle process of bidding a sanctified and peaceable farewell to my father. This explained why she was keen to mark my father's first death anniversary by visiting an ancient temple in northern Kerala, to conclude the *shraddha* (ritual for the peace of the departed soul).[5] Paying homage to one's ancestors is considered to be direct communication with them, and one of its objectives is to help the departed soul to be reborn in the same family or even the same abode. It is a striking reminder that death does not dissolve the everlasting link between the present and the past and between the living and the dead.

The ancient temple is located on a remote hillside amid a panorama of breathtaking beauty. While I was moved by the allure of this splendid ancient temple and the natural grandeur of its surroundings, I found the attitude of some of the priests acutely disturbing. There was the mercenary aspect, with some priests quite prepared to conduct "special" rituals to make an extra buck. There also was clear caste discrimination in the locations where the rituals were conducted, with prime locations provided for upper-caste Hindus and less preferable sites for the lower castes. Yet, one of the priests at this temple permitted my mother to participate in the *shraddha* ceremony from which wives of the deceased are traditionally barred. He told us that the word *shraddha* means "heartfelt respect and devotion," and felt that my mother's pure love and devotion for her departed husband entitled her to break with tradition. I saw this as a testimony of Hinduism's infinite flexibility in adjusting to human essentials and individual circumstances.

It is this adaptability that makes me hopeful about the future of this religion. Hinduism is not so much a set of religious doctrines as it is a set of values that may differ from, but do not conflict with, any other faith or community. I believe that Hinduism, the philosophy that is based on the everyday reality of the present, will prevail over Hindutva, which is not a religion but a political movement creating a Hindu identity based on the glorification of the past.

Constructing My Religious Space

My transition from a graduate student to a faculty member was both a change and a challenge. The move from rural Connecticut to Southern California was welcome. I liked the diversity of students in my classes and felt comfortable with the university community, which has considerably enriched my teaching experience. I appreciated the freedom to experiment with course content and a curriculum that moves beyond narrow Eurocentric paradigms.

At the same time, I realized that this freedom came with a tremendous sense of responsibility. Being one of the few South Asian faculty members at my college, I find myself being a spokesperson for just about anything related to India—ranging from the stereotypical caste system and the tradition of arranged marriages during casual conversation to discussing Hindu culture, tradition, and history at official forums. Topics I have been asked to address include the wider spheres of religion and globalization, such as being invited to talk about the Hindu festival of *Diwali* at the Indian Students *Diwali* program on campus, and guest lectures on related topics in classrooms. In these situations, I often find it challenging to present a complex narrative of Hinduism in India as I know it— a version that moves beyond the expected ethnocentricism and racism, yet avoids the idealistic picture of the perfect and "shining" India that Hindutva proponents tend to promote.

This aspect of Hinduism was highlighted in the California textbook controversy over the content of sixth-grade history and social science textbooks on India and Indian history. The debate started in the summer of 2005, when the California State Board of Education (SBE) requested Indian historians and members of the Indian American community to assist in the revised content; it culminated in a hotly debated public hearing in February 2006.

The main issue under contention was the proposed qualitative changes to the textual content. Two Hindutva groups wanted to do away with any mention of oppression of certain castes or female subjugation and instead present a homogenous, glorified concept of "Vedic" Hinduism, focusing on ancient Hindu philosophy as documented in the Vedas and the many achievements of Hindus in a multicultural setting. Their rationale was that teaching young students about caste distinctions and gender inequality would have a negative impact on cultural and national pride, particularly in the case of second-generation Hindu Indian Americans. These groups found strong opponents in the academic community, which insisted that this glorified and sanitized form of Hinduism was an inaccurate portrayal of the many complexities and diversities of Hinduism. They argued that such a portrayal reduced Indian history to fiction. Moreover, this monotheistic and monolithic form of Hinduism would ignore centuries of caste and gender disparities and would only misinform both Indian American and American students. In March 2006, the SBE decided to reject most of the Hindutva groups' recommendations.

The California textbook debate highlights some of the reasons why attempts to reduce Hinduism to a single, standardized religion or a monolithic culture representing the Indian American diaspora are simply not viable. First, depicting Hinduism as a faith based on sacred Vedic texts does gross injustice to the tremendous diversity of deities, myths, beliefs, rituals, and practices that differ widely, and some of which I have described earlier. Second, disassociating the caste system from the fabric of Hinduism discounts the system of social classification that was based on ancestry. Third—and possibly the most contentious issue of the public debate—removing all mention of a patriarchal society is not only a false history, but a distortion of the living Hinduism with its rich plurality of form, where women were both deified and subjugated and where the goddess-woman is depicted in folklore and epic tales. Hinduism has been and still remains a complex ideology that cannot be encapsulated into any one doctrine or set of beliefs. This form of Hinduism has no single god or scripture, but is instead a lived religion that; pays tribute to; human individuality and diversity (Kausalya 2006, Prashad 2006, Kurien 2007).

As I indicated earlier, the values I have tried to emphasize—of seeing interconnections, of flexibility, and adaptability to uphold humane practices—are counter to the patriarchal, ethnocentric ideologies being adopted by some sections of the Hindu community in the United States. Recently I had a heated debate with a cousin who accused me of being "way too idealistic." He said, "You believe in some faraway ideal, not in reality. What's wrong with you?" His words made me think on two levels. First, being called an idealist seemed to have connotations of immaturity and being foolishly unrealistic. Second, I had to examine what was "wrong with" me. I would say it was, rather, "right with" me, in the sense that I seem to have remained apart from the section of the diaspora that steadily has absorbed the Hindutva ideology.

Unlike many Hindus in the United States who glibly describe their place-bound practices as "the Indian way," I do not forget that Hinduism is expressed in thousands of ways through innumerable cultural practices developed over time to fit the needs of people in specific places. I "idealistically" value the variegated forms of Hinduism and reject the notion that one set of practices is good for everyone. If one begins at this starting point, it is easy to value all religions; so I exercise my choice, as a good Hindu, to live according to this humane principle.

Much of this "idealistic" attitude has been strengthened because of my interaction with the third group of people I mentioned earlier: a group of South Asian women—Hindu and Muslim—who have helped me to think and grow, and who have enriched my life. Some of them have authored chapters for this book. Although we are very diverse in terms of our individual inclinations, life stages, and our lived religious practices, we are able to find and share our common humanity, transcending the specific social divisions of nationality and religion. During our numerous interactions, I have come to realize that simplistic racial classifications that define us by religion or country are meaningless: We all live by humane values taught by our different religions. Our interaction is based on the easy interchange of views, beliefs, and optimism for the future. We are sufficiently strong to be openly critical of all attempts to diminish human beings (including denigrating women), and we are not hesitant about presenting our views of our religions. Together, we share a bond that transcends the superficial parameters of culture and religion.

I have developed the strength to resist internalizing corrosive ideologies because of my interactions with this group. I reject orientalist discourses about Indian women who need to be empowered; I have become active in questioning the myths about Hinduism (and Islam) constantly circulated in the media and in sections of academia. Collectively, we reject fundamentalisms and also question the role of people who uncritically imbibe ethnocentric ideologies. I see Hinduism as a way to animate concerns for human rights and as a set of obligations to help the growing trauma of people who are increasingly under high degrees of surveillance, or those who are affected by violence in their homes, communities, or countries.

While these practices are rarely recognized as "doing religion," I would assert that it is indeed through these everyday practices that I am able to uphold the religious principle that is valuable to me: interconnections with others maintained through our thoughts and practices.

Overall, my experiences in the United States and India, shaped by centuries of history, have reinforced my fundamental belief that, in my case, Hinduism gives me the tools to be tolerant and open to life's many adventures, and to understand that all of us are essentially one. But I am also convinced that we have to exercise our choice: Either we can selectively use "religious" lessons and bend them to our narrow status-maintaining ends, or we can remain open to the whole message and keep striving to be at one with all. This is the central theme of living religions.

Notes

1. Mata Amritanandamayi (which means "Mother of Absolute Bliss") is known as Amma (Mother) to her ardent devotees and as "the hugging saint" to the press. She is India's most famous godwoman, internationally renowned for her hugs, which are a form of physical and spiritual therapy. In India she has been known to hug more than 50,000 devotees in a single day.

2. In India, several female leaders have been accepted as goddesses. Foremost among them was Indira Gandhi, who first assumed the office of Prime Minister in 1966. She was often described as the goddess Durga, and the painter M. F. Hussain even presented her with triptych in oil, portraying her as such.

3. According to India's other grand epic, the *Ramayana*, Lord Ram, his wife, Sita, and his brother, Laxman, spent part of their 14-year exile at Panchavati, making it a much-venerated site.

4. Some families observe rituals for just over a fortnight (16 days), others for a month (31 days), and still others for a year. The period of official mourning is considered a time of religious hiatus with a stigma of impurity.

5. The Hindu death rituals do not end with the submergence of the ashes. To ensure the safety of the departed soul, an 11-day ritual called *Shraddha* is performed. It consists of daily offerings of *pindas* (rice balls), which provide a symbolic transitional body for the dead. During the *Shraddha* ceremony, the deceased person is believed to make the journey to the world of the *pitrs* (ancestors). Among Malayali Hindus, wives of the deceased are explicitly forbidden from performing the *Shraddha* ceremony.

11

Living Hinduism and Striving to Achieve Internal and External Harmony

Shanthi Rao

I do not wish to have my windows closed and my doors shut. I want winds from all cultures to blow freely about my home. But I refuse to be blown off my feet by any.

These words by Mahatma Gandhi sum up the model I have followed all my life, capturing the essence of what Hinduism means to me—respect for people of all races, age, gender, religion, and ethnicities in a nonviolent, nonjudgmental manner. This perspective balances openness toward all; at the same time, it shows me to be strong within my tradition. These are the core elements of Hinduism that guide my life and practice.

I grew up in Bangalore, Southern India, and moved to the United States nearly 25 years ago. How I have practiced Hinduism has been influenced by my personal, educational, social, and professional life experiences in the East (India) and the West (United States). This chapter describes my version of "Living Hinduism."

Hinduism: A Brief Overview of the Principles

Hinduism is based on a humanistic and transpersonal framework. The religion requires us to go deep into ourselves and develop an

179

understanding of who we are and how we are linked to all humankind. Hinduism is about *dharma* (law of one's being). As Swami Chinmayananda has professed Hinduism is the art of living, by which people discover in themselves the equipoise to stand up to life's situations, meeting efficiently the ever-changing world of challenges (Chinmayananda 1975). It is an individual's journey for self-actualization, self-realization, and self-transcendence. The journey moves individuals from their narrow selves to a deep awareness and appreciation of others, which in turn helps them to reach the highest potential of spiritual awareness—a sense of oneness with all humanity (*atma*).

Hinduism does not prescribe a single formula or fundamental rule to reach this point. Because individuals are different from one another, each has to discover his/her own means of attaining eternal bliss (*moksha*). In our everyday lives, we have to find and use resources or tools in order to reach this state of mind. The outcome and rewards of this journey should be a feeling of total liberation and empowerment.

There are different paths (*marga*) that we can take to reach within ourselves during our spiritual journey, but it is for us to choose the path that suits us best. These paths are called *yogas* (spiritual disciplines), of which there are four types: *Karma yoga* for people of action, *bhakti yoga* for the emotional, *jnana yoga* for the rationalists, and *raja yoga* for the empiricists (Nirvedananda 1979). Individuals choose these paths either through the advice of a spiritual guide (*guru*) or through appropriate readings and individual or family disciplines.

Two contrasting examples, *bhakti yoga* and *karma yoga*, illustrate the different ways to practice religion. Those following *bhakti yoga* may express their faith by worshipping with a temple-based community, or they could, such as the sixteenth-century *bhakti* saints, reject temples (and priest-mediated forms of worship) and try to reach god through devotional singing, humble interactions, and service to all groups of people. *Karma yogis* do not focus on devotion; they try to attain *dharma* through perfection in their work. Whatever their chosen occupation, they must do it to the best of their ability without thought of personal gain.[1]

Hinduism Through Daily Disciplines and Practices

The religious disciplines followed by my family have taught me the principles of Hinduism. The boundaries of religion and culture were not clearly marked in Bangalore, Karnataka, where I was raised in a middle-class, joint family system consisting of my parents, older brother, grandfather, and paternal uncles and aunts.

In India, Hindu families (and those of other religions) develop a set of disciplines, customs, norms, and traditions depending on their resources, support systems, and local social histories. Each family member has duties and obligations based on individual roles (which reflect their age, sex, and marital status), and my family was no exception. My paternal grandparents were considered the heads of the family, because my grandfather was the oldest sibling. My mother, the youngest of five siblings, was married at the age of 17 to my father, the oldest of seven siblings. Because my paternal grandmother had passed away by that time, my mother was elevated to the position of the senior woman in the family, despite her youth. My parents were, according to their joint role as the oldest of their generation, expected to take care of the rest of the family until my uncles and aunts were either married, or old enough to support themselves, or migrated to other parts of the country or abroad. The duties and responsibilities my parents took on may not be uniquely Hindu, yet they took on these tasks as part of their religious and cultural obligations, their *dharma*. The concept of *dharma* is not only about *pujas* (prayers and practice), it is also about doing one's duty according to one's stage of life.

Hinduism is family-specific, and there is often a great deal of variety within families. When my aunts got married, they had to learn and follow the family systems and structures already established in their husbands' families. (As families are patriarchal, men do not have to learn the ways of religious practice of their wives' families). Compared to my family, my aunts were married into families that followed a set path or trend generation after generation. For example, in one aunt's family, daily practices, customs, and disciplines were performed in a lengthy and elaborate manner, while my family followed a shorter version. My aunt's family also observed fasting on several auspicious days, whereas my family did not observe it as frequently. Also, unlike in my family, the male cousins in my aunt's family went through a religious ceremony called the *upanayana* (sacred thread ceremony), which marks the onset of adolescence.[2] My cousin's *upanayana* was performed during his sister's marriage. My brother ultimately went through this ceremony during my mother's cremation ceremony because it was considered necessary before performing a parent's final rites.

As our joint families transitioned into nuclear units, my family members had to develop their own structures to suit their circumstances. When my uncle and his family moved to North India, they discovered that Hindu religious practices there were significantly different from those in the South. They had to alter their rituals, practices, and disciplines based on whatever resources they had. For instance, in the absence of priests who were knowledgeable about South Indian traditions, women assumed the task of performing *puja*. As many women worked, they had no time to perform lengthy rituals and practices. With the continuing need to carry on these *pujas*, entrepreneurs started marketing instructive tapes for the appropriate practice and rituals for various festivals. "Traditions" were maintained in new and innovative ways to suit changed needs and match changing times and convenience.

My practices as a Hindu emerged as a part of everyday life. Apart from the daily ritual of lighting the *nanda deepa* (oil lamp) at the family altar, we offered flowers and fruits to the idols of gods, goddesses, and sages (and/or any respected elder who had passed away, as a way of showing our gratitude for their blessings). At certain times of the year, we participated in special religious festivals. *Gowri puja, Ganesha puja, Satyanarayana puja, Lakshmi puja,* and *Saraswati puja* were celebrated during September, October, and November (*Shravana Maasa*). The markets would be busy and colorful, displaying a variety of flowers and fruits. Elaborate *puja* ceremonies were performed on these days; friends and family were invited over and exchanged sweets and fruits. Schools (including Christian schools) and offices were closed to allow people to enjoy these events.

I also went to Lord Venkateshwara's temple on Saturday mornings with my parents, a distance of one-and-a-half miles. We would bathe early and take *prasadam* (flowers, fruits, and occasionally, cooked foods to offer the deity). The Brahmin priest performed the appropriate *puja* for the particular god, while devotees offered *prasadam*. Going to the temples in India is a unique experience, and there are plenty of temples to choose from within easy access of each neighborhood.[3] Mitter (2001) explains that the temple is the *devalaya* (sanctum of the deity). Certain protocols have to be observed, such as entering barefoot, as a mark of respect, and keeping the place pure (clear of the dirt of the outside world). Although temple layout and architecture vary by region, many temples have a circumlocution area that devotees use to prepare their minds to be free of anything but worship. Depending on the time of day, you hear group chanting, music, and a certain kind of vibration, and experience a sense of calmness and bliss. Oil lamps are lit within, the smell of incense and camphor fills the halls and rooms, garlands and flowers adorn the idols. It certainly is one of the most beautiful and uplifting sights to witness. Just being around this environment gave me a sense of calmness and safety.

These *pujas*, the daily prayers and traditions, and the temple visits created a sense of discipline and structure in my life and also brought a sense of faith and comfort. The chants conveyed messages of nonviolence and solidarity with all humankind. This established a solid foundation that I have continued to follow while bringing up my own family. For example, a common *shloka* (a verse that is usually chanted at the beginning of any meditative session) that I have passed on to my US-born children is:

Om Saha Naavavatu Saha Nay Bhunaktu
Saha Veeryam Karavaavahai
Tejasvi Naavadheetamastu
Maa Vidvishaavahai
Om Shaantih Shaantih Shaantihi.
  (May the Lord protect us together.
  May the Lord nourish us together.
  May we work together uniting our strength.
  For the good of humanity.
  May our learning be luminous and purposeful.
  May we never hate one another.
  May there be peace, peace, and perfect peace.)

The session ends with a peace invocation:
OM.

Sarve Bhavanthu Sukhinah
Sarve Santhu Niramayah
Sarve Bhadrani Pasyanthu
Maa Kaschit Dukha Bhag Bhaveth.
Om Shaantih, Shaantih, Shaantihi
   (PEACE
   May all be happy.
   May all be healthy.
   May all see auspiciousness.
   May none suffer.
   Peace, Peace, Peace.)

Growing Up in a Culture of Openness

I attended co-ed schools and colleges, where I encountered people
of different religions. Our school, which had an American principal and an Indian vice principal, provided a solid basic foundation
that emphasized the importance and value of both Indian and Western beliefs. The teaching models provided students with the best of
both cultures and a sense of balance. All major religious holidays
and festivals were observed and respected. At assembly, we sang
songs about various deities, as well as patriotic and spiritual songs.
I have fond memories of learning and singing songs that were either
composed by or dear to Mahatma Gandhiji, such as *Vaishna va
Janato,* Rabindranath Tagore's composition of the Indian National
anthem *Jana Gana Mana,* and Martin Luther King's anthem *We
Shall Overcome.* Themes from all these songs represented pride,
equality, and justice to all. The school embraced and emphasized
the importance and philosophy of nonviolence, tolerance, pluralism, and peace to all humankind. Christmas was observed with
Christmas carols (minus the consumer craze). The curriculum also
reflected openness to the world. We learned everything—from
William Shakespeare to India's freedom struggle. In addition, I
trained in Carnatic music through my teen years, which provided

me with an appreciation of music and later opened doors to explore diverse worlds of music in the United States.

Apart from school, my ability to be open to all religions was influenced by my family. My parents' open-doors-for-all philosophy provided me with an outlook that made me comfortable around people from various religions, communities, educational and economic backgrounds, and created a warm, nongendered, welcoming climate at home. In very orthodox Hindu families, eating foods cooked by non-Hindus is taboo. But in our family we ate a variety of foods, brought by Muslim, Christian, and Hindu students (of different castes) from the college where my father taught. Though my mother was a vegetarian (like the majority of my extended family), she never stopped us from enjoying chicken *pullao* and *biriyani*.

In sum, my memories of living my religion in India, whether it was the daily rituals or the visits to the temple, or even the major festivals, are all associated with vivid colors of flowers and fruits, and the smells and sounds of prayers. Entire sections of cities take on a festive air during these *pujas*. "Ordinary tasks" of trips to the markets, shops, and street vendors to purchase seasonal fruits, vegetables, and flowers, or going out to visit friends and family during the festive season, became memorable experiences. The festivities engaged all my senses. This is what I miss most, even after 25 years in the United States, and I crave to go back every year. When I do, my first visit is to the markets and temples of my hometown.

Recreating a Spiritual Life in the United States

Creating a religious life in the United States has been one of challenges, achievements, and change. Like many Indian women of my generation, I migrated to join my husband, who had moved to the United States to start his medical residency program. My marriage was one arranged through a network of family and friends. However, unlike the stereotype that describes arranged marriages as weddings between virtual strangers, we went out a few times to see if we were compatible. Also unlike the stereotype, my father emphasized that I did not have to agree to the marriage if I did not feel right about the relationship.

When I moved to the United States and had to set up a new home, new networks, and deal with a lack of proper education and employment opportunities, my religious foundations and disciplines provided me with a sense of comfort and structure. We did not have any family or friends from India to easily recreate the networks needed to practice our religion. We had to create a new community with people from different parts of India, by finding commonality despite differences of cultural and religious practices, including Hindu practices. Maintaining and holding on to religious traditions was a challenge.

As I started working full time and my husband was extremely busy with his residency, we had little opportunity or time to practice long daily disciplines. With very little time off from work, our trips to the temple were rare. I had to compromise and make adjustments to my daily rituals. A shelf in the apartment acted as a shrine/altar. It included Lord Satyanarayana, my family's *ishta devata* (personal god), and Lord Rama, my husband's family's *ishta devata*. Keeping the *nanda deepa* lit, as I was used to doing, became a challenge, because in the United States it is considered a fire hazard and therefore illegal in apartments.

Over time, my daily prayer practices continued, but the larger festivals and the detailed prayer ceremonies could not be replicated. I gave them up, though I continued to miss them sorely. The absence of the corner temple, the lack of specific flowers and seasonal fruits in the markets, and the lack of community for celebrating the *pujas* drained them of their festive air. It was hard to recreate the kind of community that existed all around us in India, because of the emphasis on individualism, the long hours demanded at work, and the constant emphasis on achieving.

While we lived in North Carolina, we got involved in Indian music groups. It gave us a sense of home and possibilities of starting new customs and traditions in the United States. Although there were few possibilities of forming religious communities, we held weekly gatherings in different people's houses to sing *bhajans* (devotional songs). Because the group consisted of people from different parts of India, we were further exposed to different kinds of Hinduism.

As time passed, my work and my interactions with other ethnic groups brought new meaning and excitement. I made some lasting friendships. My relationships with friends who were White Anglo Saxon Protestants, Jews, African Americans, and Italians, and with other groups, broadened my views about people.

When we moved to Connecticut, we first replicated the North Carolina pattern. Living in an affluent suburb meant we had no ethnic enclaves where we could find a community. But there were families living in various suburbs in the state, and gradually Hindu Indians, mainly from Karnataka, Kerala, and Andhra, got together at a community hall to perform *pujas* over the weekends. We would bring our *puja* materials to the hall, set up, and perform the *puja*, and then carefully remove all traces of our presence before leaving the hall. From this nascent group came the idea of building a temple, which was eventually constructed in the 1980s.

In order to explain the experience of Hinduism in the United States, it is important to describe the kind of challenges that are involved in building temples here. Unlike Christian churches, which are dedicated to Jesus, Hindus across India do not worship the same gods or goddesses (there are supposed to be 33 million faces of Brahman) and do not worship in the same way, nor follow the same rituals or the same calendar. Thus, every part of establishing this Hindu religious site had to be negotiated. The main deities in the temple are Lord Satyanarayana flanked by Sridevi and Bhoodevi. While all Hindus recognize that these idols ultimately represent the same underlying reality/truth (Brahman), with cultural practices being so different (based on who is worshipped), different linguistic communities raised money to install their special deities.

The inauguration of the temple was a remarkable experience. In India, where many temples are hundreds of years old, individuals rarely get an opportunity to be this close to the establishment of a temple. The men in the planning committee decided that the deities would be commissioned from South India. Artisans from South India also were brought over to finish the building of the temple, although this involved lobbying legislators to get them visas. The *pranaprashithapana* (the ceremony investing life in the idols) was a huge event. Brahmin priests were brought from India to conduct the ceremonies. It was a weekend affair and included feeding hundreds of people (I was involved in planning, arranging, and distributing the food). Many people sponsored *puja* to Lord Satyanarayana by donating thousands of dollars.

In the following years, other deities were added to the temple. Shaivites (followers of God Shiva) got their Shiva Linga; the Andhraites sponsored Lord Venkateshwara; the Malayalees wanted Swami Ayyapam; North Indians wanted Krishna; and the Punjabis put up Goddess Durga. The temple also has the elephant-headed Lord Ganesha, who is said to remove all obstacles that people might face.

During the initial planning phase, the temple was intended to be a place for Indians to gather and to teach our children our cultural values, and it was the permanent space to conduct our rituals. At the same time, as more and more networks centered on the temple, it inevitably became more a place for Hindus than an Indian space.

My deep involvement with the temple lessened over time. Part of the reason was a change of focus, as most people were more interested in adding deities than keeping the space as a community hall. Besides, it did not fit into our children's lives. As they grew older, they became involved with a range of activities involving their school peers, leaving us even less free time. With the demands of weekly school and work routines, our weekends were spent just trying to find some family time, which had to be balanced with "temple time." As our two daughters and son grew up, I felt they weren't getting as much out of the temple as we did. It definitely was a meeting place and a social place for us, but it was not a social node for our children. As the temple attracted larger numbers of people, the focus on meditation and *pujas* was, in my perspective, subsumed by the social networks. Every event became increasingly lengthy to accommodate everyone. It became too much of a time commitment for us. Since our needs as a family were not being met, I started more religious activities at home.

At home I have converted an alcove into an altar where I have statuettes of a few gods and goddesses given by our parents. I have a *nanda deepa*, which we light in the morning and evening (a ritual now performed by my son). I organize *Gowri-Ganesha puja* in September at home; it provides an auspicious start to the beginning of the school year. The only other *puja* we perform is for Goddess

Lakshmi, the goddess of wealth, during *Diwali*. Since firecrackers became legal in Connecticut, we light a few sparklers to mark the day. This essence of the *pujas* has become part of the next generation. When my daughters went off to college, they took along their personal deities—one chose Ganesha, the other Shiva. They do not go to temples, but they reflect on the *puja* days.

We have other abbreviated celebrations. My children get clothes for *Ugadi* (New Year), and we offer fruits and flowers to Lord Ganesha, but we cannot usually find the traditional *neem* leaves and jaggery (in India, this is eaten to symbolize the bitter and sweet in life). Here in the United States, various cultural groups get together to celebrate their New Year. Because the calendars differ, the different South Indian groups celebrate New Year at different times. Other Indian groups have their New Year celebrations at other times of the year.

Unlike us, many of our friends have stayed more closely involved with the temple. Some of them continue to volunteer considerable time to temple matters. A couple of my friends clean the temple and help with events as part of their religious discipline. My connection has been mainly through organizing the *Thyagaraja* festival. Thyagaraja was a renowned Carnatic musician, whose prolific compositions are widely known and loved in India. We began by arranging a musical evening, *Thyagaraja aradhana* (worship/commemoration of Thyagaraja through music), with artists from South India. However, we also wanted to include North Indians, so we brought in Hindustani musicians. The name was changed to *Nadaradhana* (worship of music), and it became a longer event. Children and adults perform in the mornings, while we get renowned artists for the evenings. Listening to musicians whose artistry is based on long years of discipline is an uplifting spiritual experience.

Extending beyond this musical group, I auditioned for and was invited to join a state-level choral group. Here, singing put me in touch with teachers and singers of many ethnic and racial backgrounds. Now I am part of an initiative to set up a group of multilingual singers of different races to come together to sing songs of empowerment. The varieties of music, inspired by different cultural and religious traditions, continue to connect me to a wider swath of life.

Charting a Global Hinduism

As I reflect on living Hinduism now, I try to emphasize its more universal values. Hinduism teaches peace and tolerance. It means, as I understand it, expanding to create connections with people beyond the familiar communities. It is not enough to live within one's religious community and talk about peace and tolerance. We have to take up challenges to practice this. We have been lucky to have broadening interactions with people of other religious faiths through our families and friends. For instance, one very important part of our lives is being involved with Passover every year at a friend's house. Not a single year of the past 18 years has gone by without our being part of a Seder Passover meal. Not only have our children been fortunate to have had the experience and exposure to our own traditions, customs, and practices, they also have been enriched through participating in other disciplines, customs, traditions, and practices of diverse ethnic groups. Several of my nieces and nephews have married Jews and Christians, further expanding the boundaries of who "we" are as a family. We have devised ways to teach the grandchildren both religious traditions. But creating these bridges, I feel, is what the core Hinduism principles of tolerance and peace are about: We learn from others and they, too, learn from others.

I also encounter these principles of Hinduism through the lives of my children. Each one of them, so different from the other, has been composing his/her life in different ways. My oldest daughter was a Peace Corps volunteer in Senegal; my second daughter has volunteered in Peru. Both of them have learned to take on the challenges of living very different lives. Even though they do not appear to be overtly religious, they practice the core values of connecting with people and life situations respectfully. Our interactions with their host families and friends brought new meaning to the vision of living life simply. I had seen it and experienced it in India, but those values were reaffirmed when we visited Senegal and Peru. My son has joined in many civil rights efforts in the state. They live according to this present, as we did in our time. So we have to figure out religion for our children's generation without emphasizing the status quo.

Another context for me to practice my spiritual values is through my profession and volunteer work. I returned to school for my master's degree in social work after a long gap. During this time, I was exposed to new social and political education and awareness. I also joined South Asian women's networks in my state, a civil rights group, a pan-ethnic group, and an immigrant rights group that drew me into a variety of social justice issues. As I became involved in creating multiracial coalitions to advocate for civil and economic rights of groups, I have revisited, redefined, and analyzed what Hinduism means to me.

Because I was born a Hindu, my identity as a Hindu will never change. The way I see Hinduism now is a way for me to understand the connection between who I am and all other people. The fundamental tenet of this religion is tolerance; it welcomes all other religions, and it also delves into the idea "know yourself better in order to understand others better." These principles make me reach out and understand all groups and populations. If Hinduism taught me values of peace and connecting with all, then my involvement with activist groups over the last decade has truly brought these principles to fruition. I have been involved in a number of groups, including women's networks, civil liberties, and grassroots democracy groups, as well as social service groups. These interactions have challenged me to practice interconnections beyond Indian groups and connect with others. I have volunteered for a pan-Asian group in which I have worked with refugee populations who continue to bear the scars of war-induced trauma. Yet, they draw lessons from their religious practices and live dignified lives. I have learned lessons in life from them. I also have learned lessons from the civil liberties issues I have embraced and while working for the rights of immigrants and other groups. These involvements have provided me a place to grow and learn as an individual, and for me to understand the nature of *atma,* which is not about an individual but about humanity.

Perhaps other Hindus do not follow my path of trying to reflect the principles of connecting with many groups and communities. But I see what I am doing as reaching *atma,* which involves both serving others and being one with others. Hinduism talks about *bhakti* (devotion); that is what I am practicing. *Bhakti,* to me, is not simple faith, but a devotion to a larger humanity. It is a journey of growing; we grow as individuals as we get to know others, so that our lives are always works-in-progress.

I am well aware that there is a stereotype that Hinduism subordinates women. From my experience, I know there are disparities in how it is practiced. Hinduism, like other religions, has been used in a patriarchal manner, particularly in the United States. In India, there are so many ways of practicing Hinduism that women's positions depended on region, culture, and family. In the United States, a lot of men think they know what Hinduism is all about, and they become the spokespersons for Hinduism. All initiatives about defining "Who is a Hindu?" and "What do you have to practice to be a Hindu?" have been initiated by men; women have been only followers of this process.

Conflating culture and religion is another trend in the United States. For instance, the *Bharat Natyam* dance form becomes mixed with being Hindu, so it becomes harder for people, especially the second generation, to distinguish the two. Also, as cultural groups start naming themselves, they choose religiously oriented male (often princely dynasty) names. Thus, I think gender discrepancies have increased in the United States. In the India where I was raised, religious labor was divided, but it was not a hierarchy. In the community here, men initiate all the decisions.

Outside the religiously defined community, the different types of networks I have created over the years provide me with opportunities to practice the principles in which I believe. The perspectives on life, disciplines, and interactions with diverse groups I have described are the tools that I have used to take care of my mental, emotional, and spiritual needs. For the physical aspect, I have taken up yoga. Learning the rigorous postures and breathing techniques has helped me to attain the balance between mental, physical, emotional, and spiritual well-being. To keep an open mind, I continue learning from all the networks to which I belong. At work, I learn from my small group of students. My teachers from the school of social work, with whom I keep in touch, keep me grounded in my vision of serving others. As a social worker, I learn of new worlds from my small group of clients who have immigrated as refugees; I learn from their dignity and their patience amid suffering. My colleagues from various professions and my husband and family members, each one of them has taught me the importance of having and being part of a family, being there for each other consistently. My friends have taught me how to laugh, cry, feel emotions, and keep growing as a person. All these are lessons in living that I believe reflect my religious values of respect and connection.

Conclusion

The beauty and essence of Hinduism is the diversity of its religious practices, disciplines, and doctrines. Not only does the religion that I was born into celebrate the rich diversity of all religions and humanity, it also celebrates and empowers the freedom of self and others. It can be practiced individually, or as a group or community.

Having lived and grown up in the United States longer than in India, our practices have changed to reflect the context here. Being a minority in the United States has made me realize that we need to understand the experiences and oppressions of other minority groups in the United States as well as in India. In order to interact respectfully, we need to know what they have been through and try to interact and have dialogues with them. It is important to remember that our personal identity is socially constructed, and we can control and change past patterns of behaviors. Knowing this can provide us ways to maintain our human identities under different situations or environments. We are able to develop new beginnings by facing challenges that confront us. Societies and times are constantly changing. We must learn to embrace the challenges that come with change and learn to grow from them.

One of the readings (from the Upanishads) mentions that one needs to be knowledgeable, and not ignorant, of the realities around us.

Om Asato Maa Sadgamaya
  (O Lord, please lead me from the unreal to the real.)

Tamaso Maa Jyotir Gamaya
(Lead me from darkness to light.)
Mrityor Maa Amrtam Gamaya
(Lead me from death to immortality.)
Om Shaantih, Shaantih, Shaantihi.
(May there be peace, peace, and perfect peace.)

I am also reminded of the words of Spanish American philosopher George Santayana, "Those who cannot learn from history are doomed to repeat it" (Wisdom Quotes, n.d.). I hope that I will remember this quote in the continuation and growth of my ongoing spiritual journey—to face challenges and to fulfill my *dharma* to hopefully reach the ultimate *atma*, the attainment of contentment and peace. And that is what Hinduism means to me, and that is how I choose to live it.

OM SHAANTI, SHAANTI, SHAANTIHI
(May there be peace, peace, and perfect peace.)

Notes

1. This concept is best illustrated by the *Bhagwad Gita,* when God Krishna tells the hero Arjuna, a warrior, that it is his duty to fight, and fight as best as he can. Even though there will be bloodshed, being a soldier means to fight to the best of his ability and training. However, in order to fulfill his *dharma,* Arjuna must fight without dwelling on the personal gain resulting from his actions.

2. In most traditional families, this ceremony is performed for boys before the age of 15. The boy is taught a series of readings from the Vedas by the priest and then given a sacred thread, which he will wear draped around his shoulder and underarm for most of his life.

3. There are other temples that may be distant, but attract thousands of devotees. Some of these are major temples, which have existed for a long time, supported by the donations from devotees and wealthy patrons. For example, there are major temples across India that people visit for holy pilgrimages. One of the most famous temples of Lord Venkateshwara is in Tirupati, Andhra Pradesh (see www.tirumala.org). Faithful devotees make this long trip, praying for their wishes to be fulfilled.

12

Mapping the Memories of a Nepali Woman in the United States

Shobha Hamal Gurung

This chapter is a personal account of my religious experiences, both in my homeland, Nepal, and in the United States. It examines the significant role of Nepalese women in Hindu rituals and religious observances, and whether these roles translate to women's empowerment. I describe the essential syncretism of Nepalese religious Hindu practices. I conclude with my experience of how religion helps women cope with difficult times, and the ways in which religious practices have changed over time in response to a changing environment.

Growing Up and the Construction of a Religious Identity

As a female child in a Hindu family in Kathmandu, my acquaintance with religion started with my family's religious practices and rituals. Although I had observed male members of our family participating in religious practices, it was my female relatives who introduced me to Hinduism.

My earliest recollection of identifying with religion is watching my grandmother spend several hours every morning (I later discovered she got up at 4:00 or 5:00 a.m.) and evening doing *puja* (worshipping, praying, and meditating) and then practicing *arati* (the final part of the *puja*), accompanied by the ringing of a bell. That was the sound to which I woke up. My grandmother was bedridden for the last few years of her life, during which time my mother began performing the daily *puja*. But my mother's *puja* would not start quite as early in the morning and would not involve long hours, nor would she fast as frequently. Her religious observance involved reading, discussions, and debates on various holy teachings. While much of my grandmother's religious activities remained within the home and family, with the occasional holy pilgrimage, my mother's religious activities extended well beyond the home and into the community. Along with her neighborhood friends, my mother also was active in collecting money, food, and clothing for orphans and widows. Another difference was the display of photographs and idols of Buddha, the living Mahatma, and Swami Virato in our *pujaghar* (prayer room). Just by observing my grandmother and mother in the various routines of religious practices, I learned that religious practices and the meaning of religion differs from person to person and generation to generation. I learned that devout rituals are not static; there is no one "correct" way of practicing one's faith. Although I noted the shift in my grandmother's and mother's religious practices, the essence of their *dharma* remained the same: morality, dignity, and humanity.

My childhood exposure to various aspects of Hinduism also is strongly linked to the time I spent with my maternal grandparents and their village communities. Every year, during the long school vacation, we would stay at my grandparents' village where local communities had formed a *bhajan mandali* (religious singing group) and a religious drama group. Every night, after dinner, the *bhajan mandali* would gather in my grandparents' house and sing *bhajans* (devotional songs), and we would sing along. The lyrics were about compassion, trust, devotion, moral values, empathy, discipline, and karma.

Similarly, every now and then, the people involved in the religious dramas and plays would perform different episodes of the *Mahabharata* and the *Ramayana*. Our sources of entertainment were watching *Krishna Leela* (a drama based on various aspects of Lord Krishna's life), *Ram Bhakta Hanuman, Rawaad, and Baanar Sena* (a drama on Hanuman's devotion to Lord Ram), and listening to *bhajans* and songs.

As a child, I thoroughly enjoyed visiting the Ram Janaki village temple every morning with family members and other children and eating *prasaadh* (sacred offerings). At times, priests would visit my grandparents' village; some would stay for an extended time and, during the day, they would either tell us Hindu legends or teach us morals. Occasionally, they would hold discussions with the elders on various religious issues. In the evenings, our grandmother would tell us stories about different gods, goddesses, and other religious deities. Each of her stories revolved around a particular theme and, after recounting it, she would explain its morals and messages. She used the story of Kali to demonstrate power, of Saberi to explain devotion and respect. She told us about the legendary Yudhisteer and Ram to underline the values of justice and morality, or of Arjun to explain responsibility and karma. A yearly ritual for us each February was the monthlong reading of Swasthani every evening, when we listened to the story of how the wish-fulfilling goddess Swasthani helped Parvathi obtain Lord Shiva for her husband.

Engagement in various forms of religious activities was not limited to the family and community; it extended to our school life. The boarding school I attended when I was 10 was run by a Christian family and held daily prayers before breakfast, lunch, dinner, and bedtime. On occasional Sundays, we attended services at the chapel on the school premises. Courses on moral education and Nepali literature would include religious stories and legends related to honesty, bravery, courage, responsibility, and justice. School events such as Parents' Day would include plays, such as *Siddartha Gautam* and *Paanch Paandav,* in which we would participate.

I also was raised observing Hindu temples and Buddhist monasteries existing side by side. In Nepal, Buddhism is seen as a sect of Hinduism; through *bhajans* and religious script, it is said that Buddha is the ninth incarnation of the Hindu god, Vishnu. Since Saraswati is the goddess of learning and wisdom, and Buddha is the godhead of knowledge and enlightenment, religious occasions, such as *Saraswati puja* (day of prayer and worship paying homage to Saraswati) and *Buddha Jayanti* (Buddha's birthday), were important to us, especially when we were students in elementary and high school. We celebrated these events with great enthusiasm by visiting temples and monasteries and by worshipping and praying to both Saraswati and Buddha.

Listening and singing *bhajans,* watching and participating in religious and cultural events, dramas, and plays, going to the temple, and listening to folklore and legends were an intrinsic part of our daily lives and sources of religious knowledge as well as entertainment throughout my childhood.

The Role of Women in Hindu Rituals

While growing up, I witnessed the ways in which the principles of Hindu philosophy guided the everyday cultural, social, economic, and political lives of those around me; they also were reflected in the rituals and practices associated with life-altering events, national festivals, and everyday cultural rituals. Whether it was the birth of a child or a naming ceremony, a coming-of-age or marriage ceremony, a death or a funeral, or merely a family member going away on a trip or a family moving into their new home, I was a part of many ongoing rituals and ceremonies—sometimes as an active participant and occasionally as an observer. There also are many gender-specific religious symbols and cultural rituals practiced in Hindu families, which mark the different phases of girlhood and womanhood. Female deities are central and highly valued in both the major religions of Nepal: Hinduism and Buddhism.

The predominant female deities with high symbolic power for Hindus are Durga, Kali, Chandi, Bhagwati, and Laxmi. For Buddhists, they are Vasudhara, Vajrabarahi, Vajrajogini, Bodhisattwa, Green Tara, and White Tara (both Green Tara and White Tara are Protectors from Fear). For example, White Tara "represents the collective activities of all the Bhuddhas and [is] considered the mother of the past, present, and future Bhuddhas" (Subedi 1999). Similarly, Laxmi represents wealth; Saraswati represents learning, wisdom, and knowledge; and Durga, Kali, Chandi, and Bhagwati represent strength and power.

In almost all of Nepal's major celebrations, females play vital roles both symbolically and socially. The birth of a baby daughter symbolizes the goddess Laxmi, and it is believed that she will bring wealth and prosperity to the family. When a daughter is born, the family members usually announce, "Laxmi has arrived!"

Before puberty, Hindu families give *Guniyo Cholo* (sari and blouse) to their daughters. When I was 10 years old, I was given *Guniyo Cholo* as a part of the ritual; the message is to be modest, decorous, and ladylike. A girl's first menstruation marks adulthood and requires additional rituals. Although these rules are based on the notion of purity and pollution, the women often rationalized these practices as a welcome break from tedious household chores. The rules and regulations based on the notions of purity and pollution, however, may differ from one region to another and even from one family to another.

From the engagement ceremony to moving into the groom's house, marriage involves a great deal of gender-specific rituals that hold both religious and cultural meanings and symbols. Entering the groom's house is a significant ritual. The bride enters the house by stepping on the earthen lamps and rice grains that line the main entrance to the house. She is then taken to the *pujaghar*. Her arrival symbolizes the coming of the goddess Laxmi.

Festivals also signify the important roles and the power of female deities, as well as the roles and value of girls and women in the family, community, and society simultaneously. The primary national festivals of Nepal, *Dashain* and *Tihar*, revolve around female deities. *Dashain* is based on the story of a powerful goddess who killed a demon and monsters and brought victory. On *Dashain*, people visit the various sacred sites and temples of female deities, particularly the *Navadurgas* (nine powerful female deities), to worship them. The *Malashri bhajan* (devotional songs addressed to female deities) is played every morning throughout the festival. On the ninth day of *Dashain* (called *Naawami*), most Hindu families worship nine *kanyas* (female virgins). On this day, families gather the young girls from their extended families and from their communities and the *kanyas* are worshipped. The devotees bow their heads to the *kanyas*' feet and offer them a variety of gifts and foods. This was one of my favorite festivals, particularly when we had this celebration in my grandparents' village with my cousin and other children.

Tihar, which is also called *Bhaitika/Bhaipuja*, is another major festival, and also is a festival of lights. At the center of the *Tihar* festival is the *Laxmipuja* (worship of Laxmi) and *Bhaitika/Bhaipuja* (worship of a brother by the sister). Both *Laxmipuja* and *Bhaipuja* mark the importance of the female deity. On *Laxmipuja*, people clean and decorate their homes, hang garlands of marigolds on their windows and doors, and cook *selroti* (homemade donut-like bread made with rice flour—a delicacy cooked especially for the *Tihar* festival). At night, people worship Laxmi with a multitude of flowers, garlands, colored powder, and rice grains, and by offering fruits, sweets, nuts, and homemade delicacies.

Bhaitika/Bhaipuja, which is about the love, bonding, and solidarity between brothers and sisters, takes place on the fifth day of *Tihar*. On *Tihar*, sisters worship their brothers and pray for their longevity, prosperity, and happiness; they place seven different-colored long *tika* (dot placed between the eyebrows to represent the "third eye") on their brothers' foreheads and give them a variety of sweets, nuts, fruits, and homemade delicacies, including *selroti*. Similarly, brothers place *tika* on their sisters' foreheads, give them gifts and money, and lower their head to their sisters' feet in veneration. *Tihar* signifies the value and importance of the sister-brother relationship. As a measure of the extent of a sister's power to protect her brother, it is said that even Yamraj (the god of death) cannot take a brother from his sister on *Bhaitika*. Similarly, *Tihar* symbolizes a brother's protection of his sister's honor.

Contradictions and Paradoxes

A significant personal dilemma I faced while growing up was how women have been both empowered and subjugated by their religious tradition. Blatant contradictions existed at almost every level of social interaction.

On the one hand, the arrival of a baby daughter symbolizes the goddess Laxmi, and it is believed that she will bring wealth and prosperity to the family; on the other hand, Hindu parents keep having children until a son is born. The explanation given is that it is to carry the family name through to the next generation and to ensure that rituals are performed after the parents' death. Orthodox Hindu parents worry that they will not attain heaven if, after their death, the funeral pyre is not lit by their son.

Similarly, before marriage, a woman undergoes many *Bratas* (religious fasts) in the hope of getting a good husband. After marriage, she undergoes as many *Bratas* for her husband's longevity, prosperity, and good health. I was always agitated by the fact that men never performed *Bratas* for the well-being of their women.

Most importantly, when it came to deities, the significant symbolic figuration of exemplary women emerged from the roles of epic heroines Sita and Savitri, both self-sacrificing and docile goddesses, as behavior models for women. The epics *Ramayana* and *Mahabharata* contain many tales of virtuous women whose primary duty and function in life is to love, obey, and serve their husbands. The ancient practice of *Sati* embodies this concept—by throwing herself into her dead husband's funeral pyre, a virtuous woman not only avoids inauspicious widowhood, but also adds to her husband's good *karma*. In the *Ramayana*, Sita, who is steadfastly devoted to Rama through the many years of exile, is the embodiment of wifely virtue. When her purity is in doubt after her abduction by the demon Ravana, she unhesitatingly undergoes an ordeal by fire to prove her abiding love and faith. In the *Mahabharata*, Savitri undertakes several rituals and even follows Death to reclaim her husband Satyavan, and he is resuscitated because of her chastity, devotion, and virtue.

Thus, while Hinduism venerates goddesses like Kali and Chandi, who are regarded as even more powerful than Brahma (the creator), Vishnu (the protector), or Mahesh who is also known as Shiva (the destroyer), girls are not encouraged to be like Kali or Chandi. Interestingly, even the images, coloring, and behavior of Kali and Chandi do not necessarily suggest positive connotations. Kali and Chandi are often linked with destructive behaviors and towering rage. When girls/women lose their tempers or have a public outburst, their behavior is compared to that of Kali and Chandi. Even their extremely dark complexion is considered inferior in most communities in Nepal; when seeking a bride, the family members usually look for a light-skinned girl. So, even when selecting a *Kumari* (living goddess), fair skin is a major criterion. Along the same lines, a prospective bride's beauty is measured according to how white her skin is, how large and dark her eyes are, and how black her hair is.

However, I must highlight that over the years I have come to question my own assumptions about the universal acceptance or influence of these hegemonic ideologies. Looking back, it is very clear that I was simultaneously exposed to traditions and practices that presented me with an alternative paradigm, which allowed for more active religious roles on the part of women. Thus, these gender representations are not uniform, and individuals may selectively disregard, challenge, or embrace various views and ideologies.

In fact, religion in Nepal survives largely as a result of women practitioners. It is largely women who practice, protect, and propagate the religion. Be it the daily *puja*, visits to the temple, participation in community prayer groups, or systematic adherence to rituals and fasts, it is the womenfolk's continual commitment and active involvement that contributes to the overall vitality of religious life within the home and community. In a society where adult women occupy positions of domestic authority, it is not surprising that their responsibility for the everyday welfare and well-being of their families extends beyond the economic domain and involves managing or controlling the religious domain as well. Senior women, such as my grandmother and mother, have always had the primary task of keeping their households in order, which includes keeping evil forces at bay and pacifying the gods by stringent adherence to religious practices and stipulated rituals. Furthermore, the overlap between secular and religious/spiritual roles promotes an informal, familiar relationship between the ordinary and the ordained, so that the routine of a Nepalese woman's daily existence is not ritually denigrated nor dramatically opposed to the "spiritual path." Therefore, women are not as likely to be devalued or systematically excluded from socially recognized religious roles.

Devotional practices, which are most representative of the traditional Hindu rituals, involve *puja, arati, prasad,* and *bhajans* that I have mentioned earlier, as well as dance and various other rituals as a mark of faith and obeisance. These devotional rites are largely an extra-brahminic or institutionalized form of Hinduism, a form of direct worship of the deity by the devotee-seeking divine benediction.

Hindu women have several rituals, such as religious fasts (*Bratas*), that are intended to attain specific desires. These rituals are considered acts of religious devotion that will help the devotee gain a particular desire. They may be abstentious or devotional, may seek a deity's appeasement or blessing, and are an essential part of Hindu women's religious practice. In Nepal, *Teej* is the fasting festival for women. The festival is a three-day-long celebration that combines sumptuous feasts as well as rigid fasting. Traditionally, the ritual of *Teej* is obligatory for all Hindu married women and girls who have reached puberty. According to legend, goddess Parvati fasted and prayed fervently for the great Lord Shiva to become her spouse. Touched by her devotion, he took her for his wife. Goddess Parvati in gratitude sent her emissary to preach and disseminate this religious fasting among mortal women, promising prosperity and longevity for them and their family. Consequently, the festival of *Teej* was born. Thus, while *Bratas* originated with a female deity and are practiced by women, they are not intended to benefit just women. Instead, this devotional practice represents women as agents of action, particularly as no priestly sanction or interference is required at any stage in the observance or celebration of *Teej*.

Furthermore, *Teej* also is a time when women, both married and unmarried, assemble at one place in their finest attires and dance and sing together, another important aspect of devotionalism. Drama, dance, and music always have been vehicles of religious expression in Hindu tradition. While pure music and dance (as distinguished from music and dance with devotional content) is itself said to be of divine origin and understood to lead one to the Divine, usually singing and dancing are connected with *bhakti* or devotion contained in the lyrics sung. The combination of emotional lyrics sung with abandon of devotion is said to be a path through which one can reach the divine goal of one's choice. In fact, during *Teej* women use songs and dance as an opportunity to vent their anger and frustrations of their everyday existence to their deity.

Keeping the Faith:
Hinduism in a Changing Environment

Although it is largely women's actions and their continued support of religious practices that have contributed to the vitality of religious life, they also are simultaneously experiencing changing social realities. During my study of women migrant factory-based and home-based workers in Nepal, I witnessed how forces of development and capitalism are leading to major transformations in the lives of women. However, an understanding of these political and economic forces, in trying to assess their overall impact on women's lives, should not neglect the corresponding perspective: how individual women as agents perceive these forces and how they alternatively contest, accept, or ignore the various currents that impinge on their lives.

Since I moved to the United States, I have come to realize that the experience of celebrating major festivals and performing cultural rituals away from my homeland is not the same as celebrating these festivals and rituals back home. In Nepal, *Teej*, "the women's festival," is observed in August or September and is a time for married women to go home to their parents, receive special treatment, and indulge in close bonding and joyous festivity. *Dashain*, in late September and early October, is the longest and most auspicious of the Nepalese festivals and is widely celebrated throughout the country. Marking the inevitable triumph of virtue over the forces of evil, it is a time of gift giving, family gatherings, feasts, and rituals, and is celebrated for 10 days.

Holidays and festivals in the United States may come and go, but without being able to celebrate these occasions with family members, we may not be able to fully experience and enjoy them. The vibe and charm are just not there. For example, though my brothers also live in the United States, we are all located in different cities. None of us can take time off from our jobs to celebrate *Tihar* together, the way it was meant to be celebrated. We observe it the best we can—they send me flowers and gifts, and I send them *tika*. We exchange our best wishes over the phone, but the full and true enjoyment of the festival is always lacking because we are apart.

Despite these limitations, I retain a great fondness for our festivals. By the time I moved to Connecticut with my family, I had grown accustomed to my status as a Hindu in the United States. I continued practicing my faith by observing the rituals that were ingrained in my life—maintaining a *pujaghar* (in one of the small closets in our apartment) with pictures of gods and goddesses: Ganesh, Laxmi, Kali, Shivji, and Buddha. Though I have a photograph of my grandmother in my home, I do not include it with the gods and goddesses. Though my mother placed photographs of her ancestors alongside those of the gods and goddesses in our *pujaghar* in Nepal, I somehow never absorbed this form of ancestral worship.

I recall the time and dedication my grandmother, and to a lesser extent my mother, put into the daily practice of their faith and rituals. As a Hindu in the United States, I ask myself if this deviation from tradition can be traced to the fact that I was never a formal disciple. In Nepal, a priest and monk guide the people who become their disciples. They give them a *mantra* to chant, such as the *gayatri mantra* or the *hanuman mantra*. I was never exposed to that practice. While this could be one factor, it is certainly not the only one. Identifying the other reasons answers a question I've been asked: "When there is religious freedom in the United States, why don't we practice our religion the same way we did back home?"

First, there's the time constraint. My daily schedule always leaves me short of time. The demands of work and running a house leave me with very little time to do much else, though I've always wanted to find the time to meditate. Weekends turn into a regular guilt trip over things that have been left undone. In fact, apart from the constraints I mentioned in celebrating major festivals, being a Hindu woman in the Nepalese community in the United States is liberating in certain aspects because I am justified in not being a devout practitioner of my faith. However, children who are born and raised in the United States, in particular, miss the opportunity to experience and witness everyday religious practices. They also miss the opportunities to observe and experience the ways in which certain festivals are celebrated in the family, neighborhood, and community. Many parents prefer to go home to Nepal to perform the milestone events of their children's lives, such as *Brataman* (coming-of-age ceremony for boys) and *Guniyo Cholo* (a ritual marking puberty in girls).

On the positive side, much like migrant workers in Nepal, Nepali immigrants in the United States have formed networks and social ties, refashioning their emerging and changing social order into something more acceptable and workable for them. Migrant women workers have come together through casual social gatherings and celebration of festivals to undertake a wide variety of economic, cultural, and religious tasks. They have established and created social ties that form the basis of many alliances and support networks that extend throughout the community. Similarly, being in the United States and away from home, people and communities have become surrogate kin. They have come together to form several organizations and associations to provide the Nepalese people a common platform to celebrate the major festivals and cultural and religious rituals together. As a family of friends, they share both happy and sad moments—life-altering events such as a birth, a wedding, or death.

Reflections on My Journey

Interestingly, living in the United States has further enriched my belief in the synthesis of diverse religious traditions. It was only after coming to the United States that I had an opportunity to learn about several other religions, including—surprisingly—a lot more about religions such as Buddhism, which I thought I was familiar with in Nepal. As a graduate student in Boston, I roomed with several people who belonged to several different faiths, such as Islam, Christianity, and Judaism. Interestingly, I did not find any conflict between the religions they practiced and the Hinduism I had been raised with and which had shaped my beliefs and practices. In fact, any change that took place in my belief system was positive and beneficial.

I effortlessly bonded with all my roommates when I was in Boston. We celebrated all the major Christian festivals, such as Easter,

Thanksgiving, and Christmas. It was all a lot of fun, and I gained some wonderfully fresh insights from interacting so closely with non-Hindus and learning from these experiences at a personal level. Doubtless, my interactions with friends and colleagues from various cultural backgrounds in the United States has nurtured and expanded my religious and spiritual horizons. Reading books on different religions, I was able to analyze how similar the basic principles of these spiritual disciplines are, with only the names of the religions, gods and goddesses, and rituals being different.

My recent religious and spiritual practices have become more inclusive, in the sense that I have incorporated the religious practices of several people. The longest time I shared a home was with a friend in Boston who was raised a Protestant. She exposed me to different forms of spiritual philosophy, to Sufism, Buddhism, and the writings of Rumi. Without identifying any of the religions by name, we would often share diverse religious and spiritual practices; we would first light a candle and incense, chant a few mantras, and then meditate. I was a part of her family, and our religion was an integrated philosophy.

Another friend with whom I shared a home in the United States is a practicing Muslim. I know there are Hindus who claim it is impossible for them to live with people not of their faith, particularly Muslims, but I felt no such restrictions. Today, more than ever before, there is supposed to be a gaping divide between Hindus and Muslims in terms of doctrines, practices, and ideological beliefs. I never felt any such conflict; instead I became good friends with them. During my stay with my Muslim friend, we shared common spiritual views on humanity and morality. When she left for a new job elsewhere, she gave me a laughing Buddha as a symbol of our spiritual bond.

When I ask myself why I, as a Hindu living among non-Hindus or with a Muslim, never experienced any kind of divide, I realize that the answer lies in my early background. First, while I came from a well-grounded Hindu background, my personal values did not generate anti-Hindu feelings. Second, I never was a very orthodox Hindu. The orthodox form of Hinduism, usually practiced by the older generation, lays great emphasis on the concepts of purity and pollution that I mentioned earlier. While I am aware of these orthodox practices, I have never imbibed them and retain a great interest in other faiths and peoples. Yes, I am a Hindu by birth, but my religious identity has never placed any boundaries on what religion I believe in, what faith I practice, and how I practice it in my everyday life. Being a Hindu is neither a static identity nor is Hinduism a monolithic religious practice.

Faith as Fortitude: Coping with Distressing Changes

While the recent religious violence around the world, as well as the distressing religious conflicts in Nepal, often force me to think about and ponder the dangers and absurdities of organized religion quite fiercely, I am constantly amazed to see how people continue to use religion and faith to deal with uncertainties of life and rationalize disappointments and tragedies. I have witnessed the ways religion has provided strength, devotion, faith, morality, and a routine and disciplined life to the common folk. It is their faith that enables them to overcome trials and tribulations. The religious activities they engage in help them regain their strength and attain peace and serenity during life-altering events.

My experiences as a researcher in Nepal helped me further understand the need for people to rely on religion in times of distress. Carpet-weaving women often rationalized the stress and depression they were experiencing by claiming to be possessed by spirits. The scientific view that family and work pressure can cause stress and depression provided little or no solace to these women. Women could draw solace from the understanding that their experiences are not necessarily due to their own actions, but rather due to some external force beyond their control. My field experience in Nepal prompted me to confront the fact that researchers in the field of development studies do not factor in the importance of religion and faith in people's lives. I have since learned that to understand people, it is essential to truly understand the religion/faith that defines the framework of their everyday lives and helps them make sense of it. More importantly, my experiences in two countries as a person who studies underprivileged women has shown me that creating realms of serenity, where one can be at peace with many kinds of people, is a way of resisting the forces of organized, politicized religion that demand we create an exclusive world and do so, if necessary, violently. The small acts of everyday life by unnamed millions of women have continued to maintain some peace in the world.

Conclusion

Over the years, from my grandmother's era to the present, religious practices have changed tremendously. These religious practices, norms, values, and the various teachings that I observed, absorbed, and experienced throughout the various stages of my life, however, have influenced my everyday spiritual, sociocultural, and political life. During both the happy and the difficult moments of my own life, it helps me to remember that change is the only constant. Meditation provides me with inner peace and a moment to myself for self-reflection. Hinduism continues to define my core ideology, providing the continuity and discipline throughout the variegated phases of my life. I remain cognizant of all the women in the world who use religion to reach out to others and help others support others, and do so without much fanfare, in quiet ways, fulfilling their religious obligations. I place myself in that tradition.

13

Bengali, Bangladeshi yet Muslim

Elora Halim Chowdhury

This personal essay will trace the complex and interweaving landscape of Islam through engaging its influence in my life as a
faith, an impetus for political and psychological self-determination,
an expression of feminism, and a foundation for individual and collective action spanning multiple geographies, histories, and cultural
contexts. Using Cherrie Moraga's (1983) notion of a "theory in the
flesh," I would like to chart definitive experiences that engendered
my own feminist consciousness and politics, and its link to possibilities of collective struggle. Elaborating on Moraga's work on the
intersections of the personal and the political, Paula Moya has
posited, "Implicit in these formulations [a politic born out of the
physical realities of the lives of women of color broadly defined] are
the realist insights that the different social facts of a woman's existence are relevant for the experiences she will have, and that those
experiences will inform her understanding of the world and the development of her politics" (Moya 1997, 145). Rather than assuming a self-evident relationship between social location, identity, and
experience, however, Moraga and Moya are both careful in pointing out the emergent politic as theoretically mediated through the
interpretation of experience. Following their cue, in this essay I will
chart the growth of my own feminist consciousness linked to myriad influences of religion, race/ethnicity, gender, and nationalism,
and the possibilities of feminist alliances across these categories.

211

Bengali, Bangladeshi yet Muslim

The content of my identity as Bengali, Bangladeshi yet Muslim reflects a history of cultural and activist confluences in Bangladesh and the United States. The boundaries have been marked, at times, by brutal political repression, and at other times by "genteel" exclusion. Thus my sense of "living a religion" cannot be neatly separated from a history of religiopolitics within a transnational context.

The historical context for my identity begins with the Partition of India into two nations—India and Pakistan—on the basis of religion. For those separated into Muslim East Pakistan and Hindu West Bengal in India, this partition cut at the heart of centuries-long sociocultural history of Bengal. At the same time, the Partition in 1947 not only divided East and West Pakistan by a thousand miles of Indian territory along religious lines, but also across economic, political, religious, cultural, and historic regional conflicts. Economically, East Pakistan became the "bread basket" of West Pakistan, generating more revenue yet receiving small allocation and investment of resources toward national development. Politically, the West Pakistani ruling elite formed the central government, whereas culturally Bengalis were deemed a lesser, darker, smaller race with pagan influences closer to their Hindu West Bengali neighbors (Akram 2006). According to Gendercide, the mass killings of Bengalis in 1971 were "fueled by an abiding anti-Bengali racism, especially against the Hindu minority . . . Bengalis were often compared with monkeys and chickens. Said Pakistan General Niazi, 'It was a low lying land of low lying people.' The Hindus among the Bengalis were as Jews to the Nazis: Scum and vermin that [should] best be exterminated. As to the Muslim Bengalis, they were to live only on the sufferance of the soldiers: any infraction, any suspicion cast on them, any need for reprisal, could mean their death. And the soldiers were free to kill at will" (Rummel 1994, 335, quoted on www.gendercide.org).

Bangladeshi independence from Pakistan in 1971 does not suggest drifting into a closer relationship with West Bengal, India. While Bangladeshis share the same language with West Bengal, we nevertheless became part of the Pakistan nation-state along lines of religion. Bengalis, however, were considered to be lesser Muslims, and genocide and Civil War unfolded among the same peoples who had been part of the Islamic state of Pakistan. While it also has been argued that culturally, we are closer to West Bengal, this argument does not take into consideration the intracultural variations of a nation based on space, time, or economic class. Khan argues,

> Muslim Bengalis historically defined their political orientation neither through language nor through culture as is testified to by their separation from West Bengal. Also, that the creation of Bangladesh has little to do with language and culture and much more to do with tangible factors, such as economics and social justice, is evidenced by the fact that Bengali was established as an official language of Pakistan. Therefore the fight on the language front had already been fought and won—years before the need for separation became a reality (Khan 2006).

Lamia Karim (2004) has argued that in post-independence Bangladesh, subsequent ruling parties have constructed a Bangladeshi identity with a specific Islamic wedge as a political move to garner support of Islamic parties.

Set within this historical background, what it means to be a Bangladeshi, Bengali yet Muslim is an assertion of many different intersecting layers of experience. While wide sections of the media (and others) tend to talk about "the Muslim" world, my identity can only be understood in terms of the differences of experience among Muslims from different sociohistorical contexts. I was raised in a tolerant, syncretic, diverse, and secular Islamic community. At the same time, strong nationalist feelings against mass killings of Bangladeshis because we were not "sufficiently Muslim," and the invisibility of women from the statist history of Bangladesh, forms the prism through which I reflect on the intersections of religion, nationalism, and gender in my identity.

Growing Up in Post-independence Bangladesh

My experience of a specifically Bangladeshi version of Islam has to be located within a history of Bangladesh. I was born during the war of liberation from then–West Pakistan. Growing up in post-1971 independent Bangladesh, my own consciousness was formed by the stories told and retold by my family, and the larger community espousing strong nationalist, secular, and liberatory politics. As a Bangladeshi, I was raised with an enduring sense of nationalist identity and rage against the legacies of both Pakistani and British colonialism. My father, who was an academic and political activist deeply invested in the national development of Bangladesh, was among the people whose lives were at risk in the Pakistani army's systematic killings to crush the intellectual force of the erstwhile East Pakistan. My parents, like many of their academic friends and political allies, had to flee their home on the campus of Rajshahi University—a hotbed of student insurgency—and take shelter in a remote village in Northern Bangladesh in the home of a peasant family known to them through a colleague at the university. Many a night during my childhood, and even now, my mother and aunts would regale my siblings and me with memories of the hardship and fear they endured in those nine months of war, and the incredible kindness and generosity of the people who saved their lives. As a child born during the war, I was particularly reminded of the bloodshed and destruction that gave birth to this "beloved nation." Those stories of the war, learned through the memory of the generation who lived it, instilled in me—as well as many of my generation—a sense of responsibility, awe, and respect for my previous generation whose struggles had ensured us the gift of Bangladeshi citizenship. It was perhaps because of this particular social and intellectual orientation that I was subsequently deeply influenced by the scholarship of both US women of color (writing against domestic hegemony) and Third World feminist scholars (writing against Western hegemony). The intersections of these two genres of scholarship enabled me to trace my own multiple, contradictory, and specific feminist genealogy and actively engage its implications.

Being raised in a nationalist household, I absorbed multiple narratives of the memory of 1971. Gatherings of mostly male intellectuals of my father's generation unfolded eloquent discussions on nation building, the political and strategic decisions of the nationalist leaders in the region, the government of the Awami League political party, and the legendary Father of the Nation Sheikh Mujibur

Rahman. My education about the war, however, also took place in alternate gatherings consisting of my mother, her younger sister, and the wives of my father's friends and colleagues. It is their stories—lesser known in official narratives of war—that depicted the more vivid images of "living under occupation."

It was my mother who described how her family home was destroyed in a routine raid by the Pakistani army in North Bengal. Her father, my grandfather, was a civil surgeon who had to go into hiding in Dhaka because of his role in serving the freedom fighters. His eldest son, my *boromama* (eldest maternal uncle)—also a physician serving in the army—was stationed in a prison camp in West Pakistan. His two younger sons—both students of Dhaka University at the time—and a daughter and my grandmother shuttled back and forth from their home in the village of Shirajganj to Rajshahi city and my parents' home on the campus. On one occasion, fearful of an impending raid, my grandfather along with his sons and youngest daughter, members of extended family who lived in the same household, and the domestic staff took shelter in the woods behind the family homestead in Shirajganj. My grandmother, who was ill, did not have the strength to flee with the rest of the family. The army kicked down the front door and searched every corner of the house. Unable to find anyone other than my grandmother, they started to interrogate her in Urdu. She did not understand their questions, which enraged the soldiers all the more. One of them started dragging her out of the house by the arm when she lost consciousness. Neighbors later found her after the army had left. The Pakistani army had destroyed the furniture, looted the valuables—including cash, silver, and gold jewelry—and any other items they were able to carry with them in their trucks, and set fire to the homestead where my grandmother lay unconscious on the floor. My mother also told stories how Bengalis looted one another's homes and collaborated with the Pakistani army in identifying households considered harboring freedom fighters. After the raid, for instance, her cousins went scavenging in neighbors' homes to salvage some of their looted belongings.

My mother's youngest sister was 17 at the time. She told me about many of her male cousins and acquaintances who were freedom fighters. Defying the wishes of her parents, my aunt would harbor weapons for them and provide them with food and supplies. She spoke of the special hiding place she had behind their house, under the bushes by the bank of a lake. "I know how to fire a rifle," she would tell me with pride. I learned from her that the lights would go out every night as a measure of precaution against the air raids, and she and her brothers would play games by candlelight. "You were not even born then," she would remind me. That would be my mother's cue to remind me that she was pregnant with me in 1971. My father, three siblings, my mother, and Gofraan Mama, caretaker of the family home, fled to the village on a bullock cart in the dead of night. "Gofraan wrapped all my jewelry in handker-chiefs and hid them in jars containing puffed rice (*murir tin*). We took shelter with a peasant family in North Bengal known to us through a professor colleague of your father. There was no bath-room, and we would have to go out in the fields at night. Gofraan would accompany me with an oil lamp." My second sister, four at the time, almost died of dysentery, and Gofraan Mama had to take a trip to the nearest town, which was miles away, on foot to fetch medicine. Nearly two months later, my family had to return to their home on the campus of Rajshahi University because they received news that the Pakistani army had been tipped off about their hiding place. In addition, the Pakistani government issued an order for all academics to resume teaching in their respective campuses. A pro-fessor at the university, my father's colleague and a known war col-laborator, had said "chiria to bhaag giyaa" (the bird has flown) describing my family's flight to the village hiding place. On the other hand, another collaborator saved my father on a separate occasion. During a trip by road to Dhaka from Rajshahi, an army roadblock stopped them. The Pakistani soldiers asked my father to step out of the car and show his identification papers. One member of the cadre happened to be a Bihari—non-Bengali Muslims who sided with West Pakistan in the war—who had ties to Rajshahi University and, upon recognizing my father, convinced the others to let him go.

I was born one month before Bangladesh was liberated in 1971. The night before I was born in Rajshahi Medical Hospital, my father's older brother, an engineer who worked for Radio Bangla-desh, was fatally shot in Dhaka in an apparent case of mistaken identity. He left behind his wife, my chachi, and three children 15, 12, and 5 years old. My cousin recalled the thoughts running through her mind when she saw her father's dead body, "I kept wondering what was to become of us. My father was the only earning member of the family; my mother had never worked. I felt as though time had stopped and my life was over. Who was going to take care of us?" As the eldest daughter, she had to assume responsibility. She started tutoring classes for schoolchildren to supplement the family income. "I used to cry by myself when no one was watching." Her mother took on two jobs: as a Bangla teacher in a local school and a staff artist at Radio Bangladesh. Indeed, every family in Bangladesh has stories to tell about the trauma of 1971, which is inextricably linked with our national consciousness and identity as Bengali, Bangladeshi yet Muslim.

Although women participated in the war and had diverse roles in active combat—caring for the wounded and the injured, transporting and hiding weapons, and sheltering freedom fighters—statist histories have mostly represented them as victims of systematic violence by the Pakistani army and as mothers of freedom fighters and the nation. Feminist scholar Bina D'Costa (2005) has argued that women have been important in national image making yet excluded in its official history. Statist narratives have reconstructed 1971 as "terrible and stunning violence," "the Liberation struggle," and henceforth actively engaged in realigning a nationalist and masculine identity. Societal norms of seclusion and the separation of private and public spaces broke down in 1971, and Bengali men could not live up to the role of the "protectors" of their women. The post-1971 realignment of identity of the state as protector was a response to the gendercidal/genocidal practices of the war, which targeted:

(1) The Bengali military men of the East Bengal Regiment, the East Pakistan Rifles, police, and paramilitary Ansars and Mujahids. (2) The Hindus—"We are only killing the men; the women and children go free. We are soldiers, not cowards, to kill them . . . " I was to hear in Comilla [site of a major military base]. [Comments R.J. Rummel: "One would think that murdering an unarmed man was a heroic act" (Rummel 1994, 323)]. (3) The Awami Leaguers—all office bearers

and volunteers down to the lowest link in the chain of command. (4) The students—college and university boys and some of the more militant girls. (5) Bengali intellectuals, such as professors and teachers, whenever damned by the army as "militant" (Mascarenhas 1972, 116–117, quoted in www.gendercide.org 2006).

Younger men and adolescent boys of all social classes were persecuted. Rounaq Jahan has written, "All through the liberation war, able-bodied young men were suspected of being actual or potential freedom fighters. Thousands were arrested, tortured, and killed. Eventually cities and towns became bereft of young males who either took refuge in India or joined the liberation war" (quoted in www.gendercide.org 2006). Bengali women were targeted in gang sexual assault, rape, and murder throughout the war. Girls of eight to grandmothers of 75 were sexually assaulted. The typical modus operandi of the Pakistani army included destroying schools and hospitals upon entering a town, rounding up all the men and raping the women and girls in front of them, killing the men, and taking the women hostage for further abuse in rape camps. Large-scale killing, also with gendercidal characteristics, took place following the surrender of the Pakistani army when Bengali men in the rural areas targeted those who had collaborated with the Pakistanis.

Yet, after Bangladesh's independence, the memory of 1971 has been commemorated by the state in ways that perpetuated the process of realignment of its nationalist and masculinist identity (D'Costa 2005). The state has actively constructed through ideology and practice gendered narratives in which women have been rendered the victimized/plundered role and men as the war heroes and martyrs. On the one hand, the Pakistani army operated under orders to teach the lesser breed of Bengalis a lesson by impregnating the women in a deliberate effort to create a new race or to dilute Bengali nationalism. It was understood that good Muslims would not defy their fathers (Brownmiller 1975). On the other hand, in post-liberation Bangladesh, the government responded with state-sponsored abortion and foreign adoption programs to cleanse the nation of Pakistani blood. While purity for the Pakistan nation-state meant diluting the Bengali race, for Bangladesh it meant cleansing it of all traces of Pakistan. In both contexts, women's bodies were used as the site of violence. In neither context were women's voices and realities fully understood or heard.

Shifting Identities in the United States

Growing up in post-independence Bangladesh meant negotiating a national identity—Bengali, Bangladeshi *yet* Muslim—that was distinct from the "Muslim-first" identity central to the formation of the Pakistan nation-state. But it was only when I came to the United States and had to learn the reassignment of my identity as South Asian, which erased or subsumed the particularities of a Bangladeshi identity in either the dominant Hindu Indian or the India-Pakistan conflict narrative, that I positioned myself as a self-aware Bangladeshi living in America. The complex and contradictory dynamics of inter- and intra-community relations have been well documented by researchers, and it is not my intention to rehash those here. Rather, I want to draw attention to why it is important on the one hand to carefully chart distinctive yet interconnected genealogies of subcontinentals, and on the other, the potential for feminist coalitional politics among them, particularly in the current critical juncture.

I remember my first close encounters with Pakistanis of my generation when I attended college in the United States, and the indignation I felt having to explain that I did not speak Urdu; no, we were "not all the same," and their easy declarations of "we were once one" had very different and bitter implications for those of us in the East. I remember the look of disdain from my Pakistani friends as they watched my sister's wedding video and found the Bengali Muslim wedding traditions un-Islamic, or Islamic yet unfamiliar to them, although we shared regional, national, and religious histories. I also had to remind my Indian friends that 1971 marked the Bangladesh war of liberation and not the "Indo-Pak War," and my Pakistani friends that "Dhaka did not fall" but was won with the blood of millions "of their own."

"Islam" did not provide a ready glue to override historical, political, and cultural differences with Pakistanis. Nor did my Bengali,

Bangladeshi yet Muslim identity fit easily with the current trend toward claiming "South Asian-ness" because of specific experiences
where the South Asian umbrella continues to fold important regional and historical distinctions. I think there is something to be
gained by charting our distinct genealogies yet being attentive to our
shared histories, struggles, and cultural contexts.

Having married a second generation Indian-American whose
parents have first-hand experience of the migration and dislocation
caused by Partition, the implications of physical and psychological
borders—whether national, religious, historical, or cultural—are
an undeniable reality in my personal as well as public life. On a
family trip to India, we became the object of much confusion and
interrogation by the immigration officer in Delhi International Airport who found it "illogical" that my spouse—an American citizen
of Hindu Indian descent—was married to a Muslim Bangladeshi
citizen. Using the colonial term to describe Muslims, he asked my
spouse, "Is your wife Hindu or Mohammadan?" In some ways, the
South Asian umbrella in the United States, where the general public is largely unaware of the subcontinent's political history, can
serve as a buffer from such intrusions into family dynamics. In our
everyday public lives in the United States, explanations of such nature are unnecessary, although the legacies of our colonial and nationalist histories are negotiated daily within the family and South
Asian community in matters ranging from choices of food, dress,
and forms of entertainment, observing cultural and religious traditions and holidays, and discussions of formal politics to the raising
of our children. However, in India and Bangladesh, it is in the public (as well as domestic) arena where similar negotiations are vet-
ted. In the North Indian, Punjabi community where my in-laws
reside in New Jersey, a Bengali, Bangladeshi yet Muslim identity is
in some respect alien, even threatening.

The idea of shared regional history yet distinguishing features
of a Bengali, Bangladeshi yet Muslim identity is beautifully articulated in Tareque Masud's film, *The Clay Bird* (2002). It reflects a
version of Bangladeshi Islam shaped by the region's specific social
and historical forces that Masud describes in an interview with
Sandip Roy-Chowdhury of *India Currents:*

Sufi baul tradition is a combination of Vaishnav Mysticism and Iranian sufism . . . [this] popular Islam is more inclusive, more pluralistic, more diverse and syncretic in nature, based on wisdom and common sense. This is in sharp contrast with what I call "scholastic" Islam, a bookish and modernist Islam. . . . The modernists are using this scholastic Islam for their own ends. They are trying to impose a creed and not the culture, even though clearly Islam is not just a creed; it is a culture like any other. (Roy-Chowdhury 2004)

This version of Islam challenges the view of unitary Islam; it challenges ideas about "the" Muslim world. *The Clay Bird* is set in Bangladesh in the 1960s on the eve of the Liberation struggle and portrays the fragile ties holding the two Muslim majority populations of West and East Pakistan. Says Sandip Roy-Chowdhury's review, "The heart of the film is the struggle between two definitions of Islam—one more secular and rooted in the music of the wandering baul folk singers, the other more orthodox and rigid" (Roy-Chowdhury 2004). In a 2002 interview with *Le Monde*, Masud says,

For [Bangladeshis], Islam is rooted in our own soil, it has evolved and adapted to our own traditions, including Hinduism. It has thus become our own form of Islam, a popular Islam. This is expressed through the "bahas" songs that we hear in the film. These mystical songs are still very popular, and serve to transmit much of our knowledge and heritage. They are a means of mediation and prayer. (*Le Monde* 2002)

In a powerful scene in the film set in the open under a tree, wandering folk singers (baul) debate the meaning of God in the context of competing social forces of nationalism, gender, and Islamist ideologies:

Female baul: If you want to go to heaven, keep fear of Allah in your heart.
Male baul: If you want to be close to Allah, keep love within your heart.
Female baul: I'm just your daughter's age,
I'll assume the side of Sharia.
To take an anti-Sufi stance,
Don't take what I say to heart.
You ignore the Holy Scriptures.
What kind of Muslims are you?

Why are the Mullah's always angry with you?
Keep fear of Allah in your heart.
Male baul: You need wisdom to grasp the Qur'an.
How can half-read Mullahs interpret intricate scriptures
Without knowing the text they preach to others.
The dogmatic Mullahs make a living from deception.
We don't lust for heaven.
We have no fear of hell.
If you want to be close to Allah,
Keep love within your heart.

In another scene, a conversation between two teachers in a *madrassah* unfolds, debating the merit of religious education in the context of preserving the unity of Pakistan on the basis of one religion and in the face of perceived communist and secularist threats: "Islam didn't spread here [Bengal] through the sword. It was the selfless Sufis who went to low-caste Hindus to spread Islam's message of peace and equality. The kings of Iran and Arabia conquered land but not peoples' hearts. It was thanks to the Sufis that people embraced Islam. The truth is you cannot make Islam flourish with politics or arms. It is by speaking the Islamic knowledge that Islam will prosper," opines one of the more progressive teachers. He goes on to pose the illuminating question, "If Pakistan collapses, why would Islam be endangered? Did Pakistan establish Islam or rather enforce military rule [in then-East Pakistan]?" The same question could be posed of the current political attempts in Bangladesh to create an Islamic wedge as a political move to garner support of Islamic parties by some post-independence parties (Karim 2004). Karim argues that this nationalist identity is in contrast to earlier versions, which embraced the ethnolinguistic Bengali identity.

But I do not draw on past history alone to shape my identity. I draw on particular contemporary secular and cultural platforms from a transnational sphere as a direct stance against the religious extremist fervor. Meghna Guhathakurta describes how many movements in Bangladesh always relied on the literary and folk traditions of Bengal in opposition to the Islamist politics (Guhathakurta reports in www.dristipat.org). She likens recent moves by the Bangladeshi government with Islamist party coalitions to declare out-of-bounds similar spaces commemorating nationalist struggles to students of Dhaka University who have agitated against them. According to Guhathakurta, "Cultural activism or the cultivation of secular and progressive ideals through various art forms have had a significant contribution toward the practice of democracy and freethinking in Bangladesh." Students and young people responded by ever more enthusiastic celebrations of the Bengali New Year (*Pohela Boishakh*) and first day of spring (*Boshonto Utshob*), both deemed un-Islamic by the Islamists. Protests on campus have invoked the Liberation struggle with a spontaneous performance of street theater by the students of the Fine Arts Department. "They were drawing satirical portraits of the power relations between the university administration and the ruling party cadres. [One student] later admitted that she had felt she had been transported to a *muktanchal* of the Liberation War, i.e., the areas which were liberated of Pakistani Army Occupation by the Muktibahinis (the freedom fighters)." These contemporary sites of contestation are not only reminiscent of the Bengali resistance against Pakistani repression, but also the deeply cultural spirit of democratic struggles against power etched in the consciousness of the younger generations as a result of the stories that had been told to them by family members. "A connection with a period of history which [the younger generation] had not witnessed, but was engraved deep in the collective unconscious mind of an oppressed people" (Guhathakurta reports in drishtipat .org).

Experiences Vis-à-Vis Mainstream United States

The trope of the Muslim woman as the ultimate victim of a timeless patriarchy defined by the barbarism of Islamic religion and in need of civilizing has become a very important component of Western regimes of knowledge. The need to engage pedagogically with gendered orientalism is no longer a flourish of postcolonial criticism but a sine qua non, since it is under the sign of a veiled woman that we increasingly come to recognize ourselves as gendered and heteronormative subjects, but also as located in the free West, where women are not imprisoned. (Moallem 2005, 52)

In the last five years, the racialization of Muslim South Asians in the United States has taken on new significance. Disentangling and analyzing the intersections of gender, race, nationality, and religion in such a context is a vexed proposition. As a feminist citizen of a non–Middle Eastern, democratic, Muslim-majority country, I find considerable misinformation and ignorance shaping my day-to-day interactions with mainstream America. Public understanding of Islam tends to privilege the study of texts and revolves around religion as a set of ritual practices rather than the lived experience of diverse Muslims, and to privilege the experience of Muslims in Arab countries over Muslims elsewhere. Against such a backdrop, the necessity to rigorously investigate the significance of Islam in the lives of vastly internally diverse Muslim populations across geographic, cultural, and historical spaces rather than simply presume its centrality in their lives in essentialist terms is absolutely critical.

In the fall of 2005, I was invited to attend a luncheon organized by a feminist colleague in the university where I teach in the honor of a woman journalist from Saudi Arabia, who at the time was visiting the United States as an Eisenhower Fellow. We had barely taken our seats when our host launched into a celebratory speech appreciating the "freedom" of press in the United States, and particularly the *New York Times'* critical and investigative reports. We should be thankful, she said, considering how in other parts of the world (notably the guest's) the government controlled the media and the people had few options other than swallowing the filtered information fed to them. She reminded our guest of the oppressive regime in her country that did not even allow women to drive. This came on the heels of the reports on Special Envoy Karen Hughes' statements in Saudi Arabia regarding Saudi women's lack of freedom. A *New York Times* (*NYT*) article by Steven Weisman said, "When Ms. Hughes expressed the hope here that Saudi women would be able to drive and 'fully participate in society' much as they do in her country, many challenged her" (September 28, 2005). It appeared that our host had not read the *NYT* articles that bemoaned Hughes' ill-placed remarks, and the indignant responses they invoked from the Saudi audience. Moreover, our host, declaring herself a champion of global feminism and who sat on the board of various foundations "helping" women in oppressed cultures, in an unrelated and illogical turn in the conversation, invited me to a follow up lunch with her to discuss the "issue of female genital mutilation." Although my feminist colleague at this luncheon did not know my religious and national identity, the fact that I teach "Global Feminism" led her to believe that I should be interested in such a discussion. The discourse of feminism implied in this scenario invokes a division between "feminists" and "other women"—where the assumption seems to be that feminists inhabit one world—the Western one—whereas other women live elsewhere and are *not* feminist or unequally feminist. Furthermore, the idea of internationalism is tied to the notion of America within mainstream feminism in the United States, obscuring its own fragmented communities and divisive race issues. The persistence of a unified nationalist discourse (America is democratic; American women have freedom of choice) attempts to keep alive the idea of the hegemonic white America as the "greatest nation in the world," and (white) American women as its benevolent and lucky citizens.

I refer to this conversation because I want to probe the braiding of democracy (free media in the United States, an informed public in direct opposition to authoritarian regimes, and their compliant subjects elsewhere), freedom (of women to drive and support women's oppression elsewhere manifested in FGM), and benevolent global feminism (that helps women who are victimized by their cultures, their men, and their states). At a time of militarized war and US empire building, as Chandra Mohanty (2006) has characterized the contemporary moment, it becomes ever more important to carefully examine the ways in which feminisms are deployed to further different political agendas, as well as feminist complicity and dissent to those agendas. In other words, I would like to draw attention to how global feminism is co-opted into a narrative justification of Western liberal notions of democracy, and used in the service of reconstructing/reconsolidating its civilizing mission.

Every semester, I experience a version of this brand of global feminism in my "Women in Global Perspective" course, where the discourse of human rights immediately raises a plethora of concern for oppression of veiled Muslim women, genitally mutilated African women, and impoverished Indian women, but rarely an American counterpart figure. Many students have difficulty maintaining an intersectional analysis of inter-national and intra-national gendering practices. While the intersecting axes of race/class/gender are readily applied to analyze the conditions of women's lives in the United States, in discussions of women's lives "elsewhere" that critique is often lost as women in the United States become a singular individual with freedom to choose in opposition to her singular victimized and interchangeable oppressed Third World/Muslim/Arab counterpart. I say this not to demonize students and colleagues, but rather to bring into focus enduring colonial and oriental tropes, which are enacted in the microspace of the feminist classroom and everyday conversations.

Toward Feminist Identity and Alliance

As an academic, part of the enactment of my history is in the progressive alliances I forge and the structures of knowledge I help to create, drawing upon the traditions I described in the previous section. As a conclusion, I offer two examples of the contours of such identity and alliances, drawing upon some transnational efforts to speak out against fundamentalisms, wars, and ultramasculinist, separatist reappropriations of nationalist politics.

In a recent conversation with Kavita Panjabi and Khanum Shaikh—feminist scholar/activists from India and Pakistan, respectively—about the shared struggles of South Asian women's movements yet the divisive and hostile politics of nation-states, Kavita Panjabi shared her experiences of traveling to Pakistan in 2002 with the Pakistan India Forum for Peace and Democracy, and the incredible generosity of the people and the strong kinship ties invoked despite the violent events of Partition and end of British Raj in 1947. During a previous trip to attend a regional Women's Studies Conference in 2001, she recalled the deep sorrow and nostalgia expressed by a Pakistani storekeeper in regard to the violent cessation of East Pakistan in 1971 when he met Kavita's fellow participant in the forum from Bangladesh. We—Kavita, Khanum, and I—talked about how those feelings of nostalgia were not reciprocated on the Bangladesh side of the border, where Pakistanis were viewed with unforgiving distrust for the savage and cruel forms of violence they enacted on their "own" people in then–East Pakistan. Khanum revealed how being raised in Pakistan, she had not learned in the statist national history about the genocide or systematic rape of Bangladeshi women by the Pakistan army in 1971. It was only after coming to the United States during her college years that she became aware of the underside of the nationalist history of Pakistan. This conversation, however small and insignificant, I think is a minute reflection of the South Asian feminist efforts in building regional alliances addressing the shattering consequences of communal violence and war on women.

These alliances, I believe, are particularly urgent, especially now in a world increasingly divided along religious and cultural lines and the fierce and fearsome tentacles of empire and globalization. It is relevant, too, that this conversation took place in the United States at a conference on transnational feminisms, because it begs reflection on understanding and unpacking different yet connected feminist genealogies globally.

Mary John states that while the global perspective of feminism necessarily takes one beyond national boundaries, dominant forces pre-position us to look in certain directions and not others. "Forging South-South linkages in an era of globalization has the potential of displacing the hegemony of the West as the default frame of reference" (John 1999, 202). The failure of certain global feminisms of the West that assume the right to speak for women everywhere or on behalf of "other" women elsewhere are all too well known. What is obscured in this dominant direction are the plural conversations occurring between and among "other" feminisms. One such example would be to examine alternate locations where unsuspecting alliances are being forged that are globally different. Global influences, on the one hand, have been rightly criticized as furthering the interests of the nationalist elites, but at the same time not enough has been said about how those influences also have been used by marginalized groups, such as women, indigenous people, gays, and lesbians, to articulate potentially subversive agendas. Sharpening the agenda of feminism, which previously has been narrowly conceptualized around questions of gender only, John defines this new move as "[. . . addressing] how asymmetries and structures of privilege may have prevented solidarities; and to fight on many fronts to enable the development of more viable feminisms" (John 1999, 200). Next, I offer a discussion on fledgling efforts currently under way to sharpen and give new direction to global feminism in alternative sites.

Bina D'Costa and Kavita Panjabi's work on South Asian feminist organizing efforts on reconciliation and justice around the gendered abuses of Partition and the Bangladesh War of Liberation are examples of a regional transnationalism. While women in the subcontinent contributed to the anti-colonialist and nationalist struggles, it would be an exaggeration to state that in post-independence India, Pakistan, and Bangladesh the question of autonomy and liberation of women has been adequately recognized in a national development agenda. However, it is women who have been in the forefront of retelling the history of the violent birth of India, Pakistan, and Bangladesh by retrieving the untold and suppressed stories and perspectives of millions including women and ordinary people.

Building on the common cultural and traditional backgrounds, and the shared history of nation-building, these networks have crafted innovative and groundbreaking ways of addressing the historical abuse of women and seeking reconciliation in the present. In fact, it is the South Asian feminist forum that first publicly addressed the question of gendered war atrocities, which even now remain unacknowledged by national governments in the region. Scholarship by Indian, Pakistani, and Bangladeshi feminists Veena Das, Urvashi Butalia, Ritu Menon, Kamala Bhasin, Nighat Said Khan, Jahanara Imam, and Hamida Hussain, and feminist organizations, such as Ain-O-Shalish Kendro, have initiated discussions of nation, violence, and sexuality in the region. The International Initiative for Justice in Gujarat is another instance in which national and international women's groups collectively responded to the horrific violence unleashed against the Muslim community, particularly Muslim women of Gujarat, since February 2002. Members of women's groups from India, Sri Lanka, Algeria/France, Israel/UK, Germany, and the United States came together in an exemplary international initiative that unraveled the historic, local, national, regional, and global conflicts that led to the savage violence and its explicitly gendered/sexualized nature. This initiative urged accountability of the state and national governments, the international community at the level of state, and intergovernmental and non-state organizations. They called for the utilization of international law codified in the Rome Statute of the International Criminal Court that granted avenues to prosecute sexual violence, torture, and genocide as crimes against humanity. Particularly in light of the failure of the national legal system, internationalizing the issue was of utmost importance.

Women's groups at the state, national, and international level are the ones who made explicit the ways in which women's bodies are used as battlegrounds in nationalist and communal struggles. The historical context of the Indian subcontinent, where divisions along religious and community lines have led to violence and divisiveness of mammoth proportions, generated conversations about how sexual violence against women can be effectively addressed by a legal system unequipped to deal with such crimes. The IIJ reporters framed the attacks against Muslim communities in Gujarat within the globalized and systematic attacks against Muslims particularly after September 11, 2001.

Each member of the initiative had her own history of resistance that resonated deeply with the events in Gujarat and made their participation in the panel deeply meaningful. From memories of Nazi terror to embattled Israel and Palestine; from the consequences of Muslim fundamentalism in Algeria to war crimes in Bosnia; from ethnic strife and war in Sri Lanka to the traumatic legacies of Partition and the recurring sectarian violence in the India subcontinent, Gujarat was for this group deeply personal, historical, political, and a moment to forge an alliance epitomizing women's continued struggles for survival. As Nira Yuval Davis described it, "Being part of a wonderful encompassing feminist collective experience, something I had not been part of for too many years, which helped us to find the strength and comfort with each other, and to remember to celebrate life as long as we can: [It was] feminist politics at its best." Rhonda Copelon said, "[C]ourage of the testifiers, which together with the amazing energy, solidarity, and organization of the women's groups who came together across cultural lines to organize the IIJ, and the growing significance of gender and sexual violence in international law and international arenas provides new hope." Vahida Nainar said, "The idea that it is possible to have an issue-based consensus among diverse groups was promising and exhilarating for future feminist actions against anti-democratic, nationalist, fundamentalist, and patriarchal forces." The panel collectively opined that for them participation in the IIJ was both a way of reestablishing feminist transnational solidarity and of mounting opposition to political processes that targeted minority groups.

The work of feminist politics, given the reality of global, national, and inter- as well as intra-community power relations, must address the scattered hegemonies affecting women's lives.

> It is through intersectional analyses of discrimination and oppression that the potential of "transversal politics," which crosses the boundaries created by identity, might be realized. Transversal politics understands that the subject positions on which we base our thoughts and our responses are multiple and constantly shifting. Within this context, as activists we do not represent any one group at all given times; rather, we stand as advocates of a particular understanding of a specific situation and as mobilizing and organizing agents against discriminatory and oppressive practices. (IIJG 2003, 113)

The IIJ reporters recognize in a critical way that unlike the unexamined championing of liberal notions of solidarity by some global feminist initiatives in the West, alliances between communities in South Asia with such violent political histories are forged through intense, and painful, contestations and negotiations. At the regional level, South Asian feminist movements are working toward strategies to establish and maintain cross-national connections using the parameters of international and national laws. These border-crossing networks, suggests D'Costa (2005), are seeking to access materials in government and nongovernment archives, as well as to forge dialogue among multiple groups historically involved in the wars in the region. Fragmented efforts in individual national contexts would only produce fractured versions of the shared colonialist and nationalist and postnationalist histories rather than an understanding of the region's inextricably braided evolution. South Asian feminists are beginning to craft a future of mutual respect and owning of responsibilities rather than one of mutual distrust, dislike, and suspicion. It is a step toward decolonization, moving beyond a framework where the West is always the "default frame of reference" (John 1999). This would be an alliance, a transnational resistance movement, and a feminist politic born out of "a theory of the flesh" with global transformative implications.

14

Religion as Inspiration, Religion as Action

Aysha Saeed

As I write these lines, I have been in private practice as a physician in the United States for almost seven years. I came to this
country at the age of 24, after completing my medical school in
Pakistan, and did my post-graduate residency training from the
University of Connecticut. Recollecting my past for this chapter was,
in itself, an enriching experience. It has helped me see how the past
has influenced who I am today and, by the same token, emphasized
the importance of the present moment in shaping the future.

The earliest identity I remember relating to is that of a Muslim
and a Pakistani. Now, as a US citizen, having lived in three conti-
nents (Asia, North America, and Europe), and having experienced
multiple cultures, the strongest identity I can relate to is that of a
human being. To some it might seem paradoxical, but to me, *that
is* my Islamic identity.

Medical Training

As members of the class of '98 at the University of Connecticut's internal medicine residency program, we were like a subsection of
the United Nations: We were from the United States, Nigeria, the
Philippines, Pakistan, India, Poland, Iceland, Syria, and Lebanon—
to name a few places. However, we all related to each other in our
own individual capacity as human beings, irrespective of the ethnic,

religious, or linguistic differences. We shared a common goal: taking care of patients and helping each other when needed. Nothing else seemed important except perhaps food and sleep.

While the goals were very similar during my years as a medical student, this diversity was conspicuously missing. I received my medical degree in 1992 from the Punjab University's Fatima Jinnah Medical College (FJMC) in Lahore, Pakistan. FJMC is one of two all-women medical colleges in Pakistan. All its students are women; most are Muslim and ethnically Punjabi (from the province of Punjab).

Contrary to popular opinion, I found studying in a non-coed environment in the Pakistani society an exhilarating and confidence-building experience. In this traditionally patriarchal society, having no male fellow students meant that we planned, created, and implemented all activities ourselves. We ran the Student Federation for Poor Patients (SFPP), a voluntary organization of medical students that organized blood donation drives and fund-raisers, ran a free pharmacy for indigent patients, and helped patients navigate the hospital system. We actively participated in all kinds of sports and competed at citywide, national, and international levels. Some of us took to the streets in popular political protests at that time, while others occupied themselves in fund-raising activities for charitable causes.

In Pakistan, a medical degree requires five years of schooling at most medical colleges. My family moved from Lahore to Karachi after my first year of medical school. This necessitated my moving into the college hostel. It was during the four years I spent at the hostel that I, along with some of my friends, seriously undertook the study of the Holy Qur'an—the scripture that Muslims believe to be the Divine revelation given to Prophet Mohammed (peace be upon him) in the year 610 C.E. After the evening prayers, we would all gather in one person's room and read the translation of a portion of the Qur'an each day. We would listen, discuss, and reflect on the meaning of the Qur'anic passages. I consider that time to be the real beginning of my personal spiritual journey.

During our five years of medical school, we were practically secluded from the general society. The coursework was intensive, and the remaining time was spent in clinical rotations at the adjacent Sir Ganga Ram Hospital and volunteer activities for SFPP. I did manage to keep up with my daily tennis routine that I had started during my premed college years. Our hostel had a primitive grass court, and a tennis coach was available for lessons. The ball would often spin off the uneven ground. Our coach would view that as a training strength: If we could play on this court, we could play on any court. His favorite line was *"josh say nahi, hosh say"* [Translation: Use presence of mind, not emotional frenzy (while striking the ball)]. It was, indeed, an excellent exercise in developing awareness and presence of mind.

Religious Upbringing

As is customary in Pakistan, like most children, I had finished reading the Qur'an in Arabic by the age of seven or eight. Arabic is not a language native to Pakistan. The national language of Pakistan is Urdu, although there are many other distinct languages spoken in different parts of the country. During our school years, we learned the Urdu meaning of selected passages from the Qur'an and were taught the basic tenets of the Islamic faith and its historical background. We also memorized the shorter Qur'anic *surahs* (chapters) in Arabic.

Being raised in a traditional Islamic society, the basic principles and practices of faith were passed down to us almost imperceptibly in the family: I remember standing behind my grandfather in my kindergarten years and copying his movements during *Salaat* (ritual Muslim contact prayers), repeating after him the Arabic prayers and invocations of the *Salaat*. I think that was probably how my siblings and I first learned how to pray. Muslims are supposed to offer *Salaat* at five fixed times during the day. These times include *Fajr* (before sunrise), *Zuhr* (early afternoon), *Asr* (late afternoon), *Maghrib* (just after sunset), and *Ishaa* (evening). Offering these prayers created in me a deeper connection with the nature's greater rhythm. I would listen with awe to birds that would start chirping around the *Fajr* and *Maghrib* times, starting their prayers, or so I was told. Somehow those hours of the day seemed special, and they still do.

As a child growing up, the Qur'an for me was a sacred book. It had to be handled very carefully, and ought not be allowed to fall. I would usually read it, in Arabic, during the fasting month of Ramadan. Its recitation was considered to confer blessings on the person reciting it. I do remember taking short cuts, though not without a feeling of guilt, by reading the accompanying Urdu language translation instead of the Arabic text. I would not only find the Urdu translation more interesting because I could understand it, but also would manage to finish the chapter more quickly.

My personal journey in understanding the nature of blessings conferred by reading the sacred texts has taken me full circle—from a simplistic belief in reading the sacred revealed words without understanding their meaning, to deeply studying and understanding the various available translations, to combining this understanding with the realization of the importance of the sacred language of the Qur'an. The latter appreciation was fostered by studying the concept of *Cymatics*—the study of wave phenomenon as described by Dr. Hans Jenny (1904–1972), showing the amazing power of sound to shape and transform matter that forms the substance of all living and non-living things.

Schooling at an Irish Convent

Most of my school years were spent at an Irish convent school run by Catholic nuns. The discipline of the nuns matched our rigorous upbringing at home. They would make sure our hair was cut short or neatly tied; our school uniform had to be clean and pressed; makeup of any type was disallowed. All students, including Muslims and Christians, prayed together at the morning assembly. I still remember the words of the morning prayer, "O my Lord, I offer thee all my thoughts, words, actions, joys, and sufferings of this day. Amen." During the prayer, the Muslim students would conspicuously hold their hands open, cupped together, while the Christian students would clasp them together. We jointly learned and sang the hymns during the music classes.

The nuns took great care to perfect our English, written as well as spoken. There was a lot of emphasis on character-building in our schooling. We also learned *Ikebana,* the Japanese art of flower arrangement. *Ikebana* is a disciplined art form that holds flower arrangement as a "living thing" in which nature and humanity are brought together. I still remember our instructor's emphasis on how to handle the flowers after they are clipped. She maintained that we have to actually love the flowers and handle them tenderly for the beauty to reflect in the final arrangement. To be able to love flowers was, in fact, a prerequisite for practicing *Ikebana.* I remember trying to *feel* love for the flowers as I would tenderly cut them and keep them in a bowl of water in preparation for my arrangement. Now, almost three decades later, as I attempt to understand the concept of *Hado,* or subtle energy carried by all existing things (as explained by Dr. Masaru Emoto in his book, *True Power of Water*), this energetic interaction between human beings and plants makes a lot more sense than the abstract idealistic concept.

As I look back on my childhood and school years, I only have memories of love, acceptance, and encouragement from my parents. My mother, who holds baccalaureate and master's degrees in education and mathematics, respectively, nurtured and taught us well. There was never any compromise on such basic values as respect for elders, not raising one's voice when talking, eating in silence, and never wasting any food. My father was an officer in the Pakistan army. He had a fixed income that supported a family of four children. Between my mother's frugality and my father's generosity, we always had enough to support us and to share with relatives and friends in need. I never saw my parents fight or even argue. Their relationship was based on mutual love and respect. They provided a caring environment for us to grow, and I always will be grateful for that.

I probably inherited my love of poetry from my father. Classical literary works in Urdu often have a rich Persian element. My father started studying Persian when I was in fourth grade. As Urdu is written in Persian script, my siblings and I also could read his elementary Persian language manuals. I remember all of us having a lot of fun learning the Persian vocabulary with its Urdu meanings along with our father. Mirza Ghalib's and Allama Mohammed Iqbal's poetry were his favorites. When helping us deal with difficult situations, he often would use a reflective *shayr* (verse of poetry) or two to drive his point home. Communicating through poetry, proverbs, and anecdotes was a beautiful custom passed down through generations in a society that owes much of its richness to its oral traditions. My love and fascination for Iqbal's philosophy and thought has continued to evolve since then. As my understanding deepens, my respect grows for this great twentieth century Indian Muslim thinker and philosopher.

Cultural Influences

Being raised in the seventies in Pakistan, religion, culture, and traditions were inseparably intertwined in the societal fabric. Wisdom was imperceptibly transmitted to the younger generations through stories, fables, rhymes, and family interactions.

I still have fond memories of *Taleem-o-Tarbiat* (Education and Nurturing), my favorite childhood Urdu language magazine, that we received on a subscription basis. This periodical was full of stories and anecdotes that carried Sufi wisdom, adapted for children. It was this magazine that introduced me to the ageless wisdom that showed itself through the words of mystic poets such as Rumi, Saadi, Hafiz, and the humorous and thought-provoking fables of Mullah Nasruddin.

To give you a flavor of Mullah Nasruddin's wit, let me share an English translation of one of his anecdotes:

> The dervish Nasruddin entered a formal reception area and seated himself at the foremost elegant chair. The Chief of the Guard approached and said, "Sir, those places are reserved for guests of honor."
>
> "Oh, I am more than a mere guest," replied Nasruddin confidently.
> "Oh, so are you a diplomat?"

"Far more than that!"

"Really? So you are a minister, perhaps?"

"No, bigger than that, too."

"Oho! So you must be the King himself, sir,"
  said the Chief sarcastically.

"Higher than that!"

"What? You are higher than the King! Nobody is higher than the King
  in this country!"

 "Now you have it," said Nasruddin. "I am nobody!"

Depending on who reads it, this anecdote can kindle a witty laugh or a deeper spiritual reflection on transcending one's ego, thus becoming *higher than the king* by being *nobody*.

As I sat down to pen those childhood memories, I couldn't help researching the origins of those fables. Some say Mullah Nasruddin is a mythical figure; others insist that he was a real person. Mullah Nasruddin is a name familiar to most Pakistanis from their childhood. It turns out that Mullah Nasruddin's identity is claimed by three countries: Afghanistan, Iran, and Turkey. Nasruddin's stories have been passed down for generations over hundreds of years as oral traditions. Mullah has left his indelible mark in societies extending from the Indian subcontinent, across Central Asia to Turkey. For us, it was a household name as his anecdotes used to be told at family gatherings by both adults and children, infusing Mullah's humor and wit into the natural flow of conversation.

Then there were the two popular Urdu fiction book series for children, *Tilism-e-Hoshruba* (The Stunning Magic) and *Dastan-e-Amir Hamza* (Tales of Amir Hamza). I read all of the books in those series. They were captivating books that carried you into the mythological world of magic, demons, heroes, and kings. To some, those stories were far more enchanting than Harry Potter.

At that time I did not realize that I was reading the adapted children's version of the classical Urdu literary masterpieces. *Dastan-e-Amir Hamza* was the first-ever printed Urdu language *Dastan* (a literary piece with many novels in it), first published in 1801. It is considered the longest single romance cycle in world literature with 46 volumes, averaging 900 pages each. The *Tilism-e-Hoshruba* series was completed over a period of 12 years (1883–1905), and was written by three different authors in succession. As public interest in the literary style of *Dastan* started to fade in the 1920s, these series started going out of print. Today, a complete collection of this literary treasure no longer exists, though efforts are being made to recover it. As for the availability of the children's version in Pakistan today, it is much easier to find an Urdu translation of Harry Potter than *Dastan-e Amir Hamza*.

These literary classics underscore the inseparability of local cultures, wisdom, imagination, and religion that made up the rich and beautiful fabric of the land in which I was raised. Sadly, those rich traditions are fading away fast with the growing influence of literalism and materialism, resulting in the breakdown of traditional values.

The role of oral tradition via tales and anecdotes was central in the society in which I was raised. During one's growth starting at a young age, one learns about the realities of life by finding similarities between one's own circumstances and the circumstances of the story, thus understanding the roadblocks in life's journey in a fashion that lets the lessons penetrate deep into one's psyche without bruising one's ego. As a result, these traditions and stories performed a subtle but crucial function in human spiritual and intellectual development.

In Pakistan, as religion is being detached from local culture and tradition in an effort to "purify" it, I feel a rich heritage of wisdom is being lost that had successfully nurtured generations before us. In effect, the void of imagination thus created is being filled by contemporary Western children's entertainment literature, such as Harry Potter and Superman; ethical/moral instruction has been left solely to religious education.

The combined effect of the phenomena has resulted in the breakup of the rich cultural fabric of that society. If seen from a Western lens, that society is becoming more and more extremist (*literalistic* would perhaps be a more appropriate term) in its religious interpretations; just like, from an Eastern lens, most of the Western societies are becoming totally materialistic and "godless." In reality, these are parallel developments, one feeding the other, and both existing in some form in all societies. The real clash appears to be within each civilization, not between them.

Move to the United States

I immigrated to the United States in 1992 after getting married. As is the norm in Pakistani society, ours was an arranged marriage. Azam, my husband, is a former Pakistani air force pilot, and our families knew each other well. Immigration to this country exposed me to different ways of thinking and codes of behavior. It did take a while for me to be able to "cross the cultural divide." With this transition came the realization that what we consider "Islamic" values are not much different from what Christians consider "Christian" values and Hindus consider "Hindu" values. Through this rich interaction, I have developed a deep sense of respect for other religions as well as a deeper appreciation of my own religion.

For almost a decade after I immigrated to the United States, religion remained a private aspect of our lives as Azam and I focused on our professional careers. I would offer my daily *salaat* (prayers) at home, fast during the month of Ramadan, and study the Qur'an in my spare time. All that was to change with the events of 9/11.

Looking back at my life, I see my spiritual self in a constant state of evolution: an evolution enriched by people who have shared their lives and thoughts with me, by my positive as well as negative life experiences, and by the recent world events that have brought so many human tragedies to the surface.

Post-9/11: Nationalism and the Sociopolitical Reality

September 11, 2001, altered a lot of things at individual, societal, and global levels. For most American Muslims, it became the harbinger of a new reality of existence. We were no longer the invisible minority who went about our daily lives living the American Dream. Our ethnicity, color, and names now were being identified with the ethnicity, color, and names of the hijackers whose photographs were being repeatedly flashed across television screens and newspapers all over the nation.

Although most Americans I had come in contact with previously were familiar with the name of our religion, they did not seem to know much about Islam. History has shown ignorance to be the ideal ground for the seeds of propaganda to sprout. The misinformation fed to the nation in the subsequent months helped project Islam and Terrorism as synonyms in people's minds, thus fostering an anti-Muslim sentiment among the general public. The ensuing hysteria allowed the government to "disappear" and detain thousands of American Muslims in its terrorism investigations without any charges, and without the due process that the Constitution requires. The momentum to do "something" was so strong that the U.S. Congress passed the "Patriot Act" with virtually no discussion on the various aspects of this sweeping legislation and its long-lasting implications for this nation.

However, the American nation has not completely forgotten its WWII lessons about civil rights. Unlike the Japanese Americans who were rounded up and sent to concentration camps in the 1940s, we had a lot of support from civil rights groups, activists, and churches.

While Islam has always been the central guiding force in my private life, it was the greater public scrutiny after 9/11 that brought it to center stage in our public lives. In the months that followed 9/11, the nation went through waves of shock, grief, confusion, and anger. Sadly, the mainstream media became just another vehicle to promote belligerence and jingoism. Instead of informing and educating the public about the various facets and nuances of geopolitics, especially the economic and ideological drivers of global power play, the media exploited the prevailing emotional climate to promote the image of a world that can be perfectly divided into good and evil, black and white. The unfortunate result has been that, instead of finding solutions to the complex sources of global conflict that besiege us all, the world now has been thrown into a deeper cycle of violence, something that is clearly against the interests of all the people of the world, including those of the United States.

While the mainstream media's response was disappointing, many academic and faith communities opened their hearts and doors to their fellow American Muslims. Connecticut was no exception. Azam and I joined our many Connecticut faith communities in prayers and vigils for those who died in the September 11 tragedy as well as those civilians and families that became the victims of the subsequent US bombings on Afghanistan and Iraq. We participated in various academic and faith-based forums in an effort to foster religious understanding, pluralism, and bridge building. Azam's interest and expertise in global politics, as well as his being a Muslim who was raised in Pakistan, stationed him well to moderate or speak at many such local events that desperately needed a Muslim viewpoint. Some of the areas of interest to the local non-Muslim community were quite basic, such as the rights and status of women in Islam, Islamic concept of religious pluralism and tolerance, and the concept of Jihad or Struggle (which the media often misrepresent as Holy War, a solely Christian concept). Others were more complex and required a deeper understanding of the geopolitical scene. Through those interactions, we met some wonderful people whose dedication to the human cause helps restore one's faith in the ultimate goodness of the human spirit.

My own understanding of Islam has since deepened as a result of further study and reflection. My research expanded to more extensively study the various translations of the Qur'an as well as reading the works of contemporary Muslim scholars and thinkers, such as Abu Fadl, Fazlur Rahman, Riffat Hassan, Asma Barlas, Fathi Osman, and Ahmed Hulusi, to name a few.

In September of 2002, on the first anniversary of 9/11, I remember listening to Mioyoko Matsubara's account of the Hiroshima bombing. Mioyoko was invited to speak in New Haven, Connecticut, as part of the "No More Victims Tour" organized by *September 11 Families for a Peaceful Tomorrow* and the *American Friends Service Committee*. Mioyoko is one of the survivors of the Hiroshima atomic bombing. Now in her 70s, her memory of that day was still vivid as if it had happened yesterday. The strength of Mioyoko's spirit and her resolve to be the ambassador of peace stood in sharp contrast to her frail frame. She kept asking Azam, who was moderating the event, if the United States had given any indications of actually attacking Iraq. While the nation was being rallied to gain support for invasion of Iraq under the flag of patriotism, the victims of past atrocities desperately were trying to prevent yet another human tragedy.

The year 2003 witnessed the bombing of Iraq and the flurry of patriotism that swept the nation. I remember the US tour of two Iraqi women, Amal Al-Khedairy and Nermin Al-Mufti, arranged by FOR (the Fellowship of Reconciliation) and sponsored by a number of academic as well as nonprofit institutions. Azam and I had the privilege of hosting them when they came to Connecticut. I recollect the tears that came to Amal's eyes as she showed me the photographs of her most prized possession, *Al-Beit Al-Iraqi*—her family home turned into a cultural center, now destroyed by American bombs. I also remember Nermin's passionate interview with a newspaper on the phone after breakfast the following morning. While most journalists had chosen to leave, she had chosen to stay in Iraq and fight with her pen. I respect and admire her for such courage. Given today's human condition, I find the following verse of the Qur'an enlightening:

> Call unto your Sustainer humbly, and in the secrecy of your hearts. Verily, He loves not those who transgress the bounds of what is right: Hence, do not spread corruption on earth after it has been so well ordered. And call unto Him with fear and longing: Verily, God's grace is ever near unto the doers of good. (7:55–56)

Human Place in the System of Nature

We humans seem to have forgotten our role as God's viceregent on earth as mentioned in the Qur'an:

> Behold, thy Lord said to the angels: "I will create a viceregent on earth."
> *They said:* "Wilt Thou place therein one who will make mischief therein and shed blood? Whilst we do celebrate Thy praises and glorify Thy holy (name)?"
> *He said:* "I know what ye know not." (2:30)

As we embark into the new century, this *ayat* (sign) of the Qur'an provides grounds for reflection. One starts to realize the tremendous responsibility our Creator has placed on us. One is humbled by the honor and embarrassed at the collective injustice we have done to this task. We have become the most violent specie on earth. We have caused more death, destruction, and suffering than any other specie. In the guise of *civilization,* we have colonized and destroyed traditional societies and values all over the globe. There is a lot we could have learned from those native cultures. One finds respect for the land that provides us sustenance, the plants, the wildlife, and our fellow human beings as the core values of many native cultures that are on the brink of extinction today. Human history has seen the emergence of civilizations via integration of cultural systems, and also has seen their annihilation via cultural disintegration and subjugation of societies. Integration of civilizations can be powerfully creative, allowing each to learn from the other. However, when the weaker societies are exploited by the powerful, as has been the colonization experience, humanity is the ultimate loser.

As the finest marvel of all creation, human beings possess *intelligence* and *free will.* These gifts require us to recognize our responsibility toward the rest of the creation and then to act in awareness of this. As God's viceregents on earth, it becomes incumbent upon us to protect its ecosystems and not to plunder them. As all creation is a manifestation of Divine Love and Mercy, so should love and mercy be the essence of our interaction with the rest of the creation.

The Qur'an repeatedly emphasizes the delicate balance (*Al-Mezan*) placed in nature by the Creator. As I look around, I see loss of that balance everywhere. This balance extends not only to our interaction with other human societies, but also with our environment. The concept of balance and harmony in nature, as well as respect for all life, is present in almost all the major world religions. Yet, most adherents of these religions, including Islam, seem to have collectively ignored this great responsibility. For instance, the Qur'an views animals as individuals and communities in their own right:

> Seest thou not that it is Allah Whose praises all beings in the heavens and on earth do celebrate, and the birds (of the air) with wings

outspread? Each one knows its own (mode of) prayer and praise, and Allah knows well all that they do. (24:41)

There is not an animal (that lives) on the earth, nor a being that flies on its wings, but (forms part of) communities like you. Nothing have We omitted from the Book, and they (all) shall be gathered to their Lord in the end. (6:38)

The cruel and inhumane treatment of animals in today's "factory farms," where animals are raised as mere commercial commodities without any show of respect for the sacredness of life, is in sharp contrast to the Qur'anic view that holds all life sacred. I find it very painful to see how we have broken the families and communities of animals by taking away their breeding grounds or by keeping them in cruel captivity for the purpose of human pleasure and profit.

As Dr. Ibrahim Ozdemir so reflectively explains, the ever-sustaining connection among the Divine, human beings, and the rest of the created universe as synthesized by the famous Muslim mystic, Jelaluddin Rumî: For Rumî, a force—a secret energy—lies beneath the spiritual and material world, informing the invisible, progressive change in the universe (humanity included). This force is love, and it originates in God and moves toward God. According to Rumî, love is the positive energy that is responsible for interaction between particles, thus connecting everything with everything else in the universe. So, everything in the universe is interdependent.

Furthermore, says Rumî, since love arouses every sense, increases the power of intuition, and leads to insight, love is superior to intellect in human life. In daily social life, for example, love has an important practical function: It solves disputes, eliminates selfishness and egotism, and draws aside all veils from the mind. Thus, not only is love basic and necessary for a religious and ethical life, but also for the sustainability of the cosmic order. In a nutshell, Rumî presents a deep and comprehensive understanding of the interdependence and interrelatedness of humanity and the natural world. In so doing, he affirms the reality of the world and dignity of all life, particularly of human life, which has become self-conscious and conscious of its divine origin and goal (Ozdemir 2005).

One wonders how much longer our ailing environment can support our extravagant and wasteful lifestyles. According to World Wildlife Fund (WWF) report, toxic chemicals present one of the major global challenges endangering life on earth. Wildlife, people, and entire ecosystems are threatened by chemicals that can alter sexual and neurological development, impair reproduction, and undermine immune systems. Many scientists have concluded that synthetic chemicals have damaged wildlife populations by causing decreased fertility, thyroid dysfunction, behavioral abnormalities, decreased hatching success, and feminization and demasculinization in males (World Wildlife Living Planet Report 2004). In its 2004 Living Planet Report, WWF defines humanity's challenge for the twenty-first century: *To learn to live within the means of the one and only planet that we have.* It confirms that humanity is using 20% more resources than the earth can produce, causing a rapid decline in wild animal populations. It also shows a 40% decline in terrestrial, freshwater, and marine species populations during the period between 1961 and 2000.

As is quite evident from these reports, our environmental track record has been pretty dismal. It underscores our failure to recognize ourselves as an interdependent part of nature's ecosystems that cannot survive in isolation. There is a dire need for revisiting our relationship with the rest of creation and nurturing it with love and compassion, which is the essence of all reality. Only then can we begin to realize our full potential as human beings and start the journey toward the realization of Divine attributes within our essence.

The Journey Continues

As for Azam and me, our lives continue to change as our understanding of the Qur'anic worldview improves. We feel more integrated with the rest of creation and responsible for its maintenance. In our personal lives, we make every effort to minimize our ecological footprint on this planet.

As I write these lines at the dawn of 2006, I pray for our collective consciousness to help restore the balance in nature by changing our focus from materialism to generosity of spirit, from power domination to power equity, and from wastefulness to sustainability. We have plundered the earth's resources, and this century already has started to witness the race for dominating what's left. After oil, it will be water. After earth, it will be space. How many more wars can we afford to fight?

While the hypothesis of survival of the fittest may work for the jungle where animals, devoid of free will, are still bound by the Divine order, it can spell annihilation for human beings as we have the potential to destroy the cosmic order other species cannot touch. There is a need for faith communities to step up to the challenge and start developing a world of love, compassion, and sustainability where all can have a share in nature's resources.

The technological revolution has brought the world communities closer than ever before. I feel the recent human tragedies of 9/11, Afghanistan and Iraq invasions, the Southeast Asian tsunami, Hurricane Katrina, and the South Asian earthquake have deeply touched our collective human consciousness. My faith gives me the hope of the dawn of a new day when the global human community will be able to deploy our collective consciousness toward building a future with benevolence and intent toward common good.

We have a remarkable opportunity today to build bridges of understanding between different communities and cultures through mutual respect and acceptance. This understanding can help us enrich our own lives, faiths, and cultures.

> The angel is free because of his knowledge,
>   the beast because of his ignorance.
> Between the two remains the son of man to struggle (Rumi 2000).

15

Muslim Women between Dual Realities

Rafia Zakaria

In a recent talk about her book *Looking Like the Enemy,* Kate Matsuda Grunewald recounted advice given to her by her mother while their family was in a Japanese internment camp at the onset of World War II. Using the magic of memory and the immense pliability of perspective, Grunewald's mother reminded her children that 20 years from now, the reality of their trauma would be defined singularly by how they conducted themselves during their internment. It would not be the helplessness and injustice of their surroundings, but rather the way they responded to them that would be the defining element of their story. As Grunewald's account demonstrates, we are indeed incapable of controlling the ebb and flow of life's bounty and misery. Our helplessness—at the vagaries of fate—does not, however, implicate our victimhood. It is in this interpolation of perspective, in the confrontation with the inexplicability and often unexpectedness of circumstance, that being a Muslim has sustained me.

In the Beginning . . .

When my paternal grandfather wrote my name for the first time on my birth certificate, he wrote "Dr. Rafia." No girl in our family had ever been a doctor, and it was his hope that this newest addition to his family, his first grandchild, would venture into a new sphere of achievement. My grandfather, whom I called "Pappa," also was the first person who introduced me to Islam. A few hours before he wrote those fortuitous words on my birth certificate, he had recited the *azan,* or the Muslim call for prayer, into my newborn ears. This was my initiation into faith, my entry into the world as a Muslim child. The significance of these two events surrounding my birth in many ways has defined my life. Faith and ambition always have been, and continue to be, intertwined almost inextricably in my life and have sustained and also challenged me in innumerable ways. Pappa never saw a contradiction with me being an independent Muslim woman who would chart new territory, and it is this knowledge, signified so elementally in the very first moments of my life, that has sustained me in times when circumstances and society seem to hold otherwise.

I was born into a Pakistan that was struggling with its relationship with Islam. Not long after my birth, General Zia ul Haque seized power from the democratically elected government of Zulfikar Ali Bhutto and imposed military rule on the country. In the ensuing decades, General Zia ul Haque would use Islam to try to gain legitimacy for his dictatorship. The *Zina* and *Hudood* ordinances, against which I would struggle as a woman, were introduced into law soon after I was born. They, along with the *Qisas* and *Diyat* ordinances and the *Qanun-e-Shahadat,* were defining the life of the Muslim woman in a way that was very different from the way my own family conceptualized my rights.

Pappa and the rest of my family had been in Pakistan only for a few decades when my twin brother and I came into this world. Unlike the millions of Muslims who came to Pakistan soon after Partition in 1947, my own family did not move to Karachi until the early sixties. My father, born and raised in Bombay, came to Karachi as a young boy of 14 and paved the way for the rest of the family, who would follow him. My paternal grandparents, along with my three aunts, Farida, Fauzia, and Razia, did not join him until he was 16. The Karachi to which they emigrated was one drastically different from the city of 14 million that I know today. As a child, I remember fondly all the times my father would point out the apartment on Somerset Street in downtown Karachi that they first moved into as a family recently arrived from Bombay. As a child of the suburbs, living in a villa ensconced amid lawns and fruit trees, it was especially wondrous for me to imagine living downtown amid all the hubbub and action.

My paternal grandfather came from a deeply religious family, and the mystical traditions of his religious upbringing played an integral part in my everyday life as a child. Pappa's father in India had been an adherent of the Sufi order of *Khwaja Moinuddin Chishti*, and religious practice in our home continued many of the Sufi traditions that had been a part of their religious practice in India. On certain special days, my twin brother and I, along with the rest of the family, would sit in the special formal living room on a sparkling white sheet. The adults would use dried nuts laid in the center of the sheet to repeat special prayers. These special prayers were written in special calligraphic form that also mandated how many times each was to be repeated. As a child, I remember what a struggle it was to sit quietly as my parents and grandparents picked up a handful of nuts (which were specially cleaned and used only for the purpose of counting prayers) and set them aside as they finished saying the prayer. As is the custom with many Sufi liturgical traditions, the repetition of prayers had special meditative significance. As I grew older and was able to participate in the *khatam*, I discovered the deep inner solace that an afternoon spent in prayer could provide. The most magical part of these special days was that at the end of the afternoon and after *Maghrib* (sundown prayers), my grandmother would light 12 little oil lamps to commemorate the special day. I would spend hours staring at the special silver lamps arranged on a silver tray sitting on the table in our formal living room. Even late into the night, I would find excuses to go downstairs so I could see which of the lamps stayed lit through the night. After lighting the lamps and *Maghrib* prayers, the whole family would sit down to a special meal of beef and lentil curry that my grandmother had cooked earlier. Often, the dinner conversation revolved around how the day would have been commemorated in the native Bombay. My grandmother often told stories of how as a young bride in my grandfather's family she would have to cook this special meal *every* Thursday for at least 30 to 40 people rather than every few months as we did in Karachi.

The experience of migration and the continuation of tradition in a new land was thus a constant facet of my family life in Karachi. On my father's side, we were the first children actually born in Pakistan. Our childhood narratives, told at dinner tables and over tea, thus dwelled mostly on memories of Bombay, which my father missed sorely. For me, Karachi and Pakistan were the only homes I knew, and I remember many times interjecting and insisting that it was *Karachi*, and not Bombay, that was the best city in the world. At other times, we both whined to our elders about how we were tired of listening to stories about Bombay. The sour relations between India and Pakistan, and the fact that in school we were being raised on a steady diet of nationalism, probably added significantly to our consternation at our families' constant nostalgia about what was the "enemy" nation.

If my father's side of the family lived in memories of India, the maternal side had yet another set of memories and past lives coloring their conversations. Unlike my father, my mother was born in Karachi and had been raised there, yet she, too, had lived in a satellite immigrant culture of a different sort. My maternal grandmother is Persian and met my maternal grandfather in Pune, India. The circumstances of this meeting, between my beautiful, liberal grandmother whose family had been part of the *Qajar court* in Iran and my grandfather who came from a strict bourgeois Indian Muslim family, has been a family mystery for decades. The fact that they married out of love, rather than the family-arranged marriages that are a norm in my family, was so scandalous that my grandmother has vowed to keep it a secret until she dies. Despite much coaxing and prodding, she has chosen to keep the secret to this day.

My maternal grandmother raised her four daughters to be *Shia* Muslim. True to her Iranian heritage, she taught not just her own children but also us grandchildren to celebrate *Nauroze*, the Persian New Year, as well as the Muslim celebrations of *Eid-al Fitr* and *Eid-al Azha*. My mother's childhood stories paint a picture of a home that was built quite like a microcosm of Iran. My *Nani's* (maternal grandmother) brothers and sisters followed her to Karachi, and my mother's life as a child was filled with the garrulous and often rambunctious laughter of her extended family. Her mother spoke Farsi to her brothers and sisters, and whenever my own mother got angry at us, she berated us in Farsi. Thus, sadly, my own Farsi vocabulary is limited to words like cow, donkey, lazy girl, and the like.

Interspersed so heavily with a cornucopia of cultures, migration, and the carrying of traditions to new lands, thus formed the most indelible memory of my childhood. Nostalgia and the mixing of here and there, old and new, and familiar and unfamiliar was the perpetual feature of the stories, conversations, discussions, and arguments that I heard every day. The richest part of these varied traditions was that I saw, from the very beginning, that Islam formed a central precept that was interpreted in many different ways by the traditions of each culture. My *Nani* and *Dadi* spoke different languages, wore different clothes, and cooked different food, but they prayed at the same time every day as daily life paused with the cry of the muezzin announcing the time of prayer. The varied languages of Islam and the relevance of each in appreciating the richness of Muslim culture formed an essential part of my understanding of what Islam meant to me. My mother taught me to say the ritual prayer of purification in Farsi; I learned to say my five prayers in Arabic; and when I spoke to Allah in my own personal prayers, it was always in Urdu. This constant negotiation between the differences of approaches that never compromised the unity of belief would sustain me in later years as I found myself confronted with the challenge of reconciling my faith with yet another cultural context.

When I was five years old, my twin brother and I had our traditional *Bismillah* ceremony. My memories of the event focus on the fact that I was very excited to wear a *shalwar kameez* for the very first time along with pink shoes and heels. Pappa sat us on his lap, and we read *Bismillah-hir-Rahman-ur-raheem* (In the name of Allah, the beneficent and merciful) from a large and imposing Koran that was only removed from a special cabinet for special occasions. The event marked the beginning of our Koranic education. In the weeks following, our family hired a *Maulvi Saheb* from the local neighborhood mosque to come and teach us the Koran. Every afternoon after that, we would be summoned by the doorbell that would ring at 3:00 p.m. sharp to go down into the dining room with our Korans. These 3:00 p.m. lessons were preceded by a hurried search for a cap (for my brother) and a *shalwar* and *dupatta* (for me). I was still too little to wear anything but the dress of my school uniform, but for Koran lessons I had to find a scarf and *shalwar*. After a hurried *wudu* (cleaning ritual before prayer), which probably fell far short of the thorough cleaning it was meant to be, we would rush down the marble staircase of our home to the dining room where Maulvi Saheb would be waiting. Our Maulvi Saheb, who was from the *Nakhshandi* School that is found in many parts of the Muslim subcontinent, was a kindly man who looked much like a young Santa Claus. I found out soon after our lessons began that he also was the muezzin in our neighborhood mosque. Every time after that, whenever I heard the *azan*, I imagined my Maulvi Saheb ascending a tall staircase up to the minaret and belting out the melodious call to prayer. Of course, I learned later that the *azan* is actually spoken in front of a microphone in the mosque building, but nevertheless the fantasy of our Maulvi Saheb ascending the minaret of the *masjid* never loses its allure.

One of the most cherished memories of my childhood and early girlhood are those of *Ramzan*. In Karachi, as in most Muslim countries, life comes to a sort of standstill in this holy month that Muslims devote to fasting. As a child, I remember always begging my mother to allow us to fast when *Ramzan* came around. Sometimes she would relent and let us believe that we were fasting. She would tell us after she gave us breakfast that we were now fasting. Then at lunchtime, she would say, "Okay, you have had half a fast. That is really good. Allah loves little children who try to fast," but then she would add, "A half fast is almost as good as a whole fast . . . why don't you eat a little something now?" This would go on until *we* relented and ate lunch. We were perhaps seven or eight years old when we actually kept our first *roza* (fast) and had our official *roza khushai* (celebration of the first fast). It was July in Karachi, and I remember spending what seemed like an interminably long day in my parents' air-conditioned bedroom watching cartoons.

Ramzan evenings continue to be the most festive time in Karachi. Every day, a few hours before sundown, the streets fill up with vendors selling every form of treats and delicacies that one can imagine.

Many of these, like piping hot *jalebis*, spicy *dehi baras*, sweet *ras malai*, and delicious kebabs are available only during *Ramzan*. In addition to the food sold in the streets, we and many of our neighbors would cook delicacies and exchange them during *Ramzan*. Little children bearing plates of food are often seen doing the rounds of Karachi neighborhoods a few hours before *Iftar*.

After *Iftar*, the gorging begins and often people don't stop eating again until *sehri* (dawn) when the next fast begins. The routine of the entire country changes during *Ramzan*, and shops shut during the fasting day hours and stay open late into the night. The highlight at the end of the month is of course *Eid*, and I remember waiting eagerly on *Chand Raat* (the night of the moon sighting) to see if the *Shawwal* moon would be sighted, and we would have *Eid* the next day.

Girlhood in Karachi

Like my mother and aunts, I was sent to the Mama Parsi Girls Secondary School in Karachi. The school was established in 1918 during the British Raj for Karachi's minority Zoroastrian population. Being from Iran, and hence very familiar with Zoroastrian culture and tradition, my *Nani* had chosen to send my mother and her sisters there. I followed in their footsteps. The Mama School I went to, however, now had a majority Muslim population, and our school day began, like all other schools in Pakistan, with an assembly devoted to saying Arabic prayers from the Koran. Dressed in the pristine white of our school uniform, with the brightly colored ties we retained as a relic from the school's British era, young Muslim girls from many different parts of Karachi lined up together.

The morning assembly, however, also was a period of negotiating religious differences. Unlike the majority of school-going children in Pakistan in the early nineties, I went to school with people of different faiths. I had friends who were Zoroastrian and Hindu. During an assembly, the Zoroastrian students would go to a separate assembly in another hall reserved for them. The Hindu students, and there were far fewer of them, stayed with us in our assembly. I think now of what that must have been like for many of my Hindu friends. As a child, and even as a young girl, I did not really pause to think how difficult this must have been. Indeed, this was a time in the late eighties and mid-nineties that I now know was particularly tumultuous for Pakistan's Hindu minority. The *Zina* and *Hudood* ordinances along with draconian blasphemy laws had been passed by the military regime of Zia ul-Haque. These laws, of which I was completely unaware at the time, not only made minorities liable to be tried for blasphemy under pretextual bases, but also prohibited them from political offices and judgeships.

In the sheltered oasis that was our school, however, we remained largely immune from both the religious intolerance that might have been present in other parts of Pakistani society, but also from the political vagaries of the military government. Without a doubt, faith formed an ever-present component of our identities. The Muslim girls, Parsi girls, and Hindu girls all separated during *Islamiat/Hamkara/ Ethics* classes, but that rarely if ever formed an impediment to the construction of lasting friendships and camaraderie. We never did discuss our religious differences, but I would attribute this avoidance to a steady and respectful tolerance rather than a tension-ridden aversion. We celebrated different holidays but were happy to get a day off from school regardless of whose holiday we were celebrating. The fact that at home, in my grandmother's house, we also celebrated the Zoroastrian festival of *Nauroze* impressed upon me the overlap, rather than the exclusionary distinctions, between faith and culture.

My early teen years, however, also were a time when I had to contend with how being a girl did make me different in society. Perhaps being a twin and having a twin brother made me even more attentive to the different social expectations I was now subjected to because of my gender. Puberty also brought religious obligations that had been optional during childhood. Both my grandmother and my mother prayed five times a day. I remember many times being exhorted to pray and dragging myself reluctantly away from a book, magazine article, or television show to do this. We were never punished for not praying, and honestly, with a household routine arranged around prayer times, it usually was not hard to snatch a few minutes and lay my *jai namaz* next to my mother or grandmother.

As my own world revolved around school and the home, my brother's rapidly expanded at puberty. Not only was he, unlike me, allowed to venture about on the streets, but he now was expected, religiously speaking, to go to mosque and pray collectively. At the time, until perhaps my teen years, the Pakistani weekend was Friday and Saturday. Every Friday, my father, brother, and grandfather would go to mosque for the special Friday service. A special meal of fish, rice, and vegetables would be cooked (in keeping with the coastal traditions my father's family brought back from Bombay), and at around noon, the three of them dressed in starched white *kurta shalwars* reserved for Fridays would head out for the mosque. My mother, paternal grandmother, and I would pray at home and wait for the men to return, then serve the afternoon meal. We could hear the Imam's *khutbas* from the mosque in our home, but honestly, I don't ever remember us actually attempting to listen to it. After *Jumaa,* we would all spend a lazy afternoon watching television or reading.

Negotiating the differences that my gender implicated also demanded the confrontation of certain challenges that I struggle with to this day. One of the most difficult of these was when my paternal aunt's husband took a second wife. I did not know much about the theological debates surrounding polygamy at the time, but I did know that it was allowed in Islam. My aunt at the time had been married for several years and had not had any children. Her husband's reason for taking another wife was that he wanted children and since she didn't seem to be able to conceive, he would have to take a new wife. The day she came to our house crying is etched in my memory because I had never seen her in such a state before. She stayed in my grandparents' room for days crying endlessly. I learned from snatches of conversation, which I overheard while pretending to do my homework in the next room, that both Pappa and my father, who now supported the household, wanted her to divorce him and to stay in our house instead. I remember thinking, as children perhaps in their naïveté are apt to do, how exciting it would be to have another member of the family.

But my aunt did not choose to stay. She chose to go back to her husband's home regardless of the fact that he had just celebrated another wedding with another woman. His relatives had welcomed this new woman into their midst, and she had been settled on the ground floor of the two-story home in which she lived with her husband. At the time, I remember being utterly baffled by her choice. I could not understand why she would choose to live with the man who had so blatantly disrespected her, betrayed her, and broken her heart. In retrospect, and now as a woman I realize that I did not evaluate the dynamics of her choice as she did. In many ways, her choice was between two dependencies: She could stay with us and be dependent on a retired father and a brother who already had the responsibility of supporting his own family or return to what was socially considered her "rightful" home and bear the ignominy of being one of two wives. Her choice was not an easy one, and perhaps she chose what she felt would be the least burdensome of the two on others.

The discussions of the *souten* or "other woman" that took place in hushed tones among the women of the family are instructive to consider now as I try to explain to many Westerners how Muslim women understand what seems to the West as a plain and simple case of religiously mandated oppression. These discussions always focused on the injustice of the man who had done such a thing and of his relatives who had supported him and, ultimately, the woman who had so unthinkingly ruined the home of another. Often, they would talk of how the verse in the Koran allowed four wives only under conditions that were practically impossible, emphasizing "only if ye are to be able to do justice among them." Since everyone knew that such justice was impossible, they saw the act as individually and socially contemptible rather than religiously mandated.

The repeated focus on the evil of the woman herself, and the female relatives who had actually "arranged" the match, also is telling in that my grandmother as well as my own mother blamed other women for the situation as much as they blamed the man himself. Never once did I see my aunt blame Allah for the circumstances with which she was faced. If anything, she used her faith and her belief that Allah would ultimately provide her with justice to help her through that difficult time. Indeed, she often says now that Allah did provide her with justice since her husband was unable to have any children even with his second wife.

I came of age thus with an understanding of Islam as not merely a set of rules that mandated behavior or imposed requirements of prayer and fasting, but rather as a source of deep spiritual strength that would sustain me in times of trouble. I lament the limitation in public discourse, both in the Muslim world and otherwise, in understanding Islam. It is believed that Islam is limited to the performance of prayers, the wearing of *hijab*, or the rejection of alcohol. As a Muslim woman, my guiding principle is the moral imperative of *adl*, or justice, that is at the center of the Islamic understanding of morality. It is this guiding principle, and my staunch belief that Allah never intended for religion to be used to perpetuate injustice on anyone, especially women, that sustains me in my work as a human rights activist.

Muslim in America

I remember standing in an auditorium at my law school at Indiana University two days after 9/11 and saying the words: "Please remember, the acts of 19 extremist Muslims do not mean that all of us Muslims are terrorists. I denounce this act of terror, and I also denounce the attacks on the Islamic center in Indianapolis." September 11 thrust me and many other immigrant Muslims in America into the public spotlight. Suddenly, our faith was under scrutiny and our beliefs analyzed as if they bore some secret ignored clue to the terror that had been unleashed upon American soil. Since then, the course of many lives, including mine, has been indescribably altered by the course of events and the geopolitical actions that have occurred on the world stage.

In my own case, the events following 9/11, most notably the "war on terror" in both the United States and my native Pakistan, have altered the course of my life in an indescribable way. As for most Muslims, it is alarming for me to watch the lurid and grotesque convolution of my faith into an ideology that prescribes violence, hatred, and fundamentalism. Religious extremism was a constant fact of life in Karachi, with New Year's Eve always bringing announcements from the *Ahle Sunnat* that all revelers would be shot dead and concerts cancelled because of bomb threats. However, never once were these ever-present aspects of religious extremism equated with the essence of Islam. The gravest and most devastating cost of 9/11 to American Muslims was that we were suddenly perceived as the enemy living on American soil.

The months and years immediately following brought other personal costs and challenges also. Not long after 9/11, my brother, who had just arrived in the United States from Pakistan, began to be visited by the FBI who insisted that they "just wanted to talk." My brother, who had never once in his life had any dint of religious extremism, suddenly became a suspect. I remember him, living at the time with another aunt who had migrated to Chicago, calling me, "the law student," to ask for help against these visits. Not only did they visit him, but they also made sure that everyone at his place of employment knew exactly whom they were. My brother, newly arrived from Pakistan and working desperately to take his USMLE exams, was terrified that he would have no recourse if he was fired and had to go back home to Pakistan without a job and with no hope of return.

As a law student, I began to focus my work on precisely this question. Much to my alarm, I saw law after law, such as the infamous US Patriot Act, passed into law. As a noncitizen, I had to tell my brother that he truly had no rights under American law to protest against these "friendly visits." What I did not tell him bothered me even more and kept me awake night after night. Under the US Patriot Act, not only could he not protest against such "visits," but also he could even be arrested without any probable cause and placed in detention for weeks without ever seeing a judge. I stayed awake at night thinking about scenarios of what I would do if, on one of these visits, the FBI simply took my brother away. I would have no way of finding him. What would I tell my parents?

In addition to the fear of losing my brother at the hands of an increasingly frightening legal regime, I was facing additional battles in my own life. I had come to the United States as a young bride of 18 after being married to a distant relative. After years of an abusive relationship, I now was faced with the choice of either abandoning law school or leaving my marriage. I was torn between the ideal of the Pakistani wife that my in-laws and husband expected me to be and the reality of the ambitious woman that I was. Again and again, I ran into the problem of not fitting into the stereotype

of the obedient and compliant wife that all Pakistani girls were supposed to represent. I struggled with this desperately; I had been
raised in Pakistan, but had never had my ambition thwarted because of my identity as a Muslim or a Pakistani. Suddenly, my
husband and in-laws told me that being a Muslim and being a Pakistani implied an abridgment of choices that I had never considered. I was to do what my husband commanded. These were the
hardest, most difficult times of my life and where I struggled most
every day between my own expectations and my duties toward my
husband and family.

During my second year of law school, the situation became so
dire that I found myself with my two-year-old daughter in a shelter
for abused women in a small town in Indiana. It was at this lowest
point in my life that I relied most on Allah to protect my child and
me. Nothing in my upbringing had ever prepared me to deal with
this circumstance. This time in the shelter, however, taught me more
about life and being a woman than any other experience in my life.
It was at that time that I saw perhaps the universality of the struggles that women face in life. The women here were white and American, but imprisoned in many ways by the same set of circumstances
that imprisons women in Pakistan in a cycle of dependency. Many
of the women had children, and some did not have the means or
education to leave the abusive relationships they had fled because
they would not be able to support their families on their own. However, there also were others who stayed up late into the night while
their children slept, studying for courses that would allow them to
leave their situations. After I left the shelter I filed for divorce.

Other than the physical challenges of finishing law school and
taking care of my daughter who was still a baby, the divorce imposed existential challenges in terms of my relationship with Islam.
I balked at the reality that American law provided me with more
safeguards and rights than I would have had under Islamic law. The
right of *khula,* which permits a woman to separate from her spouse,
had never been included in my original *nikahnama* when I was
married. Since I had been only 17 at the time, I had not objected or
even realized the implications of this. My family feared that this
would impede my ability to get a divorce. Furthermore, they were

concerned about how I, as a law student, would provide for my child and myself while continuing to live in the United States. Under the stipulations of *Shafii madhab* that my parents and my husband's family came from, the *mahr,* which is the money meant to safeguard the wife in case of divorce, is paid to the woman only if the husband initiates the divorce. Because I had initiated these proceedings, I had no right to support for myself.

As with all things in my life, the circumstances of my divorce imposed the most pressing questions regarding my relationship with Islam. In practical terms, realizing that my *nikahnama* would not impede my divorce, and that my ex-husband would have to pay child support regardless of who had initiated the divorce, was a victory. In terms of my existential relationship with Islam, a faith I held so dear and that formed such an integral and indelible part of my identity, I was in agony. In some ways I felt betrayed by the fact that I was considered less deserving in the eyes of Islamic law than a man. This was the beginning of a journey that continues today in my attempt to unravel how and why Muslim women came to have the status they do in the eyes of Islamic law.

The experience of personally going through this questioning of faith, and this reckoning between me and a God whom I loved and believed in completely, prompted me to begin to research and write on the issues facing Muslim women both in the West and my native Pakistan. Today as I continue to research the development of Islamic law, I realize both the potential of egalitarianism and the ossification of legal structures that were once dynamic and progressive. I realized also that my sense of betrayal came not from being less than a man in the eyes of Allah, but was due to the weight of legal tradition that consistently had been interpreted to serve patriarchal interests. The weight of this tradition, which possesses such intimidating legitimacy in the eyes of Muslims, is the ultimate challenge for Muslim women of my age. We are faced with the formidable challenge of unraveling the patriarchy inherent in this tradition without repudiating it in its entirety. And we must do this against the backdrop of a world that is intensely and often unthinkingly critical of Islam.

It is this dual reality of advocating change within Islam, but also defending Islam from the increasingly xenophobic impulses of a neoconservative agenda bent on painting all Muslims as the enemy, that defines my life today. It is a difficult journey because current geopolitics and the use of human rights to justify military invasions means that many women and men who agree with our cause are silenced because they believe that highlighting the issues within our culture is to automatically support these anti-Pakistan and anti-Muslim agendas. In terms of women's rights, we are constantly bombarded with the reality of women who have faced gang rapes, acid abuse, and rapes by law enforcement—all of whom are denied legal recourse. Yet, speaking publicly about these issues involves navigating a complex set of power hierarchies that highlight the injustices faced by women without substantiating equally detrimental orientalist stereotypes that have been used as excuses to devastate so much of the Muslim world.

Ultimately, it is this confounding reality that I believe defines the task of Muslim women today. On one hand is the urgent and imperative need to unravel the misogynistic and patriarchal interpretations of the Koran and Sunna that legitimize legal regimes that treat us unequally. On the other hand is the reality that many Muslim men and Pakistani men also are facing the injustice of being interrogated and marked as suspects in the "war on terror" that sees few limits on the infringement of human rights. We are faced with developing a voice that can advocate for change within our faith and to renounce laws like the *Zina* and *Hudood* ordinances in Pakistan, but also simultaneously defend Muslim men from being categorically and unjustly treated as suspect. In recognizing this reality, I am often saddened by Muslim women who prioritize one of these realities over another. Women such as Ayan Hirsi Ali, the Somali-born Dutch politician, prioritize women's rights but seem to deny the reality of xenophobia and discrimination that faces Muslim men. At the same time, I also lament the scores of Muslim women who, in their defensive attempt to protect Islam from critique, have uncritically accepted even overtly misogynistic symbols of repression as symbols of religiously mandated practice and expressions of Islamic authenticity.

In terms of my activism and my scholarly work, I am committed to exposing this dual challenge and the imperative of acknowledging and recognizing both of these realities. On personal terms, this imposes sometimes agonizing costs. Every time I speak at an event highlighting sexual, legal, or other abuses faced by women in Pakistan, or in other parts of the Muslim world, I am painfully self-conscious of how these narratives might be appropriated by those who have little interest in supporting the cause of justice and empowerment for women around the world. Often, when I teach in college classrooms in the American Midwest, I am confronted with students who, believing the sensationalist propaganda they see on television, unthinkingly and uncritically believe that all Muslims are terrorists and want to kill Americans.

As a Muslim woman living between these realities, I live my faith by working to eliminate both of these myths. My public expression of faith is defined by working against both of these challenges. On a personal front, my faith in Allah and the Koranic prayers, which I have mouthed since I was a small child and have sustained me in the most trying of circumstances, continue to punctuate my life today. Although in the past I may have prayed solely out of duty and a concern for my own salvation, I do so today more aware of the restorative and healing powers of faith. Halide Edib writes in her memoir regarding the innately rhythmic quality of the Muslim prayer: "You bow, you kneel, and your forehead touches the ground. Each movement is a vast and complicated rhythm, the rising and falling controlled by the invisible voices of the several muezzins" (Edib 2005, 72). Today when I pray the pauses in my day reserved for these conversations with Allah provide the regenerative peace that I need to restore my perspective. Whether they are a few snatched moments in the car, between lectures, or repeated with my daughter as I put her to bed, they are a constant reminder of the juxtaposition of the divine with the ordinary, and they sustain me in persevering in a struggle that often seems daunting and interminable.

16

Challenging the Master Frame through Dalit Organizing in the United States

Shweta Majumdar

Caste oppression has long been associated with Hinduism. Although caste-like stratifications are evident among a number of Indian—Christian (Kurien 2004), Muslim (Syed 2002), and Sikh (Khandelwal 2002)—and non-Indian groups (Blauner 1972), oppression of lower-caste people is widely viewed as a practice sanctioned by Hindu religious beliefs. Although there is a lot of significant literature on the Indian caste system, its genesis, its socioeconomic-political basis, its changes (e.g., Dumont 1970; Kaviraj 1991; Kothari 1970; Srinivas 1962), this chapter focuses on one aspect of lower caste experiences. I describe how Dalits, a group marginalized by mainstream Hindus, have been contesting public discourses about their plight. The chapter is not specifically about religious practices, but—much like the process described by Mary Katzenstein (1998) regarding women in the Catholic Church—it is about a marginalized group attempting to create a space on its own terms, to define the sources of its oppression, to name the oppressors, and to seek redress. While the other chapters of the book have been emphasizing individual experiences, this chapter documents the experiences of a group that seeks intervention by secular entities in order to claim its freedom along with one individual's journey of learning.

The genesis of this chapter lies in a personal experience. I was looking through some Web sites on Dalits in the United States when

I encountered a description of Dalit genocide.[1] I shared this discourse with two other Indian-origin sociologists, who were equally surprised to encounter this term. We analyzed the possible reasons for our lack of awareness of such an atrocity. We were uncomfortable because we believed we were or had been reasonably entrenched in progressive politics in India and such news should have gotten to us. Also, the Indian press, because of its sheer numbers and variety, is reasonably free from censorship; we should have heard of any genocide. Upon reflection, we found we had known about the killings reported on the Web site. The uprising of landless peasants—including the Tebhaga, the Dhulia, and the Naxalbari movements in postindependence India—their genesis, and their harsh repression by the state was very familiar to us. We knew about the history of the repression of very large numbers of landless peasants and marginal farmers through a class lens. Among those who were part of this discussion on genocide was an individual whose parent had been persecuted for taking part in the political struggle for the rights of landless peasants and another whose parent had been imprisoned for organizing a student agitation against a caste-segregated hotel prior to independence. Yet, we were still surprised by the discourse. On this Web site, we encountered a new frame: The history we were familiar with was being presented in terms of another facet of the identity of those killed. The people who had been killed were lower-caste and tribal populations, as they were poor, landless, and marginal farmers. These experiences were presented collectively as the Dalit genocide.

Spurred by this curiosity, I decided to delve deeper into the issue. Thus, this chapter summarizes the most pertinent findings and is an attempt to reconstruct the reality from the perspective of those who had shaped it. In the following paragraphs, I provide an overview of the Dalit movement in the United States (henceforth D-USA) to illustrate how ways of representing "reality" can be contested, shifted, and changed. The power to articulate, convey, and shape realities affects how people live. I use material from Dalit Web sites as well as interviews with several leaders of the D-USA to present the discourse and challenges framed by the Dalit movement in the United States. I will conclude by documenting the results of my encounter with the movement.

Dalits: Who Are They?

The term "Dalit" depicts people who are broken, scattered, crushed, and destroyed. The term was first used by social reformer Jyotiba Phule in the nineteenth century and gained greater importance and popularity under Dr. B. R. Ambedkar, the chairperson of the committee that drafted the Indian Constitution and the iconic champion of Dalit rights. The simplest four-fold classification of Hindus divides people into four hierarchical, ascriptive categories. The *Brahmins* (priests and scholars) are considered most superior, followed by the *Kshatriyas* (rulers and soldiers), the *Vaishyas* (traders and merchants), and the *Sudras* (agriculturalists). Dalits are the people assigned to the lowest caste. In real life, there are hundreds of castes, and the exact status of each group is dependent on local political, social, and cultural conditions (Kothari 1970; Srinivasan 1962). Only a handful of Dalits have been able to take advantage of the educational and job opportunities in independent India. The majority continues to languish under repressive circumstances, including the effects of untouchability, in their everyday lives.

The Dalit Movement: From India to the United States

The Dalit movement developed in India prior to independence, but the present movement has emerged as Dalits realized that state-mandated attempts to provide "positive discrimination" structures for them have failed to address the marginalized condition of their lives. In the words of a renowned Dalit scholar, Kancha Illaiah:

> [The] Nehruvian state did this through the process of brahminization of the state structures, which ensured that the so-called secular state became the private property of the brahminical castes . . . the Nehruvian state structure resisted the entry of the Dalitbahujans even through reservations, their entry being described as the degeneration of the system. (1999, 272)

During the 1970s, the followers of the Dalit Panther movement in the state of Maharashtra in India named themselves after the Black Panther movement in the United States and began to mobilize the "untouchables." The group named themselves Dalit to actively and consciously reject derogatory and paternalistic terms, such as *Dasa* (the slave), *Raksasa* (the demon), and *Harijan* (children of God) or untouchables, used by non-Dalits.[2]

The rise of the Dalit Panthers in Mumbai in 1972, and a militant Dalit struggle in Bihar under Naxalite leadership, marked the explosion of a new anticaste movement throughout the country, giving birth to organized movements and growing to encompass the other "backward castes" or *bahujans*. The fight was often for reservations of seats in the spheres of education, government jobs, or politics. At other times, it was against various forms of atrocities and social ostracism.

As the Dalit movement was developing in India, the United States rescinded the race-based ban on Indian migration. Under the provisions of the new immigration rules, highly educated scientists, engineers, and doctors, *including professionally trained Dalits* (among the few who had benefited from the positive discrimination efforts of the Indian government), were encouraged to migrate to the United States. The migration of Dalits from the 1960s onward is viewed as the "new" exodus.[3] The Dalits who came to America faced few constraints on their social mobility because of their caste, although they were subjected to the same race-based marginalization that affected other Indians. Almost invisible in the American mainstream, except as Indians, nonetheless they had a chance to attain goals they always aspired to (Sahoo 2005). Placed within a new structure of opportunity, the Dalits did not sever connections with their communities, which still were subjected to the inequities of the caste system in India.

While caste is less relevant in mainstream American life, sections of Hindu Indians continue to uphold caste-based barriers. They renew caste-based rituals (performed by Brahmin priests) and customs (such as sacred thread ceremonies for upper-caste males) in temples, and, as is evident from the matrimonial columns in newspapers, actively discourage inter-caste marriages with people of lower castes (Anjana Narayan provides other examples of this caste-based marking of boundaries in her chapter). The new stream of Dalit migrants in the United States—professional, educated, self-aware, and mobile—began to organize as voices for Dalits transnationally. The focus was not on reforming religion along the lines tried earlier by Phule or Vivekananda or the Brahmos in India (see, e.g., Forbes 1996), but on reclaiming the status of Dalits as human beings.

D-USA formed Volunteers in Service to India's Oppressed and Neglected (VISION) in 1975. They aligned with the Black Panther movement in the United States and highlighted their plight, which became the symbol of Dalit and black unity.[4] The efforts of the D-USA became even more visible in the late 1990s when they successfully placed "racism" against Dalits on the center stage of many international conferences. In October 1998, the first international conference of Dalits was held in Malaysia. Then again in 2001, with Amnesty International and Human Rights Watch, they worked to raise the profile of "casteism" at the United Nations' World Conference Against Racism in Durban. Their argument was primarily that casteism is illegal under a UN convention that bans racial discrimination. In response, the UN yielded to the long-standing demand of Dalits and brought out a charter noting that Indian casteism/untouchability is equivalent to racism (Human Rights Watch 2001b). This positive outcome, the ability of a marginalized group to place its cause on an international "map," is an outcome of the frames they used to mobilize people in their support.

Process of Internationalization through Framing

The process of bringing the Dalit cause to the international stage has involved the use of two frames that already had roots in the United States. The main frame equates casteism and racism. The second, overlapping frame uses the language of genocide to describe the history of oppression. Framing, as Entman suggests, is a way "to select some aspects of a perceived reality and make them more salient in a communicating text, in such a way as to promote a particular problem definition, causal interpretation, moral evaluation, and/or treatment recommendation" (Entman 1993, 52; see also

König 2006). For D-USA, changing the frame of the discourse and bringing international scrutiny to their plight were the first steps in seeking redress.

Fitting into the Racism Frame

The race-caste equation is the most recurrent and potent imagery used by the D-USA. Several Dalit Web sites use imagery of racism to convey the oppression encountered by Dalits. Even though the earlier description of Dalit migration in the United States detailed the process of dilution of caste barriers in the mainstream (and the maintenance of barriers within the ethnic group) along with the experience of racism in the mainstream, such distinctions have little relevance for the Dalits themselves. By framing caste in terms of race and by using the symbols and imagery associated with racism, Web sites seek to underscore their experiences of the dehumanization that is intrinsic to and embedded in the connotation of racism. For example, the Web site "Dalitstan," meaning a place for Dalits, depicts the centrality of the imagery. The introductory message on the Web site says:

> The Dalitstan organization is a human rights organization working for the upliftment of Dalits, the **Black Untouchables** of India. These form one of the most oppressed ethnic groups in the world, enduring the 2000-year **Sudra Holocaust**. (www.dalitstan.org)

Recurring words, such as *apartheid, negro-Dalits,* and *black untouchables,* invoke images of racism in the minds of a more international audience. In all instances, the category of Sudra used in the ancient texts is framed and translated into the specific category of "negroid race." For instance, the Web site asserts, "If a **Sudra Negroid** remembered verses from the 'holy' Vedas, he would be sawed alive," and then goes on to authenticate the assertion by quoting Gautama Dharma Sutra 12.6: "If he [a Sudra] remembers them [Vedic verses], his body shall be split in twain" (www.dalitstan.org).

In another instance, the Web site says: "The life of a **Sudroid Negro** is, as per the 'holy' Hindu law books, lower than that of an animal," and in illustration cites, "the Vaishya and Sudra are not allowed to hear it (the Vedas), much less to pronounce and recite it. If such a thing can be proved against one of them, the Brahmana will drag him before the magistrate, and he is punished by having his tongue cut off" (www.dalitstan.org).

Clearly two things are achieved here. What is most evident in the process of phrasing and rephrasing is the active process of "framing" the situation of Sudras in terms that resonate with the Western mainstream. Equally important, the *ideology* of oppression is linked directly to Hindu texts.

Among scholarly and activist circles, the conflation of caste and race has been a source of heated debate in India and the United States. T. Rajshekar's "Dalit: The Black Untouchables of India," published in 1979 and reprinted in 1987, served as the center stage for the controversy. Rajshekar claimed that Dalits are part of the African diaspora and the first settlers on the Indian subcontinent. "It is said," he writes, "that India and Africa was one land mass until separated by the ocean. So both the Africans and the Indian Untouchables and tribals had common ancestors and, consequently, similar phenotypic makeups" (quoted in Prashad 2001a, 190). Even though one could argue that the geological continuity of Africa and India predates the evolution of humans by several million years, the substantive point here, the point that resonates with the audience, is the commonality of the two groups in their experience of marginalization. There is an added implication of Dalits as indigenous people in Rajshekar's work, which creates the space for linking Dalit claims to those of indigenous groups globally.

The issue of whether caste is equivalent to race has triggered a lively debate in the scholarly community. Reflecting upon the social construction of extreme inequality in India, prominent scholars Dipankar Gupta (2001) and Andre Beteille (2001) reject this comparison, saying that the caste structure is peculiar to the Indian system and politicization of terms undermines the struggle for social equality. Gupta argued that the caste system includes multiple hierarchies within itself, and that replicating the bipolar hierarchy implicit in white versus black racism into the Brahmans versus Dalit class divide is an inaccurate way to show the various causes of Dalit marginalization (Gupta 2001; Beteille 2001). Dalit scholars, on the other hand, argue that equating caste to race is true in terms of consequences of discrimination as both groups are subjected to significant misery (Illaiah 1999).

Activists who are engaged in the process of gaining more supportive networks for the cause of Dalits are well aware of this conundrum. Dr. Bhatia,[5] a prominent Dalit activist, reflected during an interview, "Racism is the connotation [that] is easily conveyed to the western culture. The white man or a black man in a western situation can understand and relate to the issue. With the caste system, they may not know how serious or how bad it is."

In a similar vein during an interview, Dr. Sehgal reiterated, "Dalits have to make terms easy for other people to understand, to make them understand like genocide, and you know that's why these people are fighting. You know racism and casteism are two different things, but you have to translate casteism into real . . . [and convey] this is not racism, but it's worse than racism. The moment they understood this fundamental difference that casteism is worse than racism, they immediately included a paragraph in the UN charter against casteism . . . It helped in explaining their plight of the situation in front of those people who don't understand what caste-based discrimination is."

Therefore, in terms of outcome, the racism frame is more effective at gaining Western supporters, who are more powerfully positioned to influence the language and direction of human rights claims at the UN level. The extent of resonance among the Western audience of the race-caste equation can be gauged by its transmission to the media. For example, the British Broadcasting Corporation's news headline captures the dynamism of the process when it announces, "Indian 'apartheid' condemned" (British Broadcasting Corporation News 2001). While the particularities of casteism are lost in this translation, the central issue—of deeply entrenched oppression—remains alive on the international stage.

Fitting into the Frame of Genocide and Holocaust

Linking the Dalit experience to the main international discursive frame on victims of targeted violence and extermination is the overlapping mechanism that has been used by the Dalit movement. Not surprisingly, "genocide" and "holocaust" are frames that are evident on the Dalit Web sites to convey the pain and persecution of Dalits to an international audience. The Dalitstan Web site mentions:

> the **Sudra holocaust** was one of the most devastating events in world history. The indigenous **Sudra negroes** were exterminated in all of the Indus-Ganges valley. (www.dalitistan.org)

The use of terms such as "holocaust" and "genocide" helps to present the plight of the Dalits in terms that are better understood by an international audience. This language also positions the Dalit experience within the structure of the Universal Declaration of Human Rights. The Convention on the Prevention and Punishment of the Crime of Genocide (CPPCG), article 2, defines *genocide* as

> any of the following acts committed with intent to destroy, in whole or in part, a national, ethnic, racial, or religious group, as such: killing members of the group; causing serious bodily or mental harm to members of the group; deliberately inflicting on the group conditions of life calculated to bring about its physical destruction in whole or in part; imposing measures intended to prevent births within the group; and forcibly transferring children of the group to another group. (UNHCHR 1951)

Because the CPPCG does not include caste as a category, linking the Dalit experience to genocide accomplishes a major objective. Appropriation of the term *genocide* evokes heinous images of the Nazi Holocaust, Sudan's genocide, and the Rwandan massacre, and elicits feelings of horror, pity, and sympathy in the minds of the viewers for the victims of the practice. Since the convention mentions racial or ethnic groups, the framing of Dalits on those terms, as "racial or ethnic victims," does the prior work of reframing Dalits as a racial group that has been subjected to genocide.

Just as the caste-is-equivalent-to-race frame has its detractors, the use of the genocide frame also has attracted some criticism. The most persistent criticism is that "genocide" describes attempts to annihilate populations irrespective of class. The debate about Dalit genocide revolves around the issue: Have Dalits been killed on the sole basis of their low-caste status, or has class played a role as well? Critics have argued that without a clear phonotypic identity, upper-class Dalits are not easily identifiable. As Dr. Bhatia said during his interview, "Suppose I go on a train, nobody will know my caste; I am an educated man, I can speak well, I am well dressed; people think I am a Brahmin." Ambiguous last names also make caste less visible. Many last names in India often indicate caste and region, but it is harder to identify regional or caste affiliation for those with last names such as Singh. Some Dalits have changed their last names to avoid the caste-based discrimination they were otherwise likely to face.

The second argument about the fallacy of the genocide allusion among mainstream individuals is that the history of genocide has, typically, clearly pitted one group against another: The Nazis against the Jews, the Hutus against the Tutsis in the Rwandan case, and in former Yugoslavia, the Serbs against the Slavs. In each case, a bipolar relationship of extermination is established. Within the Indian caste structure, the multiple hierarchies of the caste system do not lend themselves easily to the bipolar discourse of oppression. (The argument of losing the particularities of caste discrimination mentioned in the previous section is part of the same argument). Even though Dalit Web sites present the Dalit struggle as one against "brahmanization" of Indian society, Brahmans are, in fact, a small and atypical minority in the state apparatus (Gupta 2001). Often the local struggles and killings are between higher-caste groups (whichever *jatis* make up this block in a locale) and the Dalits, but are not limited to Brahmins. As Dr. Bhatia pointed out, "Dalit men, women, and children are beaten by **landed** caste, jats, the thakurs . . . the Rajputs" (emphasis mine).

The third argument about the inappropriateness of the genocide frame in the mainstream is that genocides typically are acts of extermination condensed into short spans of time. In the Rwandan case, 800,000 Tutsis were annihilated over a period of 100 days in 1994.[6] Nazi Germany victimized close to 6 million Jews in a period of six years during World War II. About 220,000 Sinti and Roma died in the Holocaust within a span of six years.[7] In

1970–1971, 3 million Bangladeshis were killed within a space of six months (see Elora Chowdhury's chapter). In former Yugoslavia, the Srebrenica Massacre in July 1995 claimed the lives of 7,800 to 8,000 Bosnian males.[8] The Dalit Web site attempts to create a similar frame, claiming: "Mass murder and genocide of one million Dalits since the foundation of the Indian Union in 1947" (www .dalitistan.org).

We could argue that these killings have taken place over several decades, and therefore the use of the term *genocide* is inappropriate. However, irrespective of these counterarguments, using the genocide frame—which evokes imageries of brutality in the minds of the Euro-American mainstream—accomplishes the task of getting Dalit victimhood on the international stage. As strategic frames, racism and genocide have allowed Dalit groups to create links with an emerging transnational body of agents (groups, institutions, and policy makers) who are willing to listen to their cause. In the United States, Dalit groups were able to link with antiracism organizations. The collaboration between the Black Panthers and VISION is a culmination of the successful translation of caste into racial terms. Dr. Bhatia says,

> We are actually working through various church groups, human rights groups, civil rights groups, Afro-American groups, trying to educate them saying, "Look apartheid is finished, the apartheid in India is very much alive and thriving. You need to do something."

Also, getting the issues of caste on the UN platforms galvanized a series of NGOs, both at the international and national levels. These NGOs have begun to take interest in the issues related to Dalits and other marginalized sections. Amnesty International and Human Rights Watch regularly report on caste-related issues in their annual reports, keeping up the pressure on the Indian state. Indeed, Human Rights Watch has defined the commonality of caste and race by stating,

> In much of Asia and parts of Africa racism has become coterminous with caste in the definition and exclusion of distinct population groups distinguished by their descent. (Human Rights Watch 2001a)

The intervention of the United Nations Human Rights Commission, the World Bank, and other international and national institutions for maintenance of human rights of Dalits and other deprived sections collectively expresses the rising global awareness of the despicable and dehumanizing reality of casteism/untouchability.

Religion, Life Circumstances, and Change: Assessing the Outcome of Framing

The increased visibility of Dalits not only has mobilized international support, but also has redefined the contentious relations Dalits have shared with Hinduism. Given the rising importance of religion and fundamentalisms in the world today, it becomes imperative to flesh out this relationship. Though all Dalits are not Hindus, and several Dalits have converted to Christianity, Islam, Buddhism, and Jainism to protest against Hinduism, the genesis of caste-based oppression is linked to the history of Hinduism. Consequently, Dalit agitation against caste oppression is mostly framed as one against "brahmanical forces."

Dalits typically have undertaken a two-pronged strategy. They have framed their discourse to challenge "traditional Hindu religious ideology," and they have worked with marginalized groups in other religions to open up spaces for religious practice. In New York City, for instance, D-USA has found a welcoming space in the Sikh Guru Ravidas temple based on their common marginalization based on caste. The support of the Sikhs of the Guru Ravidas temple has been valuable assets in publicizing their cause as well.

Within Hinduism—unlike religions with single books in which reinterpretation of words and phrases can open up spaces for marginalized groups and indeed locate the marginalization in social customs, such as the discussion on whether the Koran supports gender hierarchies—reinterpretations of texts is a less viable strategy for Dalits to claim their freedoms. For every book that decries inhuman customs, there are others that can be selectively deployed by the oppressors to legitimize their practices.

Groups have opposed the rising power of the Dalits in different ways. Some continued to rationalize caste-based oppression as "traditional Hindu ideology." For example, Swamy (2006) writes that several Hindu supremacist organizations objected to including Dalit human rights as an agenda at the 2001 UN Conference Against Racism in Durban, South Africa, by arguing that "the abolition of the caste system would constitute a violation of Hindu human rights." Others have sought to reclaim and "reconvert" Dalits to Hinduism.

On another note, unlike the racism frame in the United States that includes indictments of capitalism and economic-political relations as a source of social hierarchies (such as in the writing of W. E. B. Dubois), the current approach of emphasizing victimization based on cultural and religious ideologies without an equally strong emphasis on economic relations is of concern to many scholars and has real-life implications for Dalits. For instance, in a personal interview, a leading Asian American academic in the United States reflected on how the material conditions of Dalits were unlikely to improve if the emphasis of the discussion—at least in the way in which it is understood in the West—is primarily based on cultural oppression. Without a significant emphasis on the capitalistic structures that intersect with cultural hierarchies to oppress Dalits, the solution to Dalit victimhood is likely to be seen in terms of cultural change alone.

The Dalit movement in India better articulates this situation. A great deal of the activism in India (often supported by political parties) is about claiming opportunities and resources. The government of India is a target of this movement as Dalits emphasize their claims to reserved seats in education, public sector jobs, and the like. So the thrust of the strategy in India is to use the political institution to claim rights that go far beyond the limits of addressing religious ideologies. It is important to note this as globalization proceeds and older support structures, such as reservations, are under siege through "free market" forces (Falk 1999). Globalization in the 1990s brought with it new uncertainties: The rolling back of state subsidies by the government in India and increased privatization has jeopardized positive discrimination. Without a concomitant emphasis at the international level about these factors that contribute to Dalit oppression, the Dalits might be materially worse off even though their plight is better recognized at the international level.

Last, but not least, what about the Dalit women? Since the international frames are set up in terms of caste (race-linked) binaries and genocide, unlike the discourse in India, the D-USA framing does not, as yet, emphasize the gendered nature of Dalit oppression, especially their sexual marginalization through violence and rape. There is some evidence that this might change. Earlier this year when progressive Indian-American groups challenged the attempts by Hindu fundamentalist groups to change the histories of India taught in the California school system, the issue of making Dalit and gender oppression invisible became a centerpiece of the challenge (see Kausalya 2006). These new conversations might kindle the lower caste/gender oppressions that have been muted in the Dalit challenge thus far.

Paying attention to the Dalit discourse reveals the inherent power structures that set the discursive frames that marginalized groups are often forced to use. Analysis of the conundrum I initiated, questioning why politically progressive people weren't aware of Dalit genocide, reveals the layers of power with which marginalized groups have to contend. Even though Dalit oppression is mostly understood in terms of religious ideology internationally, it is not about "religion" alone. Religious ideology is used as the justification to make invisible the intersecting material and political power structures that uphold such inequalities. The need for fitting into frames prevalent in the United States—an effective strategy for publicizing their plight and gaining supporters—nonetheless leaves little room for presenting the complex sources of their oppression, which arise from the intersections of economic and political structures in India and in the international sphere.

Afterword

This discussion can be concluded at two levels. The chapter outlines the barriers marginalized groups face, and the potential for using the human rights charter in ways that move beyond cultural notions of victimhood. Clearly, the global Dalit movement shows the hollowness of the sacred-secular dichotomy we continue to use in trying to understand living religions. The members of the Dalit movement have opened up a liminal space that foregrounds the ties to Hinduism (the oppressive ideology and social customs) without succumbing to "their place" in it. The emerging Dalit space is one of their own making, reflecting their experience of complex oppressions, even though currently it might be articulated and understood in mostly cultural terms. And the continued existence of the Dalit space challenges us to think about reorienting the master frames through which we think about others, even when we stand in political solidarity with them.

The second level at which I wish to conclude this chapter is at the personal level. The three sociologists engaged in this discussion came from very different backgrounds. I, for one, had grown up in a cultural diaspora in Delhi, India. The second sociologist spent her life in different parts of India, and the third was primarily based in Kolkata. Each one of us prided ourselves in being part of progressive politics including our sympathy for and support of Dalit movements. Yet we had to reorient our knowledge frames as a result of encountering the US-based movements. We were all highly critical of fundamentalist movements in terms of how these affected our lives. Now we were brought face to face with a new dimension of the renewed rejection of Dalits by the Hindu fundamentalists in the United States. We already were well aware of the insidious ways in which Hindutva ideologies are used to brutally oppress poor Dalits; now we had to rethink the connections between caste, race, class, and gender. Do our academic frames (which cast race and caste as oppressive but different systems) take precedence over the interpretation of the Dalit movement? Who speaks for whom? Whose categorization marginalizes whom? These are not questions that I can answer easily; but I can continue to search for answers as I disseminate the voices of people who draw attention to the continuing injustices done to them.

Notes

1. The Web site called Dalitstan.org was accessed between October and December 2005. This Web site is no longer in existence, but the data has been cached. According to unconfirmed Internet sources, certain Hindu groups on

the grounds of hate speech have forced this Web site off the Web. For further details, visit http://en.wikipedia.org/wiki/Dalitstan.

2. Most Dalits consider the term *Harijan* (a term developed by Mahatma Gandhi to reframe their status to indicate they were children of God) a paternalistic euphemism. They feel this term is worse than the British categorization as the depressed castes or the postindependence India's reference to them as the "scheduled castes," because it reduces them to the status of nonadults.

3. The "old" exodus composed of indentured laborers taken by the colonial powers and contractors to different countries. This diaspora is confined to south Asian and African countries (Kumar 2004). From 1870 to 1885, 41.5% of emigrants were from the "low castes" (Brereton cited in Kumar 2004, 114). The "old" exodus during colonial times was a much-favored means to escape high debts and harsh realities of the Indian caste system.

4. It is important to point out that some Dalits have converted to Christianity and there are Dalit movements among Christians in India to claim the rights of lower castes. Equally important, there are mainstream Christian groups in the United States that publicize the plight of Dalits on their Web sites to showcase the inhumane side of Hinduism. The members of the Dalit movement in the US are not Christians. Their primary identification is as Dalits, an acknowledgement of their ties to Hinduism (through oppressive ideologies and marginalizing customs) while creating new independent religious spaces of their own making.

5. Names of all the activists are fictitious.

6. http://en.wikipedia.org/wiki/Rwandan_genocide.

7. http://en.wikipedia.org/wiki/The_Holocaust#Jews.

8. http://en.wikipedia.org/wiki/Srebrenica_massacre.

17

Interpretive Intervention: Religion, Practices, and Resistances

Anjana Narayan

Where knowledge is free . . .
Where tireless striving stretches its arms towards perfection . . .
Where the mind is led forward . . . into ever widening thought and
action. (Tagore 1913b, 20)

Although the current social science literature discusses several aspects of religion, it has traditionally ignored the positive importance of religion and its rituals for women. The authors of these essays complement the existing literature by describing the religious practices, traditions, and beliefs that have had a lasting and beneficial impact on their lives and also have inspired them to pioneer social change and justice.

Although there has been a recent feminist reinterpretation of religious traditions with the emergence of feminist theology and spirituality, this literature has largely focused on the Western Christian tradition (Aquino 1994; Copeland 1996; Gudorf 1994; Reuther 1983). Islamic feminism, which gained popularity in the 1990s, is a relatively recent concept promoted by Muslim women's movements, still contested, and consequently yet to be defined (Abou-Bakr 2001; Barlas 2002; Badran 2002; Mahmood 2005; Majid 2002; Mernissi 1985; Tohidi 2002; Yazbeck et al. 2006). Within Hinduism, regardless of attempts by activists and scholars, such as Vandana Shiva who are engaged in combating patriarchal and imperialist forms of oppression from the vantage point of Hindu spiritual traditions, little attention has been paid to religion as a source of strength to challenge the status quo given the long history of libratory symbolism within the religion (for exception, see Saxena 2004).

Representing this genre of feminist interpretation of religion, the essays in this section describe religion from a personal perspective, particularly as a salubrious yet powerful force that provides the courage and confidence to combat injustice, domination, and oppression and contribute to positive social change within their sphere of influence. Shanthi Rao describes how principles of tolerance and openness within Hinduism have compelled her to understand her fellow human beings and have influenced her activist involvement with a range of social justice issues. Aysha Sayeed illustrates the Quranic worldview of *al-Mezan,* or delicate balance, as an inspiration for her environmental activism, and others like Shobha Hamal Gurung and Rafia Zakaria address the healing power of faith, religious philosophy, and beliefs which continues to provide answers to existential questions at a personal level and offers a guide to living during difficult circumstances.

However, the authors adopt a pragmatic approach and do not present religion as a unanimously liberating experience for all women everywhere. The experiences described in these essays also offer a critique of certain aspects of religions, such as practices and fundamentalist interpretations that stifle women's voices or attempt to curtail basic human rights and liberties. Rafia Zakaria describes how laws, such as the Zina and Hudood ordinances in Pakistan based on patriarchal interpretations of the Quran, have infringed the rights of women, as well as her activist efforts to expose human rights abuses in Pakistan. Shweta Majumdar writes about the Dalits (a group marginalized by Hindus) and the formal activism of the Dalit movement in the United States. Elora Chowdhury describes the violent process through which one version of Islam can be imposed on people and the efforts to combat this through cultural activism based on syncretic folk traditions of the region. And finally, Anjana Narayan explains the susceptibility of educated middle-class Indians in the United States to Hindutva ideologies and the endeavors of a small group of South Asian women to counter such patriarchal and ethnocentric beliefs.

The authors in this section provide a practical and balanced view between a romanticized religion that provides universal liberation and solidarity, and a religion that promotes oppression or intolerance. By rejecting unrealistic extremes, the authors demonstrate a more insightful, critical, and nuanced approach of how their everyday lives are interwoven with the religions they live and practice, and how their religion motivates them in their personal and professional lives. Moreover, these accounts also challenge the modernity-traditionalism dichotomy that was highlighted in the introduction. As will be demonstrated in these essays, the authors rely on their "traditional" values to embark on various forms of mobilization and change. They have been part of domestic violence activism, immigrant rights issues, building grassroots democracy, and civil rights advocacy inspired by their religious values. Furthermore, the authors refuse to fall into this one-dimensional dichotomy, especially given their minority status in the United States. They are advocates of bridges, not boundaries; as Hindus and Muslims, and as scholars and social activists, they tread the middle path between racialized, gendered, and orientalist discourses of the traditional, oppressed woman who needs to be liberated, and the equally constricting fundamentalist rhetoric and religious strictures. Rafia Zakaria describes how she deals with the dual challenge of being accused as anti-Pakistani for publicly speaking against human rights abuse of women in Pakistan and teaching students in US classrooms who believe that all Muslims are terrorists. Similarly, Elora Halim Chowdhury recounts encounters both with Western feminists in academia as well as students in classrooms and their essentialized and static construction of the Muslim woman as universal voiceless victims. Anjana Narayan illustrates, through the California textbook controversy, the challenge of activists and scholars to present a history of India that moves beyond the expected ethnocentricism and racism, yet avoids the idealistic, unblemished India that Hindutva proponents tend to promote. Finally, Shweta Majumdar shows how the conflation of caste discrimination with Hinduism by Dalit activists is being projected by Hindutva groups as a violation of Hindu human Rights.

Overall, the authors express their commitment to transforming the fundamentalist ideologies that propagate subordination, with the awareness that this commitment is not inconsistent with their religions. These essays represent the voices of women who want to maintain the best of their religious traditions, but who are also keen to challenge and change the current fundamentalist discourse, often under daunting conditions.

Finally, much of the literature on social change has focused on more public forms of activism; many of the authors indicate they are associated with formal groups. Equally important are the variety of unobtrusive ways in which women resist practices that outlive their usefulness and usher in change (Katzenstein 1995). These women are change agents; their everyday decisions and choices change the trajectories of lived practices for their whole families. While the essays by Shanthi Rao, Shobha Gurung, and Aysha Saeed talk about charting courses that are different from their mothers' ways of practicing their religion, other essays such as the ones by Anjana Narayan and Elora Halim Chowdhury demonstrate unobtrusive mobilization and discursive activism by autonomous, free-floating women's groups (Katzenstein 1995) who share common ideological objectives. These women create a space for collaborative engagement to change the discourse and meanings of how their religions (and their positions) are being discussed. These different kinds of actions cumulatively build alliances based on humane values taught by different religious traditions and shared histories.

18

Conclusion:
Human Rights, Religions, Gender

Bandana Purkayastha

When the member states of the United Nations passed the Universal Declaration of Human Rights (UDHR) in 1948, it was a revolutionary idea born out of prolonged suffering. On the one hand, the Holocaust of the Jews was a stark reminder of government-sponsored genocide against a minority group. On the other, the prolonged violence by colonial powers against their "subjects," in the guise of civilizing missions and maintenance of law and order, raised significant questions about unfettered political power in the hands of a few states globally. The human rights charter (UDHR Summary 2008), which guarantees civil, political, social, economic, and cultural rights, has been evolving through the efforts of groups worldwide, and through a series of protocols and conventions, to clarify exactly how different kinds of human beings ought to be able to access their rights. For instance, CEDAW, the Convention on the Elimination of Discrimination Against Women, was passed in 1994, many decades after the original UDHR, to address the gender biases of the original UDHR. Overall, the human rights conventions reflect two principles. First, individuals, irrespective of the political regime in which they live, are bearers of rights. Second, because the notion of rights is delinked from the exclusive focus on political systems, entities other than the government (e.g., multinational corporations, mercenaries, and hate-groups) can be identified as violators of human rights.

In recent years, with the increasing anxiety about terrorism, there are several debates about religion and human rights. Since rights are assumed to be matters of states, and religions are supposed to be separate (Bush 2007), most of the discussions about religion and human rights are framed as the negative impact of traditional institutions on modern, secular societies. Yet, as feminist scholarship has long predicted, the authors in this book show the ways in which the worlds of religion and politics overlap. From our perspective, discussions about human rights cannot be understood solely as a matter of "the" secular world. In order to promote a debate on this subject, this concluding chapter presents some major debates on political, civil, cultural, social, and economic human rights, and uses the material from this book to raise some questions about human rights, religion, and gender.

The rhetoric of clashing civilizations, which we quoted at the beginning of this book, encapsulates an important debate on political and civil human rights, religion, and gender. There are questions about the role of "some" religions in promoting violence in the world, including the role of religion in rationalizing violence against women. Do "other" religions force women to live restricted lives as orientalists suggest? An overlapping debate is about cultural rights: whether minority cultural groups should have the right to practice their cultures. Equally important, do Islamist and Hindutva groups' claims about "their" culture count as cultural human rights? Additionally, can we talk about religions when we discuss economic and social human rights? Are there links between people's need for just wages, housing, health care, education, food, and religions?

Religion, Gender, and
Questions of Political and Civil Human Rights

In his study, The International Evolution of Human Rights, Paul Lauren (1998) argues that all the major religions of the world emphasize values and principles that contribute to human rights.[1] All religions lead us to examine who we are as human beings and how we ought to relate to others, especially "whether we have any responsibilities for the well-being of other people in need or pain" (1998, 4). Every chapter in this book on living religions reflects the two religious principles Lauren identified. The idea of human rights and an interconnected humanity is apparent whether the authors carry out their religious practices in temples or mosques, at home, or through secular work. By framing the discussion of religion in more holistic terms—religions as beliefs and expectations *and* religions as they are lived—the religion is not confined to some pristine "sacred sphere." Every chapter in this book demonstrates how the private and public, and the sacred and secular, worlds intersect.

A key debate in the human rights literature is about the role of religio-nationalistic violence, though it is often discussed as violence promoted by core religious principles such as *jihad*. Violence is a staple of most forms of politicized religion since the objective is to force others to do one's bidding. As we point out repeatedly, Islamist terrorists and Hindutva proponents use a continuum of violence ranging from acts of extreme brutality (e.g., killing of hundreds and thousands of people by bombing, flying planes, or driving cars into buildings) to ongoing coercion and extreme control (e.g., restricting women's mobility, their dress, and their habits) and enforcing silence and invisibility on subalterns (e.g., Dalits and women) who dare speak out against their marginalization. And they justify their actions in terms of their "core religious principles." All the authors speak out forcefully against this violence; their reasons for challenging this violence are similar to the framework of UDHR and its conventions. If everyone has the right to life, liberty, and security of their persons (Article 3, UDHR), and everyone is born free and equal in worth and dignity (Article 1, UDHR), then fundamentalist acts that are based on distinctions between "us" and "them" negatively affect the life, liberty, security, and dignity of all persons and violate their human rights. The International Covenant on Civil and Political Rights (ICCPR) forbids propaganda advocating hatred based on religion (and other social criteria); it forbids advocating for wars—whether these are "holy" wars or wars of other kinds. The Convention on Genocide forbids killing people because of their membership in social groups (e.g., Islamist or Hindutva injunctions to kill Muslims, Hindus, Dalits, Americans, or Westerners because they belong to that group). So there are powerful justifications, from a human rights perspective *and* any religious perspective that emphasizes humane-ness and shared humanity, to label and challenge terrorist violence as heinous forms of human rights violations.

A more contentious debate focuses on the mechanisms through which violent acts ought to be controlled. In Richard Wilson's collection of papers on Human Rights in the Age of Terror (2005), many leading human rights scholars support the contemporary efforts to secure nations through the use of mechanisms, such as racial profiling, extra surveillance of some groups, and the suspension of habeus corpus when the executive branch of the government deems it necessary to do so. Other scholars (e.g., Luban 2005; Robinson 2005) point out that many of these mechanisms violate many of the same principles that terrorists violate, including life, liberty, and security of persons, and right to legal representation. And such violations by governments not only target minority groups—Muslims and Muslim-looking groups—these acts also violate the human rights of the entire society by eroding political and civil human rights in the name of security. Several authors, most notably Rafia Zakaria, Aysha Saeed, Parveen Talpur, and Salma Kamal, along with Selina Jamil, Bandana Purkayastha, Anjana Narayan, and Elora Halim Chowdhury, describe patterns of state activities that Gyanendra Pandey (2006) has described as the "violence of the modern." The authors describe how their political and civil human rights, their liberty, dignity, freedom of movement, their freedom of thought, conscience, and religion are violated. Elora Halim Chowdhury's chapter describes a prior history of "modern violence," when mass killings of intellectuals were described by the government as an issue of national security.

Fundamentalist activities introduce many levels of violence against women. Elora Chowdhury and Bandana Purkayastha mentioned genocidal violence in South Asia, where minority women are specially targeted, raped, and killed. As feminist scholars have argued such gendered violence against women is intended to signal the dominant group's hegemonic power over the women's community, because the men in the women's family, community, and nation are not "masculine enough" to protect the women of their own community. Parveen Talpur's description of Mukhtaran Mai's case provides another example, at the community level, of the same process of hegemonic masculinity in action. A key plank of feminist organizing through CEDAW and other conventions is to get governments to recognize such gendered violence as intrinsic aspects of war, ethnic, and community conflicts: to specifically recognize that women's human rights are violated even if they are not combatants themselves. Fundamentalists unleash gendered violence within their communities in other ways. Fundamentalist strictures about the separation of female and male worlds, described in the introduction, violate CEDAW's articles 15 and 16 on equal personhood. Anjana Narayan's description of attempts to rewrite history in ways that make it more homogenized and authoritarian is an example of how competing versions of culture and religion are stifled and controlled. More importantly, all the Dalitstan Web sites, which were a source of Shweta Majumdar's research two years ago, have been forced off the Web.

As Anjana Narayan points out patriarchal, authoritarian agendas also are sustained by community members who may have no formal affiliation with fundamentalist groups. These "neutral" groups contribute to the "community silence" that leads to coercion and control of women. Rafia Zakaria's chapter offers one such example. But earlier work by Abraham (2000) and Das Dasgupta (2007), among others, has documented similar private sphere abuse and violence among people of all religions in South Asian American communities.

By speaking out against ultramasculine fundamentalist projects of all religions, the authors in this book consciously challenge gendered violence in all forms and claim women's political and civil human rights. By offering historically grounded, nuanced accounts of religions, the authors claim their right to thought, expression, and conscience, and reclaim their voices and authority for writing about their lives. Through acts of defying religious boundaries in their everyday life as Shobha Hamal Gurung's chapter shows, they insist upon acknowledging their shared humanity. And, through the "public" act of writing together, they insist upon maintaining an arena in civil society where people of all religions can come together.

Cultural Human Rights, Gender, and Religion

The notion of cultural human rights has gotten mired, almost exclusively, on debates about the *hijab*, honor killings, stoning rape victims (along with genital mutilation, forced marriages, and polygamy). Cultural human rights were developed to protect minority cultures from extinction in the midst of a powerful majority culture. The world's indigenous people, for instance, have sought cultural human rights protection to revive and sustain their identities. Yet, most of the discussions of cultural human rights do not focus on organized attempts to promote cultural extinction. Nor do many "transnational" feminist activists who claim to speak for "global women's rights" systematically consult with local groups that actually work on these issues (Tripp 2006). Mirroring the discussion on political and civil rights, cultural human rights discussions focus on women's bodies and attire to discuss how traditions impinge upon and impede modernity and freedom. As the control of women's bodies becomes the battleground for cultural human rights discussions, the *hijab* has become the symbol of enforced traditionalism (e.g., Pollitt 1999). Yet, for some Muslim women, wearing the *hijab* is a sign of protest against Western cultural hegemony (Al-Hibri 1999). For others it is something they are forced to wear. But the substantive point about the *hijab*, which Parveen Talpur points out—wearing the *hijab* is a matter of local culture, and that Islamic societies differ on this issue—is lost in the debates. The authors in this book do not embark on hijab debates, but they collectively provide an insight that is relevant to this debate. Selina Jamil, Salma Kamal, Parveen Talpur, Elora Chowdhury, Aysha Saeed, and Rafia Zakaria show that Islam is not a changeless ahistorical homogenous, monolithic religion. Instead the key principles are practiced in different ways, depending on local histories and cultures. These descriptions should make pundits pause before continuing to equate the *hijab* to an expression of gendered repression within Islam, and therefore an automatic reason for denying cultural human rights.

The authors in this book focus on two cultural human rights issues that are important to them. Bidya Ranjeet's description of the impediments to carrying out her brother's funeral rites in the appropriate manner is an excellent example of a group's inability to practice, as Article 15 of the Convention on Social Economic and Cultural Human Rights suggests, their cultural life. Many authors describe the problems of arranging religious celebrations because of the lack of the formal right to celebrate religious events. Providing stratified rights—the dominant groups get holidays, the marginalized ones do not—is a cultural human rights violation. The accounts by Salma Kamal and Monoswita Saha starkly show how their lives as Americans are limited. Their freedom to claim their cultural human rights—where "American" continues to be defined as primarily white and Christian—and identify themselves as American Hindu or Muslim becomes an uphill battle (see Joshi 2006 for a detailed discussion on this subject).

While the United States is more open to multiple cultures now, people expect cultures and religions of others to be matters of the private sphere. Since Christian practices and beliefs are taken for granted as the normal way of living, most Christians do not recognize the special privileges they enjoy in the political and civil spheres of life. Despite being a secular nation, minorities are expected to acculturate and assimilate by changing their religious practices, as Bandana Purkayastha described, to fit the form that is reflective of Christian practices. An alternative model of secularism is available in India, where the state stays out of religiocultural matters by allowing minority religious groups to follow their own normative practices in matters of birth, death, marriage, and inheritance; Indian "family laws" vary by religion (and region). For many years, liberal feminist groups in India have lobbied for a uniform civil code, arguing that women of minority religions are placed in a disadvantaged position compared to the majority Hindu women. But recently, Hindu fundamentalists began to make the same demand for a uniform civil code, claiming India did not have to be any different from Western democracies on this matter of cultural rights.

Merry (2006) points out Indian liberal feminist groups realized how an exclusive focus on women qua women can put them on the same political side as fundamentalists who wanted to force minorities— Muslims and Christians—to adopt the ways of the majority. Many of the cultural human rights barriers the authors have described here would be breached if the United States adopted a more inclusive concept of secularism.

However, providing cultural rights is not simply a matter of making provisions for multiple sets of "personal and family" civil laws based on the idea that religions and cultures are unchanging and nondiverse. These same laws have been used by men to subordinate women in "their" communities (Hussain 2007). Some of these claims can be challenged by vigorous enforcement of criminal laws when people's lives are in danger (see Kumar 1993; or Abraham 2000 for some examples of "culture" and domestic violence). A multifaceted strategy, proposed by groups such as Ain-O-Shalish Kendra in Bangladesh (Husain 2004), Women's Action Forum in Pakistan (Afzal-Khan 2007), and Women's Action Research and Laws for Women (WARLAW) in India (Sundar 2007), offers lessons for claiming cultural human rights in the United States. These organizations have reviewed and interpreted laws (including "religious laws") in ways that make patriarchal interpretations and gendered inequalities visible. They have lobbied governments for the enforcement of CEDAW principles in different arenas of life. Groups like BAOBAB (Imam 2004) or Women Living Under Muslim Laws (Afkami and Vaziri 1998) have long argued that groups invested in maintaining local patriarchal powers are, in effect, supported by "W"esterners (media and pundits) who believe Muslim laws are uniform and incapable of change or reform (Tripp 2006).

The issues emphasized by the authors in this book can be placed within the larger stream of human rights activism that pierces the notion of religious sovereignty and determinism. Breaking away from "W"estern liberal notions of human rights,[2] these women are demanding their human rights *and* their ability to practice their religions, an idea that Sundar (2007) has described as "freedom with identity" (see also An-Na'im 1992). The diversity documented in this book is an important corrective to claims of "the" religious tradition in matters of cultural human rights. Listening to the voices of these women, as authorities on the subject of laws and their lives, is germane to understanding how to get out of the cultural rights debate impasse. But who speaks for "the culture" has to include the marginalized within each group. As Dalit activists point out, and Shweta Majumdar describes in her chapter, well–intentioned, middle-class women within cultural groups fail to listen to the ways in which the marginalized frame their own lives. Using these more complex definitions of cultures—cultures that are shaped by histories, politics, and unequal social and economic power—is necessary for addressing patriarchal power and ethnocentrism in matters of cultural human rights.

Social and Economic Human Rights, Religion, Gender

Mary Robinson (2005) points out the world has focused on the 25,000 deaths due to terrorist violence over the last six years and directed billions of dollars for "security." Yet, a holistic understanding of human security should lead us to examine the 250,000 deaths *each year* due to hunger, malnutrition, and preventable diseases as central questions of human rights and security. How are we to assure life, liberty, and security without thinking about food, shelter, health care, education, and just pay for work, which are some key claims of social and economic human rights? Our understanding of social and economic human rights intersects with matters of gender and religion in two ways. First, paying attention to the basic needs of survival and a free life emphasizes the role women play in a million "informal" ways to provide care, income, and community building, which are key to ensuring these rights (Poonacha 1995). Yet, these contributions are gendered, meaning they are made invisible as matters of the private sphere, and women's capabilities are ignored in many discussions of human rights (for an exception, see Martha Nussbaum 2002). Equally important, people are often inspired by their religious beliefs to act for social justice. Whether it is engagement in humanitarian initiatives, sharing of resources and charitable giving as a part of religious duty, protecting

the environment, or standing up for the rights of the most marginalized, religion can be the inspiration for action to address social
and economic human rights. Shanthi Rao and Aysha Saeed's description of their activism are examples of such principled actions.

Many recent studies show that the absence of conflict is a pre-
condition for better access to economic and social human rights.
When the poor Hindu and Muslim women who are part of the
Self Employed Women's Association (SEWA) in Gujarat, India,
maintained their bonds amid the genocidal violence unleashed by
Hindutva supporters, they did so because they understood as marginalized workers they had much in common even if they practiced
different religions.[3] They began to celebrate Diwali and Ramadan
Eid together (SEWA newsletter 2005), because they "believe in the
Gandhian philosophy of Satya (truth), ahimsa (nonviolence), sar-
vadharma (integration of all faiths and all religion), and Khadi
(preparation of local employment and self-reliance) as the basis for
claiming their economic and social human rights." Other studies
by Nandy et al. (1997) and Shiva (2005) demonstrate the same link;
the need for peace to access economic and social human rights. To
build a global world with more money for food, shelter, education,
health care, and other social support systems, we need mechanisms
to arrest the violence of modernity that diverts huge sums of money
to wars and conflicts to promote religio-nationalistic and "patriotic"
causes. Equally important, as Tripp argues, we need powerful voices
in the West to work through their governments on matters such as
food and medicine prices, instead of pouring most of their energy
into cultural human rights issues. Understanding and appreciating
the kind of diversity presented in this book, the everyday actions that
are needed for building a shared humanity and tasks that are often
gendered and made invisible, are crucial for accessing social and economic human rights.

Conclusion

The human rights charter and the associated conventions provide
a framework for living lives that are not circumscribed by single

identities. In the introductory chapter, we presented Amartya Sen's argument for acknowledging our multiple identities. These multiple identities allow us to maintain many different kinds of networks and ties to keep us cognizant of our shared humanity. In order to enact our multiple identities in our everyday lives at the current historical moment, with its toxic mixture of fundamentalist and "security" driven claims about religions, it is important to problematize the concept of religion, to emphasize blurred boundaries, showcase internal diversities, challenge patriarchal/racist interpretations, and to use it as a tool to achieve our political, civil, social, and economic human rights.

Notes

1. These multicivilizational roots is a subject of debate. Many scholars believe human rights are a Western invention, and they draw a straight line from the human rights discourse today back to Enlightenment. Missing in these accounts are the histories of colonialism, genocide, and other large-scale human rights violations that also are a part of the legacy of Western civilization. Nor do these accounts acknowledge other histories of rights. Sen (2005) has pointed out the role of the second century (B.C.E.) Emperor Ashoka in rejecting violence as a state practice, or sixteenth century Islamic Emperor Akbar's attempts to create a state where all religions had equal freedom. There are many dictators and fundamentalist groups around the world who seek protection from human rights standards by stating these are "Western" inventions. Recognizing the multicivilizational, including plural, religious roots of human rights challenges ethnocentric claims.

2. Sen (1998) also has pointed out that many dictators have argued that human rights are a Western cultural tradition and claims to universality are neo-imperialism in disguise. This argument conveniently ignores the universal contributions to the development of the charter on human rights (see Lauren 1998 for a short history). Many Western scholars also trace human rights to Western Enlightenment alone, conveniently overlooking the gaps in their own history between earlier visions and intervening realities reflected in histories of racism, genocide, and colonialism (Nandy 1998).

3. SEWA members are Hindus and Muslims; one-third are Dalits, so the insistence of emphasizing their class-based bonds offers an excellent example of weaving many identities together.

Appendix:
Methodological Notes

This book presents women's experiences of living Hinduism and Islam. We invited women to contribute chapters that describe how they live their religions, including practices they grew up with, values that are important to them now, and any other subject related to living religions about which they are passionate. Instead of following an interview format where the information, even under the best of circumstances, gets refracted through the lens of the researcher, we let the participants describe in their own words whatever they considered to be important. Leaving the definition of "religion" open was methodologically important to us, as we discussed in the introduction. We achieved this goal by asking generic questions with no directions about what we were looking for. If the different emphases of the chapter do not appear to follow the arguments of the introductory chapter that is exactly what we intended. We wished to draw our interpretations from what the authors provided to us—as the interpretive chapters show—instead of editing the chapters to fit into the frames we emphasized. The diverse interpretations in this book testify that this strategy worked. This method also addresses some concerns about insider versus outsider knowledge in research settings. Some have argued co-ethnic researchers are best positioned to understand and convey cultural nuances their participants describe. Others have argued participants assume co-ethnic researchers "know" what they are talking about and are less likely to describe what they take for granted; outsiders are better positioned to seek explanations and clarifications of social phenomenon. By asking our co-participants to write about their experiences we effaced ourselves from the process as the authors wrote for a general audience.

But there are some limitations of this research strategy. By asking for written narratives, we could only ask women who have the time, resources, and ability to write for collections such as this one. Statistically, these highly educated middle-class authors represent the average South Asian American Hindu or Muslim woman (Narayan 2004a, 2004b; Pews 2007). Their social locations are reflected in their descriptions. Even though several authors are very conscious about the influence of their social locations on their writing, we would caution readers about generalizing these collective accounts to represent the universe of practices of all Hindu and Muslim women. We are acutely aware that the leaders of most women-led religious reform movements in South Asia were women of lower classes and castes; if there are similar leaders in the United States, their voices are not present in this book. We tried to ensure geographic variability of our co-participants. We consciously contacted women who lived in different parts of Bangladesh, India, Pakistan, and Nepal; they now live in different parts of the United States. The participants are of different ages and generations. Because we were missing the voices of the marginalized lower caste groups among Hindus, we invited one author to contribute a chapter on the Dalit movement in the United States. Instead of adding one token voice, the chapter describes a movement and interrogates our progressive views on the movement. In the end, the collective accounts presented here reflect a pragmatic compromise of who could write and who was available to write.

As feminists we are very much aware of the other implications of our academic work. First, these essays show that subaltern women of South Asian origin can speak. But when we do, pundits are quick to claim we found our voices through our encounter with modern US society. The authors reinterpret religious texts, provide alternative interpretations, and use different epistemologies and scholarly lineages to write accounts that challenge such stereotypes.

Second, a collection by middle-class authors is also a challenge to fundamentalist groups and the middle-class women who serve the fundamentalist cause. Fundamentalisms are rarely about including the poor and the dispossessed; rather such movements are often conceptualized and organized by middle class groups who feel they are losing some of their hereditary (race, gender, caste, or class) advantages. Fundamentalists have been challenging feminists by showcasing the voices of "their" women and arguing that "their" women represent the authentic voices of women who actually practice "their" religion. These accounts interrupt that process of myth-making.

Third, there are many differences between Hinduism and Islam. Nonetheless, as the authors show, there are also, depending on the socio-historical context, many similarities and convergences between the religions. The creation of three nation-states—Bangladesh, India, and Pakistan—and the increasing visibility of religious politics in the process of nation-making is often interpreted by the media and scholars in terms of adversarial relations between these countries. We follow the path of gender scholars in South Asia to collectively trace our historical similarities *and* differences. This book, by women who trace their origins to four countries, indicates our ability and commitment to coexist and be enriched by our unity in diversity.

Bibliography

Abou-Bakr, Omaima. 2001. Islamic Feminism: What's in a name? *Middle East Women's Studies Review* 15: 4 and 16: 1–4.

Abraham, Margaret. 2000. *Speaking the unspeakable: Marital violence among South Asian Americans.* New Brunswick, N.J.: Rutgers University Press.

Abuza, Zachary. 2007. Political Islam and violence in Indonesia. *Sidel Journal of Islamic Studies* 18: 449–452.

Achebe, Chinua. 1959. *Things fall apart.* New York: Anchor.

Afzal-Khan, Fawzia. 2007. Betwixt and between? Women, the nation and Islamization in Pakistan. *Social Identities* 13: 19–29.

Ahmed, Durre (ed.). 2002. *Gendering the spirit: Women, religion and the postcolonial response.* London: Zed Books.

Ahmed, Syed Jamil. 2000. *Acinpakhi infinity: Indigenous theatre of Bangladesh.* Dhaka, Bangladesh: The University Press Limited.

Afkhami, Mahnaz and Vaziri Haleh. 1998. *Claiming our rights: A manual for human rights education in Muslim societies.* Bethesda, MD: Sisterhood is Global Institute.

Akram, Tanweer. 2005. "Bangladesh and Pakistan." Available at: http://www.virtualbangladesh.com/history/overview_akram.html, May 1, 2005.

Al-Hibri, Azizhah. 1999. Is western patriarchal feminism good for Third World/minority women? In *Is multiculralism bad for women?* Princeton: Princeton University Press, 41–46.

Ali, Ayaan Hirsi. 2007. *Infidel.* New York: Free Press.

Alvarez, Sonia. 2000. Translating the global: Effects of transnational organizing on local feminist discourses and practices in Latin America. *Meridians* 1: 29–67.

Amos, Valerie and Pratibha Parmer. 1984. Challenging imperial feminism. *Feminist Review* 17: 3–20.

Andersen, Margaret. 2005. *Thinking about women: Sociological perspectives on sex and gender* (7th edition). Boston: Allyn and Bacon.

An-Na'im, Abdullahi. 1992. *Human rights in cross-cultural perspective.* Philadephia: University of Pennsylvania Press.

Apffel-Marglin, Frederique and Julia Jean. (in press). Weaving the body and the cosmos: Yantric homologies at a goddess temple in northeastern India. In *Shaktika on the ascent.* Delhi: Oxford University Press.

Aquino, Maria Pilat. 1994. *Our cry for life: Feminist theology from Latin America*. New York: Orbis Books.

Ba-Yunus, Ilyas. 1997. Muslim of Illinois, A demographic report. *East West Review (Summer)*, Special Supplement, 9.

Baca Zinn, Maxine and Bonnie Thornton Dill (eds.). 1994. *Women of color in U.S. society*. Philadelphia: Temple University Press.

Bacchetta, Paola. 2004. *Gender in the Hindu Nation: RSS women as ideologues*. Delhi: Kali for Women.

Badran, Margot. 2002. "Islamic feminism: What's in a name?" *Al-Ahram Weekly* 10: 17–23.

Barlas, Asma. 2002. *Believing women in Islam: Unreading patriarchal interpretations of the Quran*. Austin: Texas University Press.

Baron, Kevin. 2006. "Bush brings faith to foreign aid." *Boston Globe*. October 8.

Barry, Brian M. 1995. *Justice as impartiality*. Oxford: Oxford University Press.

Beane, Wendell. 1977. *Myth, cult and symbols in Sakta Hinduism*. Leiden: Brill.

Benford, Robert D. and David A. Snow. 2000. Framing processes and social movements: An overview and assessment. *Annual Review of Sociology* 26: 11–39.

Begen, Peter. 2001. *Holy War Inc.: Inside the secret war of Osama bin Laden*. New York: The Free Press.

Beteille, Andre. 2001. "Race and caste." In *World conference against racism, racial discrimination, xenophobia, and related intolerance*. Available at: http://wcar.alrc.net/mainfile2.php/For+the+negative/14/.

Bhargava, Rajeev (ed.). 1999. *Secularism and its critics*. New Delhi: Oxford University Press.

Bhaskarananda, Swami. 1994. *The essentials of Hinduism: A comprehensive overview of the world's oldest religion*. Seattle, WA: Viveka Press.

Blauner, Robert. 1972. *Racial oppression in America*. New York: Harper and Row.

Brah, Avtar. 1996. *Cartographies of diaspora*. London: Routledge.

British Broadcasting Corporation News. 2001. "Indian apartheid condemned." February 23. Available at: http://news.bbc.co.uk/2/hi/south_asia/1186101.stm.

Brownmiller, Susan. 1975. "Against our will: Men, women and rape." Available at: www.drishtipat.org/1971/war-susan.html.

Burke, Mary Louise. 1983. *Swami Vivekananda in the west: New discoveries: His prophetic mission*. Vol. 1. Calcutta, India: Advaita Ashram.

———. 1996. *Swami Vivekananda in the west: New discoveries* (second edition). Vols. 2, 4, 5. Calcutta, India: Advaita Ashram.

Bush, Evelyn. 2007. Religion in global society. *Social Forces* 85:1645–1665.

CAIR (Council on American Islamic Relations). 2006. *American Muslim voters: Demographic profile and survey of attitudes.* Washington, DC: CAIR.

Caldwell, Sarah. 2001. *Oh terrifying mother: Sexuality, violence, and worship of the Goddess Kali.* New Delhi: Oxford University Press.

Capra, Fritjof. 1972. *The Tao of physics: An exploration of the parallels between modern physics and eastern mysticism.* Suffolk, UK: Fontana Collins.

Carlyle, Thomas. 1985. The hero as Prophet: Mahomet and Islam. In *On heroes, hero-worship and the heroic in history.* Oxford: Oxford University Press.

Carnes, Tony and Fenggang Yang (eds.). 2004. *Asian American religions: The making or remaking of borders and boundaries.* New York: New York University Press.

Census 2000. Data on ethnic groups. Available at: www.factfinder.census.gov/ethnicity.

Chakraborty, Amiya (ed.). 1961. *Fireflies: A Tagore reader.* New York: The Macmillan Company.

Chakraborty, Uma. 2003. *Gendering caste: Through a feminist lens.* Calcutta: Stree Publishers.

Chinmayananda, Swami. 1975. A Manual of Self Unfoldment. Napa, CA: Chinmayananda Foundation.

Clinton, Hillary R. 1999. Remarks by First Lady Hillary Rodham Clinton in Tunis on women's rights. Available at: http://usembassy-amman.org.jo/3firstL.html.

Coburn, Thomas. 1991. *Encountering the Goddess: A translation of the Devi Mahatmya and a study of its interpretation.* Albany, NY: SUNY Press.

Cohen, Stephen. 2004. *The idea of Pakistan.* Washington, DC: Brookings Institution Press.

Conde Nast Traveller. 2008. A conversation with Ayaan Hirsi Ali. Available at: http://www.concierge.com/cntraveler/articles/detail?articleId=11919.

Copeland, M. Shawn. 1996. Wading through many sorrows: Towards a theology of suffering in womanist perspective. In *Feminist ethics and the Catholic moral tradition.* New York: Paulist Press.

Dannin, Robert. 1996. Island in a sea of ignorance. In *Making Muslim space in North America and Europe.* Berkeley: University of California Press.

Das Dasgupta, Shamita (ed.). 2007. *Body evidence: Intimate violence against South Asian women in America.* New Brunswick, N.J.: Rutgers University Press.

Das, N. K. 2006. Cultural diversity, religious syncretism and people of India: An anthropological interpretation. *Bangladesh e-Journal of Sociology,* Vol. 3 (2). Available at: http://www.bangladeshsociology.org/BEJS%203.2%20Das.pdf.

Davis, Grace. 2006. Borders, boundaries and frontiers in the study of religion: A sociological response. *Social Compass* 53: 243–249.

Dawood, Nessim Joseph. 1993. *The Koran.* (Translated). London: Penguin.

D'Costa, Bina. 2000. "(Dis)Appearing women in nationalist narratives: (Part 1) Interview with Respondent A." Available at the website of Drishtipat: Voice for human rights in Bangladesh at http://www.drishtipat.org/1971/docs/interview1_bina.pdf.

———. 2002. (Dis)Appearing women in nationalist narratives: Interview with Dr. Geoffrey Davis (Part 2). Available at the website of Drishtipat: Voice for human rights in Bangladesh at http://www.drishtipat.org/1971/docs/interview2davis_bina.pdf.

———. 2005. Coming to terms with the past in Bangladesh. In *Feminist politics, activism and vision.* London: Zed Books.

———. n.d. "War babies: The question of national honour." Available at the website of Drishtipat: Voice for human rights in Bangladesh at http://www.drishtipat.org/1971/docs/warbabies_bina.pdf.

Demerath, N. J. III. 2001. *Crossing the Gods: World religions and worldly politics.* New Brunswick, N.J.: Rutgers University Press.

Dempsey, Corinne G. 2001. *Kerala Christian sainthood: Collisions of culture and worldview in South India.* New York: Oxford University Press.

Dimock, Edward C. 1966. *The Bauls of Bengal. The place of the hidden moon.* Chicago and London: University of Chicago Press.

Donnelly, Jack. 1982. Human rights and human dignity: An analytic critique of non-western conceptions of human rights. In *The American Political Science Review* 76: 303–316.

Dumont, Louis and Homo Hierarchichus. 1970. *An essay on the caste system.* Translation by Mark Sainsbury. Chicago: University of Chicago Press.

Easwaran, Eknath. 1985. *The Bhagavad Gita.* Tomales: Nilgiri Press.

Ebaugh, Rose and Janet Saltzman Chaftez. 2000. *Religion and the new immigrants: Continuities and adaptations in immigrant congregations.* Walnut Creek, CA: Altamira Press.

Eck, Diana. 1993. *Encountering God: A spiritual journey from Bozeman to Banaras.* Boston, MA: Beacon Press.

———. 1994. *On common ground: World religions in America.* New York: Columbia University Press; CD-ROM edition.

Edib, Halide Adivar. 2005. *Memoirs of Halide Edib.* Charlottsville, VA: Gorgias Press LLC.

Eliot, T. S. 1968. *Murder in the cathedral.* London: Faber and Faber.

Entman, Robert M. 1993. Framing: Toward clarification of a fractured paradigm. *Journal of Communication* 43, no. 4: 51–58.

Ernst, Carl W. 1997. *The Shambala guide to Sufism.* Boston, MA and London, UK: Shambala.

Espiritu, Yen. 1997. *Asian American women and men: Love, labor, laws.* Walnut Creek, CA: Sage.

Fadiman, James, and Robert Frager (eds.). 1997. *Essential Sufism.* New York: Harper San Francisco.

Falk, Richard. 1999. *Predatory globalization: A critique*. Cambridge: Polity Press.

Forbes, Geraldine. 1996. *Women in modern India*. Cambridge: Cambridge University Press.

Forsythe, David P. 2000. *Human rights in international relations*. Cambridge: Cambridge University Press.

Foucault, Michel. 1986. Of other spaces. Translation by Jay Miscowiec. *Diacritics* 16: 22–27.

Fuller, Lon L. 1969. *The morality of law*. New Haven/London: Yale University Press.

Fyzee, Asaf A. A. 1978. *A modern approach to Islam*. Lahore, Pakistan: Universal Books.

Gans, Herbert. 1979. Symbolic ethnicity: The future of ethnic groups and cultures in America. *Ethnic and Racial Studies* 2: 1–20.

——. 1994. Symbolic ethnicity and symbolic religiosity: Towards a comparison of ethnic and religious generation. *Ethnic and Racial Studies* 17: 577–591.

Gellener, David. 1991. Hinduism, tribalism and the position of women: The problem of Newar identity. *Man* 26: 105–125.

Gendercide. 1971. "Case Study: Genocide in Bangladesh." Available at: http://www.gendercide.org/case_bangladesh.html.

Gerson, Judith M. and Kathy Peiss. 1985. Boundaries, negotiation, consciousness: Reconceptualizing gender relations. *Social Problems* 32, no. 4: 317–331.

Gewirth, Alan. 1996. *The community of rights*. Chicago/London: The University of Chicago Press.

Gewirth, Alan. 1998. *Self-fulfilment*. Princeton: Princeton University Press.

Glenn, Evelyn Nakano. 2002. *Unequal freedoms: How race and gender shaped American citizenship and labor*. Cambridge MA: Harvard University Press.

Grillo, Thomas. 2001. "Baptist Book Spurs March by Hindus." *The Boston Globe*. November 22.

Grunewald, Mary Matsuda. 2005. *Looking like the enemy: My story of imprisonment in Japanese American internment camps*. Troutdale, OR: New Sage Press.

Gudorf, Christine.1994. *Body, sex and pleasure: Reconstructing Christian sexual ethics*. Cleveland, OH: Pilgrim Press.

Guhathakurta, Meghna. 1971. War of symbols: How today's generation remembers. Available at the website of Drishtipat: Voice for human rights in Bangladesh at http://www.drishtipat.org/1971/war-meghna.html.

Gull Hasan, Asma. 2000. *American Muslims: The new generation*. New York: London Continuum.

Gupta, Dipankar. 2001. "Caste, race, politics." Available at: http://www.india-seminar.com/2001/508/508%20dipankar%20gupta.htm.

Haddad, Yvonne and Adair T. Lummis. 1987. *Islamic values in the United States*. New York: Oxford Press.

Hansen, Thomas Blom. 1999. *The saffron wave: Democracy and Hindu nationalism in modern India*. Princeton: Princeton University Press.

Hassan, Riffat. 1995. Are human rights compatible with Islam? The issue of the rights of women in Muslim communities. Available at: http://www.religiousconsultation.org/hassan2.htm#intro.

Hassan, Riffat. "Members, one of another: Gender equality and justice in Islam." Available on the website of Religious Consultation on Population, Reproductive Health and Ethics at: http://www.religiousconsultation.org/hassan.htm.

Hill Collins, Patricia. 1990. *Black feminist thought*. New York: Routledge.

Hossain, Hameeda. n.d. The lessons we never learn. Available at the website of Drishtipat: Voice for human rights in Bangladesh at http://www.drishtipat.org/1971/docs/war-hameeda.htm.

Hosseini, Khaled. 2005. *Kite Runner*. New York: Penguin.

Hubel, Teresa. 1996. *Whose India? The independence struggle in British and Indian fiction and history*. Durham: Duke University Press.

Human Rights Watch. 2001a. End Caste Discrimination. Available at: http://www.hrw.org/campaigns/caste/.

―――. 2001b. Caste discrimination: A global concern. A Report by Human Rights Watch for the UN World Conference Against Racism, Racial Discrimination, Xenophobia and Related Intolerance. Durban, South Africa. Available at: http://www.hrw.org/reports/2001/globalcaste/index.htm#TopOfPage.

Huntington, Samuel. 1998. *The clash of civilizations and the remaking of world order*. New York: Touchstone Books.

Husain, Shahanara. 2004. Women's networks and social change in Bangladesh. In *The power of informal networks: Lessons in social change from South Asia and West Africa*. Lanham, MD: Lexington Books.

Hussain, Sabiha. 2007. Reflections on Islamic identity, citizenship rights and women's struggle for gender justice: Illustrations from India. *International Women's Studies Journal* 9: 63–79.

Illaiah, Kancha. 1999. *Why I Am Not a Hindu: A Sudra Critique of Hindutva, Philosophy, Culture, and Political Economy*. Kolkata, India: Bhatkal Books International.

Imam, Ayesha. 1991. The Muslim religious right (fundamentalists) and sexuality. In *Dossier (Women Living Under Muslim Laws)* 17: 7–25.

―――. 2004. Fighting the political (Ab)use of religion in Nigeria: BAOBAB for women's human rights, allies and others. Available at: www.wluml.org/english/pubs/pdf/wsf/15.pdf.

The Institute of Islamic Information and Education. Human rights in Islam. In *III&E Brochure Series: 7*. Chicago: The Institute of Islamic Information and Education (III&E). Available at: http://www.usc.edu/dept/MSA/human relations/humanrights.

Ishaque, Khalid M. 1980. Islamic law: Its ideals and principles. In *The challenge of Islam*. London: The Islamic Council of Europe.

IIJG (International Initiative for Justice in Gujarat). 2003. Threatened existence: A feminist analysis of the genocide in Gujarat. Available at: http://www.onlinevolunteers.org/gujarat/reports/iijg/.

James, William. 1900. *Psychology: The briefer course*. New York: Henry Holt and Company.

John, Mary E. 1999. Feminisms and internationalisms: A response from India. In *Feminisms and internationalisms*. Oxford: Blackwell Publishers.

Jones, Owen. 2002. *Pakistan: Eye of the storm*. New Haven: Yale University Press.

Jones, Peter. 1994. *Rights*. Basingstoke, UK: Macmillan.

Joshi, Khyati. 2006. *On America's sacred ground*. New Brunswick, N.J.: Rutgers University Press.

Jullundhri, Rashid Ahmed. 1980. Human rights in Islam. In *Understanding human rights*. Dublin: Irish School of Ecumenics.

Kamguian, Azam. 2004. Islam and the liberation of women in the Middle East: Separation of mosque and state is the only answer. Available at: http://www.islam-watch.org/Azam_Kamguian/Islam-Liberation-Women-in-Middle-East.htm.

Kancha, Ilaiah. 1999. Dalitism versus brahminism: The epistemological conflict in history in Dalits and peasants. In *The emerging caste-class dynamics*. Delhi: Gyan Sagar Publications.

Karim, Lamia. 2004. Democratizing Bangladesh: State, NGOs, militant Islam. *Cultural Dynamics* 16: 291–318.

Katzenstein, Mary. 1995. Discursive politics and feminist activism in the Catholic church. In *Feminist organizations: Harvest of the new women's movements*. Philadelphia: Temple University Press.

———. 1998. *Faithful and fearless: Moving feminist protest inside church and military*. Princeton: Princeton University Press.

Kausalya. 2006. The battle over California's textbooks. *Samar 22*. Available at: http://www.samarmagazine.org/archive/article.php?id=212.

Kaviraj, Sudipta. 1991. On state, society and discourse in India. In *Rethinking third world politics*. London: Longmans.

Kaya, Ilhan. 2007. Religion as a site of boundary construction: Islam and the integration of Turkish Americans. *US Alternatives* 6: 139–157.

Kelly, Jan. 2001. Indian Sikhs appeal for tolerance. *Herald Sun*. October 26.

Khan, Abdul Gaffar. Biography. Available at the website of the Sevagram Ashram at: http://www.mkgandhi.org/sevagram.

Khan, Zeeshan Rahman. 2006. "The state we are in." *Star Weekend Magazine 5*, no. 90.

Khandelwal, Madhulika. 2002. *Becoming Indian, becoming American.* Ithaca: Cornell University Press.

Khanna, Simar. 2001. "Fear at home." *The San Francisco Chronicle.* September 24.

Kishwar, Madhu. 1998. *Religion in the service of nationalism.* New Delhi: Oxford University Press.

———. 1999. A Horror of "isms." Why I do not call myself a feminist. In *Off the beaten track,* by Madhu Kishwar. New Delhi: Oxford University Press.

Klosterman, Chuck. 2003. *Sex, drugs and cocoa puffs: A low culture manifesto.* New York: Scribner.

König, Thomas. 2006. "Frame Analysis: A Primer." Available at the website of the department of Social Sciences: *New methods for the analysis of media content,* Loughborough University at http://www.lboro.ac.uk/research/methods/resources/links/frames_primer.html#b_s_2000.

Kosmin, Barry and Seymour Lachman. 1993. *One nation under God: Religion in contemporary American society.* New York: Harmony Books.

Kothari, Rajni (ed.). 1970. *Caste in Indian politics.* New Delhi: Orient Longmans.

Kumar, Radha. 1993. *A History of doing.* London: Verso.

Kumar, Vivek. 2004. Understanding Dalit diaspora. *Economic and Political Weekly* 39 (1): 114.

Kupperman, Joel. 2001. *Classic Asian philosophy: A guide to the essential texts.* New York: Oxford University Press.

Kurien, Prema. 2004. Christian by birth or rebirth? Generation and difference in an Indian American Christian church. In *Asian American Religions.* New York: New York University Press.

———. 2007. *A place at the multicultural table: Development of an American religion.* New Brunswick, N.J.: Rutgers University Press.

Lal, Vinay 1991. Literature from below, review of *The Folktales of India,* ed. Brenda Beck et al., and William Crooke's A Glossary of North Indian Peasant Life, *Indian Literature* 34 (3): 111–118.

———. 2002. *The history of history: Politics and scholarship in modern India.* New York: Oxford University Press.

———. 2006. "Palpable Falsehoods." Available at: http://www.sscnet.ucla.edu/southasia/Diaspora/palpable_falsehoods.pdf.

Lauren, Paul. 1998. *The evolution of international human rights.* Philadelphia: University of Pennsylvania Press.

Le Monde. 2002. Interview with Tareque Masud. Available at: http://www.ctmasud.web.aplus.net/filmmakers/interview_LeMonde.htm.

Levitt, Peggy. 2007. *God needs no passport: Immigrants and the changing American landscape.* New York: The New Press.

Liptak, Adam. 2008. "When God and the law don't square." *New York Times,* February 17.

Luban, David. 2005. Eight fallacies about liberty and security. In *Human rights in the war on terror.* Cambridge: Cambridge University Press.

Luo, Michael. 2008. A host disparages Obama, and McCain apologizes. *New York Times,* February 27.

Mahmood, Saba. 2005. *Politics of piety: The Islamic revival and the feminist subject.* Princeton: Princeton University Press.

Maira, Sunaina. 1999/2000. Ideologies of authenticity: Youth, politics, and diaspora. *Amerasia Journal* 25, no. 3: 139–149.

Majid, Anouar. 2002. *The politics of feminism in Islam.* Chicago and London: The University of Chicago Press.

Mascarenhas, Anthony. 1972. *The rape of Bangladesh.* Delhi: Vikas Publications.

Massey, James. 1997. *Downtrodden: The struggle of India's Dalits for identity, solidarity and liberation.* Geneva: WCC Publications.

Maududi, Abul A. 1977. *Human rights in Islam.* Lahore: Islamic Publications.

Mayo, Katherine, Mother India, 1925. In *Selections from Mother India,* by Mrinalini Sinha, 1998. New Delhi: Kali for Women.

McKay, Robert. B. 1979. What next? In *Human dignity, the internationalization of human rights.* New York: Aspen Institute for Humanistic Studies.

Mernissi, Fatima. 1985. *Beyond the veil: Male-female dynamics in modern Muslim society.* Bloomington, IN: Indiana University Press.

———. 1987. *The veil and male elite: A feminist interpretation of women's rights in Islam.* Reading: Addison Wesley.

Merry, Sherry Engle. 2006. *Human rights and gender violence: Translating international law into local justice.* Chicago: University of Chicago Press.

Miller, Barbara (trans.) 1986. *Bhagavad-Gita.* New York: Bantam Books.

Mitchell, Claire. 2006. The religious content of ethnic identities. *Sociology* 40: 1135–1152.

Mitra, Sukumar. 1989. *Bharater swadhinata sangrame jessore o khulna.* Kolkata: Kalanter Press.

Mitter, Partha. 2001. *Indian art.* Oxford: Oxford University Press.

Moallem, Minoo. 2005. Am I a Muslim woman? Nationalist reactions and postcolonial transgressions. In *Shattering the stereotypes: Muslim women speak out.* Fowlerville, MA: Olive Branch Press.

Moghadam, Valentine (ed.). 1994. *Identity, politics and women: Cultural reassertions and feminisms from an international perspective.* Boulder, CO: Westview Press.

———. 2003. *Modernizing women: Gender and social change in the Middle East.* Boulder, CO: Westview Press.

Mohanty, Chandra Talpade. 1994. Under western eyes: Feminist scholarship and colonial discourses. In *Colonial discourse and post-colonial theory.* New York: Columbia University Press.

Mohanty, Chandra. 2006. U.S. empire and the project of women's studies: Stories of citizenship, complicity and dissent. *Gender, place and culture,* 13, no. 1: 7–20.

Mookerjee, Ajit and Madhu Khanna. 1977. *The tantric way: Art, science, ritual.* London: Thames and Hudson.

Moraga, Cherrie and Gloria Anzaldua (eds.). 1983. *This bridge called my back: Writings by radical women of color.* New York: Kitchen Table/Women of Color Press.

Moya, Paula. 1997. Postmodernism, "realism," and the politics of identity: Cherrie Moraga and chicana feminism. In *Feminist genealogies, colonial legacies, democratic futures.* New York: Routledge.

Muhaiyaddeen, M. R. Bawa. 1987. *Islam and world peace: Explanations of a Sufi.* Philadelphia: The Fellowship Press.

Mujahid, Abdul. 2001. Muslims in America: Profile 2001. Available at: http://www.soundvision.com/info/yearinreview/2001/profile.asp.

Mukherjee, Nayanika. 2003. Ethical issues concerning representation of narratives of sexual violence of 1971. Available at the website of Drishtipat: Voice for human rights in Bangladesh, at http://www.drishtipat.org/1971/docs/war_nayanika.pdf.

Mukhtaran, Bibi. 2007. Biography. Available at: http://www.en.wikipedia.org/wiki/Mukhtaran_Bibi.

Mulhall, Stephen and Adam Swift. 1992. *Liberals and communitarians.* Cambridge, MA: Blackwell Publishing.

Mynott, Adam. 2001. Couple hanged for forbidden love. *BBC Online.* August 8. Available at: http://news.bbc.co.uk/1/low/world/south_asia/1480302.stm.

Nandy, Ashis. 1993. *Illegitimacy of nationalism.* New Delhi: Oxford University Press.

———. 1998. The politics of secularism and the recovery of religious tolerance. In *Secularism and its critics.* New Delhi: Oxford University Press.

———. 1999. The politics of secularism and the recovery of religious tolerance. In *Secularism and its critics.* Edited by Rajeev Bhargava. New Delhi: Oxford University Press.

———. 2002. *Time warps: Silent and evasive pasts in Indian politics and religion.* New Brunswick, N.J.: Rutgers University Press.

———. 2005. Creating a nationality. In *Exiled at home.* New Delhi: Oxford University Press.

Nandy, Ashis, Shikha Trivedy, Shail Mayaram, and Achyut Yagnik. 1997. *Creating a nationality: The Ramjanmabhoomi and fear of the self.* New Delhi: Oxford Paperbacks.

Narayan, Anjana. 2004a. Asian Americans in Connecticut, Census 2000: Citizenship, employment, poverty, income and education. Asian American Studies Institute, University of Connecticut.

———. 2004b. Asian Americans in Connecticut, Census 2000: Race and ethnicity, household, family. Asian American Studies Institute, University of Connecticut.

———. 2006. Ethnic Organizations and Ethnic Identities: Websites as a Tool to Create Transnational Gendered Identities. Unpublished Ph.D. dissertation. University of Connecticut.

Nietzsche, Friedrich. 1967. *The will to power.* Translation by Walter Kaufmann. New York: Vintage.

Nirbedananda, Swami. 1979 (1944). *Hinduism at a glance* (1st edition). Calcutta: Ramkrishna Mission Calcutta Students Home.

Numan, Fareed H. 1990. The Muslim population in the United States. Available at: http://www.islam101.com/history/population2_usa.html.

Nurbaksh, Javed. 1990. *Sufi women.* New York: Knopf.

Nussbaum, Martha. 2002. Women's capabilities and social justice. In *Gender justice, development, and rights.* Oxford: Oxford University Press.

Okin, Susan Moller. 1999. *Is multiculturalism bad for women?* J. Cohen, M. Howard and M. Nussbaum (eds.). Princeton: Princeton University Press.

Omvedt, Gail. 1995. *Dalit visions.* New Delhi: Orient Longmans.

Orwin, Clifford and Thomas Pangle. 1984. Philosophical foundation of human rights. In *Human rights in our time.* Boulder/London: Westview Press.

Osella, Filippo and Carolina Osella. 2003. "Ayyappan saranam": Masculinity and the Sabarimala pilgrimage in Kerala. *Journal of the Royal Anthropological Institute,* 9: 729–753.

Osho. 2004. *Buddha: His life and teachings.* Osho International Foundation. Lewes, UK: The Bridgewater Book Company Ltd.

Oyewumi, Oyeronke. 1997. *The invention of women: Making an African sense of western gender discourses.* Minneapolis: University of Minnesota Press.

Ozdemir, Ibrahim. 2005. Commentary—*Creative love, nature and Mawlana Jelal al-Din Rumi.* Today's Zaman. Available at: http://en.wikipedia.org/wiki/ brahim_Özdemir.

Pandey, Gyanendra. 2006. *Routine violence: Nations, fragments, histories.* Stanford, CA: Stanford University Press.

Panikkar, Raimundo. Is the notion of human rights a western concept? In *Breakthrough.* New York: Global Education Associates.

Panjabi, Kavita. 2005. *Old maps and new: Legacies of the partition.* Calcutta: Seagull Press.

Pew Charitable Trust. 2005. Available at: http://www.pewtrusts.org/our_work_report_detail.aspx?id=32854.

Pew Charitable Trust. 2007. Muslim Americans: Mostly Middle Class, Mainstream. http://www.pewtrusts.org/our_work_report_detail.aspx?id=25650.

Pollitt, Katha. 1999. Whose culture? In *Is multiculturalism bad for Women?* Princeton: Princeton University Press.

Poonacha, Veena. 1995. *Gender within the human rights discourse.* Bombay: Women's Center for Women's Studies, SNDT University Publication.

Prabhabananda, Swami and Frederick Manchester. 1957. *The Upanishads: Breath of the Upanishad.* Hollywood: Vedanta Society of Southern California.

Prashad, Vijay. 2000a. *The Karma of brown folk.* Minneapolis: University of Minnesota Press.

————. 2001. Afro-Dalits of the world, unite. *African Studies Review Special Issue on the Diaspora,* vol. 43 (1): 189–201.

————. 2006. "Debating the California textbook controversy: In the shadow of Saraswati." Available at: http://www.littleindia.com/news/135/ARTICLE/1134/2006-03-13.html.

Purkayastha, Bandana. 2002. Contesting multiple margins: Asian Indian community activism in the early and late 20th century. In *Women's activism and globalization: Linking local struggles and transnational politics.* New York: Routledge.

————. 2003. Looking beyond the individual: Interaction of structural factors and human agency in the empowerment of women. In *Conditioning and the empowerment of women: A multidimensional approach.* New Delhi, India: Gyan Publishing House.

————. 2005. *Negotiating ethnicity: Second generation South Asian Americans traverse a transnational world.* New Brunswick, N.J.: Rutgers University Press.

Purkayastha, Bandana and Anjana Narayan. Forthcoming. Bridges and chasms: Orientalism and the making of Asian Indians in New England. In *Asian Americans in New England.* Lebanon, NH: University of Press of New England.

Radhakrishnan, Sarvapalli and Charles Moore. 1957. *Sourcebook of Indian philosophy.* Princeton: Princeton University Press.

Radice, William (ed.). 1999. *Vivekananda and the modernization of Hinduism.* New Delhi: Oxford University Press.

Raisuddin, A. N. M. 2005. "Sufism." Available at the website of Banglapedia at: http://search.com.bd/banglapedia/HT/S_0580.htm.

Ramusack, Barbara and Sharon Seivers. 1999. *Women in Asia: Restoring women to history.* Bloomington: Indiana University Press.

Rashid, Ahmed. 2001. *Taliban: Militant Islam, oil and fundamentalism in Central Asia.* New Haven: Yale University Press.

Rayaprol, Aparna. 1997. *Negotiating identities: Women in the Indian diaspora.* Delhi: Oxford University Press.

Reuther, Rosemary Radford. 1983. *Sexism and God-talk: Toward a feminist theology.* Boston: Beacon Press.

Rhodes, Katherine. 2006. *God's troublemakers: How women of faith are changing the world.* New York: Continuum International Publishing Group.

The Rising Nepal. 2001. (Reforms in Buddhism.) Available at: http://www.nepalnews.com.np/contents/englishdaily/trn/2001/apr/apr07/.

Robbins, Susan, Pranab Chatterjee, and Edward R. Canda. 1998. *Contemporary human behavior theory: A critical perspective for Social Work.* Boston: Allyn & Bacon.

Robinson, Mary. 2005. Connecting human rights, human development and human security. In *Human rights in the war on terror.* Cambridge, UK: Cambridge University Press.

Rose, Kalima. 1992. *Where women are leaders. The SEWA movement in India.* New Delhi: Vistaar Publications.

Rotto, Rich. 2000. Malla Period (1200–1769 C.E.) Available at: http://internet .cybermesa.com/~rotto/hist3.html.

Roy-Chowdhury, Sandeep. 2004. A boy, a nation, and a clay bird. *India Currents.* June 14. Available at: http://www.indiacurrents.com/news/view_ article.html?article_id=1a1ef527262e67c758fd372ac2c7179c.

Rumi, Fihi Ma Fihi. 2000. *The Rumi Collection—Edited By Kabir Helminski.*

Rumi, Jalalu'l-Din. 1950. *Rumi: poet and mystic.* Translation by Reynold A. Nicholson. London: George Allen and Unwin Ltd.

Rummel, Rudolph J. 1994. *Death by government.* New Brunswick, N.J.: Transaction Publishers.

Sahoo, Ajaya Kumar. 2005 "Some Reflections on Dalit Diaspora." Available at: http://www.geocities.com/husociology/dalits7.htm.

Said, Edward. 1979. *Orientalism.* New York: Vintage Paperbacks.

Saikia, Jaideep. 2004. *Terror sans frontier: Islamic militancy in North East India.* New Delhi: Vision Books.

Salomon, Carol. 1995. Baul Songs. In *Religions of India in practice: Princeton readings in religion.* Princeton: Princeton University Press.

Santayana, George. n.d. In Wisdom Quotes. Available at: http://www.wisdom quotes.com/002322.html.

Santos, Fernanda. 2008. After the war, a new battle to become citizens. *New York Times,* February 24.

Sardar, Ziauddin. 2004. *Desperately seeking paradise: Journeys of a skeptical Muslim.* London: Granta Books.

Sarkar, Tanika and Urvashi Butalia. 1995. *Women and the Hindu right.* Delhi: Kali for Women.

Sarna, Jonathan and David Dahlin. 1997. *Religion and state in the American Jewish experience.* Notre Dame: University of Notre Dame Press.

Saxena, Neela Bhattacharya. 2004. *In the beginning is desire: Tracing Kali's footprints in Indian literature.* Delhi: Indialog Books.

———. 2002. Border in the courtyard: Partitioned India and my mother's "home." *Nassau Review* 8, no. 3: 22–32.

———. Forthcoming. Beauty, wonder, and knowledge in the Mahavidya icon of Chinnamasta. In *Hinduism and the feminine.*

Schimmel, Annemarie. 1975. *Mystical dimensions of Islam.* Chapel Hill: University of North Carolina Press.

———. 1982. *Islam in India and Pakistan.* Leiden, The Netherlands: Brill.

Schneider, Miriam (ed.). 1972. *Feminism: The essential historical writings.* New York: Bantam Books.

Sehgal, Meera. 2007. Manufacturing a feminized siege mentality: Hindu nationalist paramilitary camps for women in India. *Journal of Contemporaray Ethnography* 36: 165–183.

Sen, Amartya. 1998. Universal truths: Human rights and the westernizing illusion. *Harvard International Review* 20: 40–43.

———. 2005. *The argumentative Indian: Writings on Indian history, culture, identity.* New York: Farrar, Strauss, Giroux.

———. 2006. *Identity and violence: The illusion of destiny.* New York: W.W. Norton & Co.

Sen, Amiya. 2000. *Swami Vivekananda.* New Delhi: Oxford University Press.

Sen, Ilina. 1990. *A space within the struggle.* New Delhi: Kali for Women.

Sengupta, Somini. 2006a. 3 Indian scientists protest in getting visas." *New York Times,* February 24.

———. 2006b. Braids of faith found at Baba's temple. A Hindu-Muslim Idyll. *New York Times,* March 17.

SEWA newsletter. January 2005. Available at: http://www.sewainternational .org/dynamic/modules.

Shah, Lalon. 1964. *Songs of Lalon Shah.* Translation by Abu Rushd. Dacca: Bengali Academy.

"Shab-e-barat." 2008. Available at: http://www.surfindia.com/festivals/shab-e-barat.html.

Shaikh, Nermeen. 2004. "Interview with Tareque Masud." Available at the website of *Asia Source: A resource of the Asia Society* at http://www.asiasource .org/news/special_reports/masud.cfm. Kolkata, India: Asia Society.

Sharma, Anup. 2001. *Ke Unihari Sukhi Chan?* Space Visesa (Saturday Supplement) *Spacetime Nepali Daily,* July 30.

Shiva, Vandana. 2005. *India divided.* New York: Seven Stories Press.

———. 2006. *India divided: Diversity and democracy under attack.* Boston: South End Press.

Simon, Rita and Susan Alexander. 1993. *The ambivalent welcome: Print media, public opinion and immigration.* Westport: Praeger Press.

Srinivas, Mysore N. 1962. *Caste in modern India, and other essays.* Bombay: Asia Publishing House.

Subedi, Salil. 1999. *Poubha: The ancient art of Kathmandu Valley.* Kathmandu: Jagadamba Press.

Sundar, Madhavi. 2007. Piercing the Veil. *The Yale Law Journal,* 112: 1399–1472.

Swamy, Raja. 2006. "Yankee Hindutva: Indian Jim Crow in 'victim' garb." Available at: http://www.dissidentvoice.org.

Syed, Ali. 2002. Collective and elective ethnicity: Caste among urban Muslims in India. *Sociological Forum* 17: 593–620.

Tagore, Rabindranath. 1913a. *Sadhana.* Calcutta: MacMillian.

———. 1913b. *Gitanjali.* Calcutta: MacMillian.

———. 1931. *Religion of man.* London: George Unwin.

———. 1961a. *Samagra rachanabali* (Collected works of Tagore). Calcutta: Visva Bharati Publications.

————. 1961b. Santiniketan. In *Samagra Rachanbali* (Collected works of Tagore). Calcutta: Visva Bharati Publishers. Vols. 7–8: 110–117, 445–450.

Tattwajnanadana, Swami. 2001. *A symphony in architecture: A visitor's guide towards better understanding of the spirit and architecture of the temple.* Belur, India: Ramakrishna Mission.

Tharoor, Sashi. 1998. *India from midnight to the millennium.* New York: Arcade Publishing.

"The Clay Bird." Directed by Tareque Masud, Audiovision, 2002.

The Holy Bible: New International Version. 1984. Colorado Springs: International Bible Society.

"The Los Angeles Time poll of US Jews." *Los Angeles Times* 1998.

Tohidi, Nayereh. 2002. Islamic feminism: Perils and promises. *Middle East Women's Studies Review* 16: 1–6.

Tripp Alili-Marie. 2006. Challenges in transnational feminist mobilization. In *Global feminisms: Transnational women's activism, organizing and human rights.* New York: New York University Press.

UDHR Summary. 2008. A Summary of United Nations Agreements on Human Rights. Available at: http://www.hrweb.org/legal/undocs.html.

United Nations. 1998. A United Nations priority: Universal Declaration of Human Rights. Available at: http://www.un.org/rights/HRToday/declar.htm.

UNHCHR. 1951. Convention on the prevention and punishment of the crime of genocide. Available at: http://www.unhchr.ch/html/menu3/b/p_genoci .htm.

Van der Veer, Peter. 2003. Religious radicalism in South Asia. *South Asian Journal,* 3–6. Available at: http://www.southasianmedia.net/Magazine/ Journal/previousissue2.htm.

Vanita, Ruth. 2002. *Queering India: Same sex love and eroticism in Indian culture and society.* New York: Routledge.

Vivekananda, Swami. 1974. *Chicago Addresses.* 17th Impression Calcutta: Advaita Ashram.

————. 1978. *Inspired talks.* Collection of talks by Vivekananda. New York: Ramakrishna-Vivekananda Center.

————. 2003. *Karma yoga: The yoga of action.* Kolkata, India: Advaita Ashram.

Waldron, Jeremy. 1995. The cosmopolitan alternative. In *The rights of minority cultures.* Oxford: Oxford University Press.

Weisman, Steven. 2005. "Saudi women have message for U.S. envoy." *New York Times,* September 28.

Wilson, Bryan. 1979. *Contemporary transformations of religion.* Oxford: Clarendon Press.

Wilson, Richard (ed.). 2005. *Human rights in the war on terror.* Cambridge, UK: Cambridge University Press.

World Almanac and St. Martins Press. 2001. *World almanac book of facts 2001.* Mahwah, NJ: World Almanac Books.

World Conference against Racism. 2001. If caste is not a form of racial discrimination, Jupiter is not one of the planets of the solar system. Available at: http://wcar.alrc.net/.

World Wildlife Fund Report. 2006. WWF Living Planet Report. Available at: http://www.worldwildlife.org/toxics/.

Yang, Fengyang and Rose Ebaugh. 2001. Transformations in new immigrant religions and their global implications. *American Sociological Review* 66: 269–288.

Yazbeck, Yvonne, Jane I. Smith, and Kathleen M. Moore. 2006. *Muslim women in America: The challenge of Islamic identity today.* New York: Oxford University Press.

Yuktananda, Swami and Evelyn Guha. 1989. *Values and ourselves.* Calcutta: Vivekananda Nidhi.

The Contributors

Elora Halim Chowdhury is Assistant Professor of Women's Studies in the University of Massachusetts, Boston. She holds a Ph.D. in Women's Studies from Clark University, Massachusetts (2004). Her teaching and research interests include critical development studies, third world/transnational feminisms, globalization and women's organizing in Bangladesh. Her work has appeared in the *International Feminist Journal of Politics; Meridians: Feminism, Race, Transnationalism; Violence Against Women: An International and Interdisciplinary Journal; Frontier: A Journal of Women Studies* and in edited anthologies. She is currently working on a book manuscript titled, *'Transnationalism Reversed': Engaging Development, NGO Politics, and Women's Organizing in Bangladesh.*

Shobha Hamal Gurung specializes in gender and labor, globalization, comparative family and community, and development and cultural studies. Her current scholarship focuses on human trafficking and the sex trade, and in the lives of Nepali female migrants working in the informal economic sectors in the US. She has worked professionally as well as voluntarily for a number of national and international organizations and agencies in different capacities. Some of these include Boston Women's Health Book Collective, the World Conservation Union, and Maiti Nepal.

Selina Jamil received a Ph.D. for her dissertation on Henry James from Michigan State University in 1997 and is an Associate Professor at Prince George's Community College in Largo, Maryland. Two of her articles on Tagore are forthcoming in the *Journal of Commonwealth and Postcolonial Studies* and in a book entitled

Rabindranath Tagore in the New Millennium—Questions of Gender, Nation, Science and Tradition. Apart from her interest in South Asian literature, her areas of work include research in American literature. She has published an article on Stowe's *Uncle Tom's Cabin* in *Harvest: Jahangirnagar Studies in Literature* (1992). Her book on Henry James is forthcoming from the University Press of America. She has also published poetry in literary magazines, and two of her poems are forthcoming in *Ariel: A Review of International English Literature.*

Salma Kamal was born and raised in Hackensack, New Jersey. She graduated with honors in political science and minors in history, human rights, and women studies from the University of Connecticut. She co-chaired PIRG's (Public Interest Research Group) committee on Hunger Awareness, and was later elected treasurer of the local and state executive board. She has also worked with the Violence Against Women Prevention program. She lives and works in Conneticut as a project manager for a Chicago-based marketing research firm and is involved with a local violence prevention shelter to provide counseling and services to women in need.

Shweta Majumdar is a graduate student in Sociology at the University of Connecticut. She received a master's degree in International Development from the University of Pittsburgh. She also has a master's degree in Sociology from Jawaharlal Nehru University in New Delhi. Her research interests include gender, human rights, and immigration. She has been actively involved with several development projects in India and has also worked as Program Management Intern at Management Systems International in Washington, D.C.

Anjana Narayan is an Assistant Professor at California State Polytechnic University at Pomona. Her recent research deals with transnational ethnic identities on the web and the racialized and gendered components of these identities. She is a recipient of several university-wide awards including the 100 Years of Women's Scholarship Award and received a citation from Governor Jodi Rell for her scholarship, activism, and commitment to women's issues. She also has a postgraduate degree in Social Work from the Tata Institute of Social Sciences (TISS) in Mumbai, India. She was associated with a range of innovative initiatives in the field of women and development in India.

Bandana Purkayastha is an Associate Professor of Sociology and Asian American Studies at the University of Connecticut. She was educated at Presidency College (India), the University of Massachusetts, and the University of Connecticut. Her current research and publications focus on the intersection of racialized ethnicity, gender, and class. She has published chapters and articles in the United States, United Kingdom, Germany, and India on multiple marginalities that affect Asian American women. She is the author of the book titled *Negotiating Ethnicity—Second Generation South Asian Americans Traverse a Transnational World* (Rutgers University Press 2005), and the co-editor of *The Power of Women's Informal Networks—Lessons in Social Change from South Asia and West Africa* (Lexington Books 2004). She is also Deputy Editor of the journal *Gender and Society*. She has been invited to speak on gender and globalization at universities like Hofstra, Yale, and Visva Bharati (India) and has won several awards including University of Connecticut Women of Color Award for Excellence in Leadership, Achievement, and Service.

Bidya Ranjeet is the Director of the University of Connecticut's Student Support Services (SSS) program in the Center for Academic Programs. Through her work at UConn she has been integral in providing access to higher education for students from Connecticut's urban centers. In collaboration with other departments, Bidya has made a significant contribution to the university's mission of promoting diversity; she is the primary force behind the creation of study abroad opportunities for students who normally would encounter too many obstacles, both financial and familial, to consider participating. Bidya is involved, in varying capacities, in the Women's Center Advisory Board and Diversity Committee, the UConn Nepali Student Association, and the Asian American Faculty and Staff Association. Outside of the university, Bidya has devoted her spare time to advocating on behalf of South Asian women and assisting them. Specifically she is involved in TSAT (The South Asian Tree) and is a board member for the Nepali Women's Global Network. Most notably Bidya is one of the first women to confront, through written publications and presentations, issues regarding domestic violence against Nepali women living in the United States.

Shanthi Rao was born in Bangalore, India. She immigrated to the United States from India in 1977 and has been living in the Hartford area. She received her master's degree in Social Work from the University of Connecticut. Her interests and strengths in community activism came from working with various ethnic groups and populations, both internationally and domestically. Her involvement with organizations such as the Connecticut Immigrant and Refugee Coalition, American Civil Liberties Union of Connecticut, and Asian Family Services gave her insightful experience into effective development work with local immigrants, refugees, and minority populations. Presently she works as a consultant facilitating community and hospital-based prenatal and parenting groups. She volunteers for a local shelter running a support group for victims of domestic violence. She is a member of the Asian Pacific American Coalition working toward the creation of an Asian American Pacific Commission in Connecticut. She is trained in Indian classical music and has been training in Western classical music. She is also a trained Reiki practitioner. Her hobbies include gardening and reading a variety of literature.

Aysha Saeed was born and raised in Pakistan. She completed her postgraduate training in Internal Medicine at the University of Connecticut and practices medicine in Meriden, Connecticut. She has a special interest in environmental protection issues and has been involved in interfaith and human rights initiatives.

Monoswita Saha is an Economics and English double major at the University of Connecticut. She is a University Scholar, the highest recognition for academic excellence for undergraduate students at the university. She has won several grants and awards including the UConn Humanities Institute Fellowship and the Hira and Sunita Jain outstanding student award. She has worked on several research projects (of her own design) in India. The most recent was a study of globalization, studying people of different social and occupational strata in three major urban areas in India. A 1.5 generation individual who came to the United States when she was four years old, Monoswita also has been active in the Vedanta society.

Neela Bhattacharya Saxena is an Associate Professor of English at Nassau Community College in Garden City, NY. Besides British and American literature, she teaches South Asian literature as well as multidisciplinary history of ideas and women's studies courses. Her book *In the Beginning IS Desire: Tracing Kali's Footprints in Indian Literature* was published in 2004. Some of her recent publications include "Gaia Mandala: An Eco-Thealogical Vision of the Indic Shakti Tradition" (*InterCulture,* April 2006) and "The Funhouse Mirror of Tantric Studies" (*Evam: Forum on Indian Representations* Vol. 4, No. 1 and 2, 2006). Her forthcoming essays include "Gynocentric Thealogy of Tantric Hinduism: A Meditation upon the Devi," scheduled to appear in *Oxford Handbook of Feminist Theology* and "Beauty, Terror, and Knowledge in the Mahavidya Icon of Chinnamasta" to appear in *Hinduism and the Feminine: Reclamations and Reconstructions.*

Parveen Talpur is a Historian/Writer living in Ithaca, New York since 1990. Originally from Pakistan, Parveen contributed essays and feature articles in the country's major magazines and newspapers listed below. She worked as a sub-editor in *Dawn* and as an assistant editor in *Tribune.* In Ithaca Parveen was a Visiting Scholar at Cornell University and worked on two research projects: Decipherment of the Indus Valley Seal Symbols (2500–1500 B.C.) and pre-colonial Sindh (1784–1843).The results of her research have been published as three separate texts. Parveen taught South Asian History at Cornell University, Binghamton University, Elmira College, and the University of Sindh (Pakistan). She has written ficton and non-fiction, including two books on Pakistan's archeology and history (*Evidence* *of Geometry in Indus Valley Civilization* and *Talpur Rule in Sindh*), a children's novel (*Mystery of Three headed Bull*), a book of poems (*Footnotes*) and several short stories.

Rafia Zakaria is an attorney currently completing her doctorate in Political Science at Indiana University where she is the John Edwards Fellow (2007–2008). Her research focuses on Muslim identity specifically as it relates to Sharia law initiatives and multiculturalism in Western states. She teaches courses on US Constitutional Law, Political Philosophy, and Islam and Politics and her dissertation is entitled "Constructing Identity: Feminism, Multiculturalism and the Muslim Woman." Rafia also works on the Middle East Country Group of Amnesty International USA. She is the Associate Executive Director of the Muslim Alliance of Indiana, and a board member of Ibtida (an NGO that builds schools in rural Pakistan) and ANAA (an NGO dedicated to advocacy for female victims of violence in her native Pakistan). Rafia is a weekly columnist for *Daily Times* in Pakistan and an associate editor at www.altmuslim.com.

She writes frequently for US and international publications, her work has appeared in *Frontline India, The Nation, Reason, Arts and Letters Daily,* and numerous other publications. She has been quoted by the *New York Times, Fox News,* and the *Indianapolis Star.*

Index

Also from Kumarian Press...

Women & Gender:

The Hidden Assembly Line:
Gender Dynamics of Subcontracted Work in a Global Economy
Edited by Radhika Balakrishnan

Women and the Politics of Place
Edited by Wendy Harcourt and Arturo Escobar

Cinderella or Cyberella?
Empowering Women in the Knowledge Society
Edited by Nancy Hafkin and Sophia Huyer

New and Forthcoming:

Hollow Bodies: Institutional Responses to
Sex Trafficking in Armenia, Bosnia, and India
Susan Dewey

Reluctant Bedfellows:
Feminism, Activism and Prostitution in the Philippines
Meredith Ralston and Edna Keeble

Peace Through Health:
How Health Professionals Can Work for a Less Violent World
Edited by Neil Arya and Joanna Santa Barbara

Visit Kumarian Press at **www.kpbooks.com** or call **toll-free**
800.232.0223 for a complete catalog.

Kumarian Press, located in Sterling, Virginia, is a forward-looking, scholarly press that promotes active international engagement and an awareness of global connectedness.